HISTORY
OF RUSSIA

Sergei Mikhailovich Soloviev

The Academic International Press Edition of Sergei M. Soloviev's History of Russia From Earliest Times. Peter von Wahlde, General Editor.

Contributing Editors:

HUGH F. GRAHAM

SERGEI M. SOLOVIEV

History of Russia

Volume 9

The Age of Vasily III

Edited, Translated and With an

Introduction by

Hugh F. Graham

Academic International Press

1976

The Academic International Press Edition of S. M. Soloviev's *History of Russia from Earliest Times* in fifty volumes

Volume 9 *The Age of Vasily III* Unabridged translation of the text of Volume 5, Part II, Chapters I-II and Volume 6, Chapters I-II of S. M. Soloviev's *Istoriia Rossii s drevneishikh vremen* as found in Volume III of this work published in Moscow, 1962-1966, with added annotation.

Copyright © 1976 by Academic International Press

All rights reserved. The reproduction or utilization of this work in any form or by any electronic, mechanical, or other means, now known or hereafter invented, including xerography, photocopying, and recording, and in any information storage and retrieval system, by any individual, institution or library, is forbidden under law without the written permission of the publisher.

Library of Congress Catalog Card Number: 75–11085
ISBN O-87569-O66-1

By publisher-direct subscription to the work as published

Typography by Susan D. Long
Title Page by King & Queen Press

Printed in the United States of America

A list of titles published by Academic International Press is found at the end of this volume.

ACADEMIC INTERNATIONAL PRESS
Box 555 Gulf Breeze FL 32561

CONTENTS

WEIGHTS AND MEASURES

Linear Measure

Verst: 500 sazhen, 1166 yards and 2 feet, .663 miles, 1.0668 km
Sazhen: 3 arshins, 7 feet, 2.133 m
Arshin: 16 vershoks, 28 in. (diuims), 72.12 cm
Chetvert: ¼ arshin
Fut: 12 diuims, 1 foot, 30.48 cm
Vershok: 1.75 in., 4.445 cm, 1/16 arshin
Diuim: 1 inch, 2.54 cm
Desiatina: 2400 square sazhens, 2.7 acres, 1.0925 hectare
Chetvert (quarter): ½ desiatina, 1.35 acre (sometimes 1.5 desiatinas or ca. 4.1 acres)

Liquid Measure

Vedro (pail): 3.25 gallons, 12.3 liters
Bochka (barrel): 40 vedros, 121 gallons, 492 liters
Chetvert (quarter): ¼ bochka, 32.5 gallons

Weights

Berkovets: 361 lbs., 10 puds
Pud: 40 funts, 36.113 lbs. (US), 40 lbs. (Russian), 16.38 kg
Funt: 96 zolotniks, .903 lb.
Korob (basket): 7 puds, 252 lbs.
Rad: 14 puds, 505.58 lbs.
Chetvert (quarter: basic grain dry measure): ¼ rad, 3.5 puds, 126.39 lbs.
Chetverik (grain measure dating from 16th century): 1/8 chetvert, 15.8 lbs.
Zolotnik: 1/96 lb., 4.26 grams

Money (15th and 16th centuries)

Muscovite Denga: 200 equals 1 ruble
Novgorod Denga: 100 equals 1 ruble
Altyn: 6 Muscovite dengas
Grivna: 20 Muscovite dengas, 10 grivnas equals 1 ruble
Poltina: ½ ruble
Poltora: 1½ rubles
Peniaz: 10 equals one grosh (Lithuania)
Kopa grosh: 60 groshas, one Muscovite poltina
Chetvertak: silver coin equal to 25 kopecks or ¼ ruble (18-19th centuries)
Kopeck: two Muscovite dengas

Note: Weights and measures often changed values over time and sometimes held more than one value at the same time. For details consult Sergei G. Pushkarev, *Dictionary of Russian Historical Terms from the Eleventh Century to 1917* (Yale, 1970).

RUSSIA UNDER VASILY III

PREFACE

This book is an unabridged translation of the text of Volume V, Part II, Chapters I-III, and Volume 6, Chapters I-II, which are, respectively, pp. 218-352 and 395-454 in Volume 3 of the multi-volume edition of Soloviev's *Istoriia Rossii s drevneishikh vremen,* published from 1959 through 1966 in Moscow.

The present translation endeavors faithfully to reflect Soloviev's thought. No attempt is made to reproduce his style; literary felicity was not among Soloviev's many strengths. A primary consideration has been to render his history readable, and certain devices conducive to that end may be mentioned. Technical terms employed to describe administrative functions are the despair of translators. Many histories of Russia in English leave these terms untranslated in the body of the text to mar almost every page. The extent of the difficulty may be gauged by examining the invaluable reference work by Sergei G. Pushkarev, *Dictionary of Russian Historical Terms from the Eleventh Century to 1917* (1970), which has been consulted extensively during the preparation of this translation. In keeping with the purpose of the *Dictionary* the compiler has for the most part defined and explained terms, but has seldom provided precise equivalents for them. In this translator's opinion it is possible to locate appropriate English words and phrases to serve as succinct, accurate equivalents of almost all the technical terms Soloviev employs. No device for rendering the terminology of a bygone era into another language can secure universal approbation, but this translation has sedulously striven to find suitable equivalents in its concern to facilitate the flow of Soloviev's narrative without awkward interruptions.

To focus upon particular problems, something should be said about *boyar, voevoda* and *diak,* three words that appear with high frequency in this portion of Soloviev's *History.* They are difficult to render precisely and uniformly because the administrative concepts underlying them impinged upon the new central apparatus, in a state of flux, which had begun to evolve during the sixteenth century in a country where the appanage principle of local independence and autonomy had long predominated. The same man will hold different offices, for no concept of separate civil and military services could as yet be said to exist.

The *boyars* (this term has been fully anglicized) form the group referred to most frequently in any discussion of the early history of Russia. They were the most prominent and powerful individuals in the grand duchy of Muscovy, the grand princes' chief coadjutors, advising the ruler on basic issues singly, in groups, in their council (*duma*), or at his call, and executing major policy. *Boyar* was the highest rank a grand prince could confer (and he did so sparingly), in contrast with the title *prince* (*kniaz*), which was hereditary. A prince might be a boyar; a boyar could not become a prince, but the same persons were usually both. Two gradations in this rank may be noted. Next to the boyars stood *okolnichie,* whose duties Soloviev examines on more than one occasion. Since *okolnichie* frequently performed duties connected with the ceremonies of the court this rank can be rendered by the term *lord-in-waiting. Junior boyars* (*deti boiarskie,* pl., *syn boiarskii,* sing.), a large and amorphous group, were, as the name implies, concerned with carrying out the orders of their superiors. They might aspire as high as a seat in the boyar council, but they normally performed routine civil or military tasks in the provinces or on the frontiers. Accordingly, they are rendered as *junior boyars, junior officers,* or *junior officials,* depending on context.

A *voevoda* was usually a high-ranking military officer, a *commander,* when on active service. As a *commandant* his duties might overlap those of a garrison officer, or a provincial *governor* or *lord-lieutenant* or *vicegerent* (*namestnik*), who discharged both civilian and military responsibilities. Princes and boyars normally held this office.

Diaki (plural) first became important in the sixteenth century. They supplied the growing need for the literate skills lacked by many princes and boyars but required by the nascent chancery system developing to sustain the central authority. They discharged preponderantly civilian duties; a *diak* very rarely led an army. The increasing tension between the grand princes and their leading boyars, a problem to which Soloviev devotes much attention, was a further reason for the rise of *diaki.* In need of servitors whose first loyalty was to the royal house, the grand princes began promoting men of non-boyar, non-princely origin (Adashev is a good example) as a counterpoise to the power and strength of the great traditional houses. It was unprecedented for a man of rank to serve as a *diak.* Accordingly, the term is rendered as *secretary* when the context emphasizes the incumbent's clerical responsibilities, or as *official* or *state secretary* when reference is more general.

Transliteration of proper and geographic names is always a problem. This translation has used initial *ya* and *yu*, and terminal *y* and *i* to designate various endings, such as *ii* and *yi*. A few common names have been anglicized, but most are retained in their original form. Soloviev calls Ivan the Terrible *John*, a practice that has not been followed. The ubiquitous soft-sign has been omitted. Distances have been given in miles when that term is employed by the author, although the English mile is not necessarily meant; otherwise *verst* has been preferred. Units of measurement are given their English equivalents (see Table of Equivalents), and the monetary units of Muscovy and Lithuania are uniformly rendered in rubles and kopecks. Country of origin determines the form of foreign names, except for Tatars, whose names are reproduced as Soloviev wrote them. Thus names of Polish origin such as Jan or Stanislaw are reproduced in Polish form. Lithuanian names retain their Russian form, a procedure which seems an appropriate way to reflect the official status the Russian language enjoyed in the grand duchy of Lithuania in the sixteenth century. Capitalization as found in quotations is retained, as are the author's italics. The translator has added certain explanatory notes of a general nature to the chapters, and has given a few of Soloviev's notes, most of which, however, have been omitted due to their highly specialized bibliographic character.

I wish to thank Ms. Jacalyn Kenneth of the MTST center of the California State College, Bakersfield, who cheerfully and efficiently typed the manuscript. My wife, Ann Lett Graham, provided warm encouragement as I wrought "only a translation," a labor more arduous than some suppose.

Hugh F. Graham

INTRODUCTION

Sergei Mikhailovich Soloviev (1820-1879) deserves the reputation he has acquired as an outstanding historian of Russia. The scope of his work, the exhaustiveness of his treatment, and the sweep of his design have expanded and deepened general awareness and appreciation of Russian history. Succeeding generations of historians owe a considerable debt to him. It is thus appropriate to preface the first English edition of a segment of S.M. Soloviev's *History of Russia from Earliest Times* with a few remarks about the man, his ideas, and his era.

In spite (or perhaps because) of the best efforts Tsar Nicholas I could make during the second quarter of the nineteenth century to inhibit expression and exchange of ideas, those decades, the formative years in Soloviev's life, were filled with ideological ferment. Champions of the existing order articulated their beliefs in the vague formulation of Orthodoxy, Autocracy and Nationality, but concerned members of Russia's burgeoning intelligentsia, in growing numbers and with increasing insistence, demanded thoroughgoing reform. All factions agreed that abolition of serfdom constituted the preliminary step to further action, although the political reforms they contemplated ranged from peasant socialism to limited constitutional monarchy. Consideration of such practical questions inevitably led to more abstruse issues, such as the nature of Russia's mission and destiny. Two contradictory trends of thought emerged, and at risk of over-simplification they may be designated the positions adopted by Westerners and Slavophiles. Each side possessed ardent advocates.

The reign of Peter the Great was pivotal in the formulations of both groups. Praising him for having compelled Russia to join Europe, the Westerners asserted that their own time required firmer commitment to the principles Peter had enunciated. The Slavophiles took an opposing view. By callously seeking to destroy the unique civilization Old Muscovy had devised, Peter had distorted and perverted Russia's subsequent development. The solution lay in rededication to the spirit which the Slavophiles assumed to have been present in Old Muscovy before Russia became contaminated by contact with foreigners and their institutions.

The intensity with which the debate was conducted encouraged pamphleteers and publicists to adopt extravagant positions based on flimsy, misleading, or unsubstantiated evidence. Such practice contained important implications for the study of history: in order to determine what Russia's future should be, one must know what Russia's past had been. Responding to this need a growing number of serious scholars, among whom Soloviev took a prominent place, worked to fill the void. The government was not immune; it facilitated the historians' task. The nineteenth century was a golden age of archival exploration. Commissions ransacked public and private repositories, where they discovered a mass of documents, the publication of which substantially increased the fund of primary source material available for the study of Russian history.

Although Soloviev never stood apart from questions agitating society in his own time and often wrote articles and made speeches on topics of current interest, he was the quintessential scholar. He spent his entire life in the university, the library, the archive, and at his writing-desk. The son of a priest, Soloviev obtained a secular education in a Moscow gymnasium, where he first manifested an interest in history. Entering Moscow University in 1838, he completed the history curriculum in 1842. Upon graduation he went abroad for two years as tutor in the family of the wealthy Count Stroganov. He attended lectures by leading scholars in Berlin and Paris, where he had an opportunity to become familiar with the main trends of contemporary historical thought in Western Europe.

On his return to Moscow Soloviev submitted his master's thesis, entitled *Novgorod's Relations with the Grand Princes.* His reputation was now such that the university authorities assigned him to teach a course in Russian history, and his academic career was launched. In 1847 he brilliantly defended his doctoral dissertation, a major study known as *A History of the Relations among the Princes of the House of Rurik.* In that year he also was appointed professor of Russian history at the university, where he trained the next generation of historians. The most distinguished among them was V.O. Kliuchevsky, who eventually succeeded to Soloviev's chair.

In 1851 Soloviev began to compose his *History of Russia from Earliest Times,* which was to engross him for the remainder of his life. Producing a volume each year during the next twenty-nine years, he reached 1775; only death prevented him from bringing the account down to his own time. Although the hectic tempo of publication denied Soloviev an opportunity to refine and polish his narrative, the *History* remains a monument of Russian historiography. One salient characteristic, which set it apart from the work of his predecessors, was Soloviev's determined, if not always fully realized, attempt to submit a welter of disparate facts to an overall design. It is instructive to consider certain underlying assumptions Soloviev utilized in pursuit of his goal.

Soloviev believed that historians must rigorously eschew the form assumed by the debate on Russia's role in the world prevalent in his own time. By this he meant that the past may not be judged by the present and that it is improper to evaluate the past in the light of contemporary aspirations. He insisted that historical narrative be based on primary sources. While an undergraduate he had criticized certain of his professors for what he considered to be their lack of method and critical approach to their topic. His views led him to the conclusion that a historian, conscientiously utilizing the available sources of a bygone era, must make every effort to understand and appraise the period he studies solely in terms of its comprehension of itself. Soloviev had, however, no intention of implying that past epochs were isolated; each one has formed an integral strand in the chain of the total development of history, which is in a state of constant evolution. In this Soloviev's debt to Hegel is obvious; it comes as no surprise that Soloviev was a long and close student of Hegel's *Philosophy of History.*

Soloviev used this unifying principle as an organizational device around which to structure the history of Russia. By fusing Hegelian concepts with the theme of Russia's unique mission inherent in the thought of the Slavophiles, which was freer from the assumption of Russian inferiority than that implicit in the formulation of the Westerners, Soloviev was able to approach Russia's past in an optimistic spirit. However, he never shrank from criticizing the Slavophiles for the vague generalizations about Old Muscovy, unsubstantiated by the sources, which they were prone to make, and Peter the Great, the reforming tsar, was one of his chief heroes.

Soloviev identified three phenomena which he believed had exercised a decisive influence in shaping Russian history. Geography was a basic factor. The absence of natural boundaries rendered the European Russian plain vulnerable to attack, and it was exposed to depredations by successive waves of steppe nomads, which culminated in the Mongol-Tatar invasion of the mid-thirteenth century. The ensuing two hundred and fifty years of Tatar domination proved costly to Russia, since the country suffered a perpetual drain on its resources while striving to throw off the foreign yoke. The encounter did not end then. Soloviev termed this contest and Moscow's subsequent strife with the Tatar principalities to regain lost territory the struggle of the forest with the steppe. It assumed a variety of forms, two of which Soloviev discusses in the present section: the clashes with the Tatars of the Crimea and Kazan, and the activity of the cossacks on the southern frontiers.

Soloviev's second conviction, undoubtedly a fruit of his sojourn abroad, was that no people could develop in isolation; Russia was part of Europe. This is the reason why Soloviev devotes the considerable attention to Russia's relations with Lithuania and Poland that he does in this part of his *History*. The third factor Soloviev considered important derives from the preceding two. He rejected rigid periodization in favor of Hegel's notion that history is a series of comings-to-be and passings-away: what has gone before leads imperceptibly to what is to come. Nevertheless, certain developments could be discerned within this scheme. The kinship system on which society was based in Kievan times was steadily breaking down, and it continued to dissolve after the focus of power shifted to the northeast. The rise of Moscow corresponded to the beginnings of governmental centralization, a tendency which representatives of the old kinship order were bound to resist, but with increasing lack of success, until Muscovite society had been largely transformed by the reign of Vasily III. In this context Soloviev saw geography determining social order; the forest's struggle with the steppe, and Muscovy's later contest with Lithuania and Poland rendered centralized administration a pre-condition for survival. Soloviev considered the process beneficial, as may be inferred from the strictures he passes on the boyar regime in the present section.

This approach may seem to be a justification of the existing order, but Soloviev was not a member of the statist, or juridical school of history espoused by some nineteenth-century Russian writers, who regarded the state, and the ruler who exemplified it, as an uncontrollable independent force that determined the destiny of the people. He considered a state to be no more than a distillation of the experience of the people who inhabited it, through which they expressed themselves in their own idiom.

Soloviev's line of reasoning has led to the assertion that he was a determinist, who allowed little scope for the role of a strong creative personality. Careful perusal of his *History,* including the present section of it, militates against this assumption. A dichotomy exists between Soloviev's views and the way in which he presents them. Advancing his narrative almost exclusively in terms of the statements, pronouncements and activities of grand princes, kings and khans, and concentrating mainly on political, diplomatic and military issues, Soloviev allowed the history of Russia to unfold through the eyes of its rulers, and never clarified the ambiguous relationship between the specific and the general. The present section provides an example. Soloviev sketched a psychological portrait of the young Ivan the Terrible in considerable detail because he saw the ruler's temperament as the key to his subsequent actions. In many other instances as well Soloviev depicted the grand princes and other rulers as leaders whose conscious decisions informed, shaped and controlled the destinies of their peoples rather than as men simply reacting to the operation of impersonal forces.

Soloviev's *History* set a new critical standard for detailed sober analysis, which subsequent historians were quick to emulate. His uncompromising insistence that historical narrative must be based on primary sources won wide acceptance. Anyone who pauses to reflect on the number of common assumptions about Russian history which Soloviev was the first to articulate will soon recognize how influential he has been in forming modern attitudes to Russia's past.

It is hoped that these general observations will aid in consideration of the portion of Soloviev's *History* presented here. Next, a few comments on Vasily III's reign will be followed by reference to main themes which Soloviev develops in the five chapters that comprise this segment of his *History*.

The first four decades of the sixteenth century usually receive cursory treatment in general histories of Russia. A good reason for this has been advanced by George Vernadsky, who owed much to Soloviev in terms of his conception of Russian history and the organization of his work. In *Russia at the Dawn of the Modern Age* (New Haven & London, 1959, p. 134) he wrote:

Vasili III's personality, as well as the significance of his rule, has been obscured by the period of constructive achievements of the preceding reign (his father, Ivan III) and by the intense drama of the subsequent age (his son, Ivan IV). Hemmed in between the two Ivans, Vasili seems at first glance a colorless character, and his reign is often characterized merely as a continuation of his father's or a prelude to his son's. One is inclined to speak of his age as a period of transition, a term to which the historian often has recourse when not willing to take the trouble to analyze properly a stage of historical development.

As the present chapters demonstrate, Soloviev took the trouble to make an exhaustive analysis of Vasily's reign. In the process he provided rich information about the grand duchy of Moscow and its three major (and dangerous) neighbors, the grand duchy of Lithuania, and the khanates of the Crimea and Kazan. Foreign relations, diplomacy and war predominate, but Soloviev has not neglected other topics. He discusses church affairs, intellectual life, legal systems, forms of land tenure, economic conditions, and kinds and degrees of local governance, and includes detail concerning the life of the people. He has not ignored the peasants, although his inquiries into their status were not as comprehensive as later trends in Russian historiography have been inclined to demand. An outstanding feature of his *History* is the extensive use Soloviev has made of direct quotations from original sources, most frequently chronicles, but also diplomatic notes, decrees, statutes and charters. He has revised the archaic language of the original documents while preserving their spirit and flavor.

In the last two chapters Soloviev discusses the childhood of Ivan the Terrible. His presentation of the ways in which the experiences of Ivan's formative years affected his character has won wide acceptance. Other views exist, but Soloviev's interpretation has stood the test of time well. It is also instructive to compare Soloviev's analysis of Vasily's reign with a recent study by a leading Soviet authority on the sixteenth century, A.A. Zimin's *Russia on the Threshold of a New Era* (1972). Zimin criticizes Soloviev for viewing Vasily's epoch exclusively through the eyes of the grand prince and the great boyars, but perusal of his monograph reveals that Zimin has covered much the same ground in much the same way. This constitutes impressive testimony to the validity of the approach to Russian history that Soloviev pioneered, and which succeeding generations of historians have in large measure come to accept.

The first chapter in this portion of Soloviev's *History* is entitled *Pskov*, but the range of material contained in it reaches much further. The chapter is actually a study in the foreign relations of the grand duchy of Muscovy during the earlier period of Vasily's reign. As such, it concentrates attention on the constant clashes between Muscovy and its three chief foes, the Tatar enclaves of Kazan and the Crimea, and the grand duchy of Lithuania. Kazan not only barred Muscovite expansion to the east and south along the Volga, but continued to make punishing raids into territories adjacent to it controlled by Moscow. More serious was the danger from the Crimea. Operating from their secure and secluded base far to the south, the Crimean Tatars both interdicted Moscow from the steppeland and restricted the grand prince's hegemony to a narrow area extending no more than twenty or thirty miles south of Moscow itself. There Vasily had to maintain an elaborate and costly system of defense lines along the Oka river, which were not always effective in preventing Crimean raiders from ranging further north in search of plunder. Simultaneously, the growing convergence of ruling forces in the kingdom of Poland and the grand duchy of Lithuania made increasing military strength available to the latter to deploy in the struggle with Moscow that religious differences constantly exacerbated.

One theme in this chapter is the alternating rhythm of Moscow's relations with its enemies. When the Tatars were quiet Vasily proceeded against Lithuania, but when the Tatars were menacing he came to terms with Lithuania. Another theme is the contrast between old and new. Moscow's contest with the Tatars represented the old involvement of the forest with the steppe, as Vasily struggled to maintain parity with these antagonists. The destructive plundering raids and the insults which Moscow's envoys to the Crimea were patiently forced to endure are forceful reminders of the great amount of energy Moscow was obliged to expend upon the Tatar problem.

Moscow's developing struggle with Lithuania represents the new, European aspect of Russia's position. One of the major merits of Soloviev's *History* is the close attention the work devotes to this region, which the author calls West Russia. Carefully examining the composition of this hybrid state Soloviev provides glimpses of the fatal religious division that was to play so large a part in its destruction. The fascinating career of Prince Mikhail Glinsky, which Soloviev carefully analyzes, demonstrates how the destinies of the eastern and western halves of the European Russian plain were inextricably linked, far more than the two rulers, each seeking to embarrass and discomfit the other, were able to comprehend.

Soloviev devotes the last part of this chapter to Pskov. Vasily's actions are shown to be the final fruition of his father's policy of incorporating into the grand duchy of Muscovy adjacent realms possessing potential to become alternative power centers. Ivan III had subdued formidable Novgorod; now his son deals with Novgorod's "younger brother." Soloviev's detailed description of the grand prince's actions draws attention to the policy of centralization which Moscow was striving to establish throughout the territory over which the grand duchy had asserted its jurisdiction.

The second chapter, like the first, is devoted to foreign affairs. Moscow's capture of Smolensk, the important West Russian city affording Lithuania control of the upper Dnieper river region, and Vasily's inconclusive struggle with the Tatars of Kazan constitute the most significant events in the series of successes and reverses Muscovy experienced at this time. Soloviev capaciously analyzes these and other developments, each of which contributed to the final phase of the "gathering of the Russian lands" and the emergence of Muscovy as an autonomous power center in Eastern Europe. The capture of Smolensk serves as well as any incident to illustrate the growing strength of Muscovy. The Lithuanians acknowledged their awareness of it by the fierce attempts they made to recover the city and the intransigent position they adopted in negotiations concerning it. Soloviev employs Vasily's equally determined insistence on holding Smolensk as a means to demonstrate what he considered to be the extraordinary tenacity displayed by the grand princes of Muscovy in acquiring their "patrimony," which, they believed, comprehended no less than the entire territory once under the control of the original Kievan state. Vasily manifested a comparable spirit in dealing with the Tatars. His envoys to the Crimea and Kazan might endure insult and danger, or even lose their lives, but a combination of patience and diplomacy, and a judicious use of force enabled Vasily to dissipate the threat posed by an alliance of the major Tatar enclaves directed against Moscow.

A related point deserves attention. At the battle of Orsha in 1514 the Lithuanians inflicted severe losses on the Muscovite army and Mohammed-Girey's raid in 1521 caused heavy damage to Moscow itself, but in neither instance were the Lithuanians or the Tatars able to profit from their success. Moscow quickly rebounded; defeats that might previously have proved unqualified disasters now amounted to no more than temporary setbacks.

Muscovy had not yet fully entered the emerging concert of European powers. Moscow's involvement with other European countries was still conditioned by its relations with Lithuania, as Soloviev reveals in his account of the negotiations between Vasily and representatives of Maximilian, the Holy Roman Emperor, whose concern was to resolve, if he could, the conflict between Moscow and Lithuania. The emperor's principal negotiator was Baron Sigismund von Herberstein, whose *Commentary* on Muscovite affairs, which first appeared in 1549, entitles him to be considered as the first foreign Slavic scholar. Soloviev foreshadows Moscow's future prominence when he quotes Maximilian's statement that he was not anxious to help Russia at the expense of Poland-Lithuania, and when he analyzes the reasons for assuming that conflicts between Russia and Turkey would eventually take place.

Soloviev portrays Vasily as a shrewd and vigorous monarch, under whose administration Muscovy continued to advance and consolidate its position. It is a record of success; Soloviev handles his narrative well, and this chapter does much to retrieve Grand Prince Vasily from the obscurity to which his presence between his distinguished father and his turbulent son consigned him. Woven into the analysis are parenthetic allusions to a problem to which Ivan the Terrible eventually devoted a good part of his life in search of a solution, the growing boyar alienation from the new order based on the grand princes' sovereign authority. When describing quarrels over precedence in rank, provoked by jealousy, in which commanders in the field indulged, Soloviev shows that the way in which the Muscovite army was organized on the genealogical principle contributed to its defeat at Orsha and had much to do with the failure to bring the Kazan campaign to a satisfactory conclusion.

In the long third chapter Soloviev abandons his concentration on Muscovy's foreign relations in order to provide descriptive detail concerning the life of the peoples inhabiting Muscovy and Lithuania in the first half of the sixteenth century. He tries to make Grand Prince Vasily come alive to the reader, although he acknowledges the considerable difficulty involved in doing so. This is strikingly revealed in the lengthy account, based on a document that described, at times in agonizing detail, the grand prince's final illness and death. Soloviev also explores Vasily's relations with members of his family and mentions his amusements and recreations. To round out the portrait the author makes an interesting attempt to locate Vasily's position in Russian history, and this in turn leads him to evaluate the careers of certain previous grand princes. This analysis serves as a sterling illustration of Soloviev's view that the course of Russian history constituted a slow and inexorable forward movement that triumphed over every obstacle. Another example is Soloviev's observations on the rise of the cossacks. They reflect the historian's admiration for the bold independent frontiersman, whose settlement of the borderlands played a vital role in the forest's return to the steppe. Soloviev displays the religious convictions that formed part of his temperament when he praises the grand princes for encouraging missionary activity among the pagan tribes of the far northeast, and he reveals his sensitivity to Russia's relationship with Europe when observing in this connection that the princes did so while they themselves were seeking "to appropriate the fruits of European civility."

In his discussion of church and related intellectual affairs, to which he devotes considerable attention in this chapter, Soloviev quotes from Nil of Sorsk's writings on mystic communion and the arguments advanced against monastery landowning by Vassian Patrikeev, but his portrait of Joseph of Volokolamsk, an ardent champion of the existing order, appears fuller and more sympathetic. Quoting extensively from primary sources, such as official charters and decrees, Soloviev provides valuable information about Muscovy's natural resources and economy and affords glimpses of peasant and merchant life.

Soloviev performs an important service by stressing developments, legal or otherwise, in the grand duchy of Lithuania. The examples he furnishes again reveal the essential homogeneity of East and West Russia, although its people were politically separated. His observations facilitate an understanding of why Ukrainians and other West Russians were able to carve a niche for themselves in the Russian empire and exercise considerable influence on its development after the bulk of this region passed under Moscow's control a little more than a century later.

Soloviev also provides a mass of information about a host of other disparate subjects, which, taken together, sketches a revealing picture of what society was then like in the European Russian plain. However, the modern reader may experience some frustration over the historian's failure to group his vignettes around central themes, and may question the necessity of including the uncompromisingly long lists of items which are scattered throughout the chapter.

The fourth chapter deals with the first phase of Ivan IV's minority, which lasted to the death of his mother, Grand Princess Elena, in 1538. It is a chronicle of intrigue; in Soloviev's perception it is the beginning of the final round in the contest between the monarchy, determined to complete administrative centralization, and representatives of the great houses, who endeavored to take advantage of the ruler's minority to advance their own interests in the name of the traditional prerogative of princely independence. The first challenge during this phase of the struggle emanated from the grand prince's close relatives, the clearest example of which was the abortive revolt of his uncle, Prince Andrei of Staritsa, in 1537. It is a measure of Ivan's good fortune that so dangerous an opposition movement was led by weak, indecisive men—Prince Andrei in this instance and his son Vladimir, facing the mature Ivan two decades later.

In this round the contestants were limited to achieving power behind the throne by influencing the regent. Like other early rulers of Muscovy, Elena is featureless; the laconic sources provide no picture of her individual character and temperament. Soloviev is charitable to her. Contemporaries frequently attributed the swift rise of Telepnev-Obolensky to the same causes that advanced the interests of the Orlov brothers at the court of Catherine the Great.

The internecine rivalries, the constant disturbances, and the defection of such able and determined intriguers as Prince Semen Belsky might have been expected to weaken Moscow's ability to conduct an effective foreign policy, but, as the appropriate sections in this chapter demonstrate, Muscovite military power and diplomatic skill were as strong and supple as ever. The state continued to enjoy success in the struggle with Lithuania and managed to prevent the Tatars from taking advantage of a fortuituous turn of events that enabled the Crimea and Kazan temporarily to make common cause.

True to his principles, Soloviev closely adheres to the sources, chronicles and official documents. They refer constantly to what the grand prince did or said, but this statement, taken literally, is obviously inapplicable to a ruler less than ten years of age. The boyars who composed the documents, which scribes copied, remain unknown.

Soloviev integrates foreign affairs and domestic developments somewhat more fully in the last chapter of this part of his *History* than he has done before. He continues to analyze Moscow's contest with Lithuania, the Crimea, and Kazan while developing two main themes in domestic politics. He shows how the great boyar families, particularly the faction led by the Shuisky princes, formed combinations and resorted to violence in order to acquire power, and describes the maturing of the young ruler Ivan until he attained a position of decisive influence in the power equation.

The chronic uncertainty and strife in the capital still did not seriously affect Moscow's relations with neighboring states. Lithuania deemed it advisable to avoid war and renewed the truce. Raiders harried the eastern borderlands, but Moscow succeeded in keeping Kazan off balance by pitting one dissident faction in that city against the other. Prince Semen Belsky, the renegade of whose colorful career Soloviev gives highlights, persuaded the Crimean khan to lead a large force to attack the Oka defense line, but the brief unstable regime headed by Prince Ivan Belsky and Metropolitan Ioasaf scored a considerable victory over the Tatars in 1541. As was true of Elena's regency, no matter who held power for the moment in the capital, Moscow's capacity to mount an effective foreign policy remained impressive.

On the domestic scene Soloviev approaches what he saw as the final stage in the transformation of Russia into a centralized autocracy superseding the congeries of autonomous and semi-autonomous principalities of which the country had been originally composed. The monarchy was the catalyst and the boyar factions represented the forces of the old kinship order. Their behavior during Ivan's minority, which is described in considerable detail, furnished the author with abundant material for his condemnation of the boyars as men of anachronistic, anarchic views, opponents of the basic thrust of Russian history, whose endeavors were thereby doomed to failure.

In sketching the early years of the future Ivan the Terrible, to which he devotes considerable attention, Soloviev stresses the view that events occurring during Ivan's childhood played a decisive role in moulding the young tsar's nature and temperament. Pertinent in this context were the death of his parents, which prematurely thrust Ivan into the conduct of affairs, and the indifference, neglect and arrogant behavior of the boyars, who encouraged Ivan to throw off restraint. The boy was endowed with what Soloviev considered to be a bright, passionate and irritable temperament, and the combination of lack of supervision and fostering indulgence made the tsar suspicious, secretive, and unstable. Soloviev was impressed with Ivan's quick intellect, his voracious reading, and his theoretical formulation of the principles of autocracy.

Ivan's increasing alienation from the boyars left him open to other influences, such as the positive ones exercised by the priest Silvester and Alexis Adashev. With Ivan's summary arrest and execution of Prince Andrei Shuisky, the leader of the major boyar faction, the stage was set for the final development of a genuine monarchy in Russia. On this note this portion of Soloviev's *History* logically comes to a close.

History of Russia

Volume 9

The Age of Vasily III

I

PSKOV

Death prevented Ivan from punishing his tributary, the ruler of Kazan, for his rupture with Moscow. Coming to power in autumn, 1505, Vasily planned to launch an expedition by water against Mohammed-Amin the following spring.[1] In April of 1506 the grand prince's brother, Dmitry Ivanovich, and the commander, Prince Fedor Ivanovich Belsky, set out with a land and river force while a cavalry detachment proceeded overland under the command of Prince Alexander Vladimirovich Rostovsky. The land and naval force anchored off Kazan on May 22, and in spite of the intense heat Prince Dmitry lost no time disembarking his men and marching against the city. The Tatars came out to engage them, while another unit of the Kazan forces rode secretly to their rear and cut them off from their vessels. The Russians sustained a severe defeat. Many soldiers were killed, many were captured, and many drowned in Lake Pogany.

As soon as he learned of the disaster the grand prince told Prince Vasily Danilovich Kholmsky and other officers to proceed to Kazan, and instructed his brother not to renew the attack until Kholmsky arrived. When the cavalry led by the prince of Rostov came up on June 22, Dmitry threw restraint to the winds and ordered his armies to attack the city. At first successful, subsequently he was defeated and forced to withdraw after losing his artillery and siege engines. The story goes that the people of Kazan had lost all hope of defeating the Russians in the field and resorted to subterfuge. They made a camp and then abandoned it, pretending to be overcome with terror. Hoping for booty the Russians began plundering the camp, and the army of Kazan took advantage of the situation to destroy them. Prince Dmitry retired to Nizhny Novgorod. Another unit of the Muscovite army, led by the Tatar prince, Yan-Ali, and Commander Kiselev, was on its way to Murom when it was overtaken by the forces of Kazan.[2] They were beaten back, and the detachment reached Murom in good order.

Preparations for the next spring's campaign were underway when, in March of 1507 Mohammed-Amin, seeking to avoid hostilities, petitioned Moscow and asked Vasily to make peace and restore the friendly relations that had existed during the reign of the latter's father, Grand Prince Ivan. In return he pledged to free ambassador Yaropkin and all prisoners he had taken during the course of the war. Vasily took counsel with his brothers and his boyars and agreed, because peace would enable him to secure the release of Christian souls fallen into Muslim hands and advance the general good of Christendom.

WAR WITH LITHUANIA

The grand prince had other compelling reasons for concluding peace and restoring the previous relationship with Kazan. Urgent business required all of Vasily's attention in the west. Alexander of Lithuania had set great store by Ivan's death, particularly because the general view in Lithuania was that the party supporting Ivan's grandson Dmitry had acquired considerable strength and would oppose Vasily's accession to his father's throne.[3] The factionalism anticipated between uncle and nephew would afford Alexander a splendid opportunity to recover the Lithuanian lands Ivan had seized.

On learning of the death of his father-in-law, Alexander informed Plettenberg, master of the Livonian Order, that now was an opportune moment for them to join forces in attacking the *enemy of the Christian faith,* who had done such damage to Lithuania and Livonia alike. The master replied that, favorable as the moment was, he felt constrained to wait for the expiration of the formal sworn truce. It was imprudent to launch a sudden attack on so formidable a foe without clearly ascertaining what attitude the appanage princes might adopt. Plettenberg expected that they would fall out amongst themselves, and their action would furnish an excellent pretext for war.

Alexander and his council acknowledged the justice of these observations, thanked the master for his good advice, and asked him to be sure to provide Lithuania with any information he could obtain concerning disputes among the Muscovite princes. Alexander also told Plettenberg that he was conducting levies in the hope of persuading Muscovite princes living along the frontier and the grand prince's brothers, who lived on small appanages, to come over to him once they witnessed this activity. He asked the master to carry out a similar muster in Livonia in order to alarm the prince of Muscovy and dispose him to make concessions.

As Alexander was preparing his forces for war, reports arrived that all was quiet in Muscovy. Vasily sat on his father's throne and Ivan III's grandson Dmitry remained in close confinement. All hope disappeared that internal dissension would force Vasily to make concessions. When Alexander's envoys declared that there could be no peace until Vasily restored all the Lithuanian territory Ivan had acquired, the boyars answered as they had before: the grand prince held no land not his own and could not yield what he did not have. As his father had done, Vasily reminded Alexander that he must not force Elena[4] to become a Catholic.

Alexander failed to derive any advantage from Ivan's death and died himself in August, 1506. Vasily tried to take advantage of his brother-in-law's death without issue in order to bring about a peaceful union of Lithuania and Muscovy. He told his sister to ask the bishop, the magnates, the council, and the entire people to choose him, Vasily, as their ruler, and to serve him. He told them they need not fear for their faith, as he had no intention of attacking it. The situation would remain as it had been during Alexander's reign, and he was prepared to make further concessions. Vasily made the same appeal to Prince Voitekh, bishop of Vilna, Lord Nicholas Radziwill and to the whole council, calling upon them to make him ruler of Lithuania. Elena replied that Alexander had designated his brother Sigismund as his successor, but serious domestic disturbances broke out in Lithuania of which Vasily hoped to take advantage.

GLINSKY

Prince Mikhail Glinsky had been a favorite of the late King Alexander. A descendant of a Tatar prince who settled in Lithuania in Vitovt's time, he was marshal of the court and had spent considerable time abroad, in Italy, Spain, and at the court of Emperor Maximilian. Everywhere he went he won favor and respect for his intelligence, education, and military skill; not surprisingly he surpassed the other Lithuanian nobles and won Alexander's full confidence. The owner of enormous estates and many fortresses, which amounted to almost half of Lithuania, Glinsky had acquired a large number of adherents, most of whom were Russians. Such might aroused the envy of the rest of the Lithuanian nobles, who feared that Glinsky would win control of the whole grand duchy and transfer its capital to Russia. This was the source of the hostility which the other members of the council of Lithuania manifested towards Glinsky.

Their enmity intensified when Alexander acceded to Glinsky's request to take the town of Lida away from the nobleman Ilinich and give it to Andrei Drozhzha, one of Glinsky's supporters. Ilinich complained to the Lithuanian magnates who previously had figured in Muscovite affairs: Voitekh Tabor, the bishop, and Nicholas Radziwill, the commander, of Vilna, Jan Zaberezski, or Zabrzhezinsky, the commander of Trokai, Stanislaw Janowicz, the governor of Samogitia, Stanislaw Glebowicz, commander of Polotsk, and Stanislaw Petrowicz Kiszka, governor of Smolensk. When these men elevated Alexander to the throne of Lithuania they obliged him not to deprive any individual of his estate unless he were charged with criminal acts involving loss of rank or life. Basing their position on this understanding, the magnates refused to allow Andrei Drozhzha to take possession of Lida and restored the town to Ilinich.

Alexander was furious and Glinsky naturally did all he could to inflame the king's anger. The story goes that he kept telling the king that the grand duchy would have no peace as long as these nobles lived in Lithuania. He so aroused the king that Alexander summoned the nobles to a diet in Brest, where he planned to confine them to a fortress and condemn them to death. Warned of their danger by Laski, the chancellor of Poland, they refused to enter the fortress and thus frustrated the king's intention. Alexander had to content himself with removing Jan Zaberezski, Glinsky's chief enemy, from the command of Trokai, arresting and imprisoning Ilinich, and banishing the others from his presence. The Polish magnates later prevailed upon the king to forgive them.

ALEXANDER'S DEATH AND SIGISMUND'S ACCESSION

This was the situation when Alexander was stricken with a fatal illness. The final act of his life was to place an army under Glinsky's command to attack the bands of Crimean Tatars ravaging Lithuania. Glinsky brilliantly defeated the invaders, but his victory, which delivered the country from the savage Tatars, made Glinsky even more dangerous in the eyes of the Lithuanian magnates. As soon as Alexander died a dispute broke out concerning the place of his interment. Laski, the Polish chancellor, wanted to bury the king in Cracow, in accordance with the deceased's own wishes, but the Lithuanian magnates insisted that Alexander be buried in Vilna. They feared that Glinsky would take advantage of their absence, while they were escorting the body to Cracow, to seize Vilna with his Russian troops.

Their alarm was without foundation. Sigismund, Alexander's brother, soon arrived in Vilna, and Glinsky was the first to greet him. Aware that the new grand prince had been warned against him, Glinsky made a fulsome speech, in which he sought to clear himself of suspicion of plotting to seize the grand ducal throne, and promised to be a faithful servitor. In a courteous reply Sigismund thanked Glinsky for his expressions of loyalty. The joyful haste with which the Lithuanian nobility recognized Sigismund and proceeded to crown him in Vilna can readily be imagined. The Polish diet quickly followed suit and declared him king.

Plettenberg's perceptive advice, Vasily's untroubled accession to his father's throne, the Tatar attacks, and finally illness had caused Alexander to postpone war with Muscovy. Sigismund considered circumstances early in 1507 propitious for celebrating his accession with a successful war against the foe. Vasily's campaign against Kazan had not gone well and the grand prince was again obliged to make substantial efforts to improve his position in the east. Relations between Moscow and the Crimea had deteriorated; the khan was now prepared to assist his stepson, the ruler of Kazan, and to cooperate with Lithuania against Muscovy. Meeting on February 2, 1507, the Vilna diet ordered a troop muster on Easter Sunday. The diet's resolution declared: "We have decreed so short a period of time in order to prevent the enemy of our sovereign, when he learns of our sovereign's desire to wage war to recover his lands, from stealing a march upon us and attacking first."

Sigismund informed Plettenberg that he had concluded an alliance with the Crimean khan against Muscovy, and envoys of the khan of Kazan were urging Lithuania to take advantage of the splendid opportunity to join them in an attack on Moscow: their ruler had defeated the Muscovite forces four times, routed the grand prince's brother and his army of 50,000 men, and was constantly ravaging Muscovite territory. Sigismund also told Plettenberg he had dispatched envoys to the Crimea and Kazan to arouse the Tatars against Vasily and ordered his subjects to be ready to move on Easter Sunday. He wished to attack the enemy with all his strength, because he was convinced that conditions for war with Muscovy had never been more favorable.

After making these arrangements Sigismund sent envoys to ascertain how matters stood at the court in Moscow. They informed Vasily of Alexander's death and Sigismund's accession, and in the latter's name declared that Grand Prince Vasily Vasilievich and King Casimir had concluded a perpetual peace, the terms of which bound both signatories not to occupy the lands and waters belonging to the other. They went on to say that King Casimir had scrupulously adhered to the terms of the treaty but the Muscovites had violated its provisions. The honorable behavior of Kings Casimir and Alexander was universally recognized;

thus, Sigismund was calling upon Grand Prince Vasily to cede all the Lithuanian towns, estates, lands and waters his father had occupied during previous wars and free all Lithuanian prisoners, in an effort to staunch the flow of Christian blood. His cause was just, and the king placed his hopes in God. This amounted to a clear threat that if Vasily refused to meet these demands, a declaration of war was imminent. As a final item the envoys complained that Muscovites had seized four estates in the Smolensk district, and the forces inhabiting the Dorogobuzh region were creating incidents along the Lithuanian frontier.

Sigismund was as mistaken as Alexander had been in his belief that this was an auspicious moment to attack Muscovy. Prior to the arrival of the king's envoys, representatives from Kazan had brought a peace proposal to the grand prince. Freed from anxiety in this quarter Vasily was encouraged to return to Sigismund's envoys the traditional reply: "We hold no towns, estates, lands or waters belonging to Sigismund or to his ancestors. By God's will we hold our ancestral towns, estates, lands, and waters, which our father, the grand prince, graciously bequeathed to us, and which God gave us. Since the days of our ancestors the whole Russian land has been our patrimony."

Vasily went further. Replying to Sigismund's haughty summons he issued a stern call to war of his own, unless the king chose to accept terms agreeable to him. He said to the envoys: "Like our father, we too swore an oath to our brother-in-law Alexander when we made the peace treaty, and we fully adhered to its terms until his death, but we have no treaty with King Sigismund. You say King Sigismund desires to maintain good and peaceful relations with us. We too wish peace with him, but only on terms that are agreeable to us." Vasily listed the affronts the Lithuanians had given the Russians, such as the occupation of more than one hundred hamlets and villages in the Briansk district, robbing merchants from Kozelsk, Aleksin, Kaluga and Pskov, and seizing estates belonging to Prince Belsky. He told them to inform the king that the latter must fully atone for all these actions otherwise he, Vasily, would take matters into his own hands. Dismissing the envoys the grand prince personally told them to remind Sigismund that his [Vasily's] sister, Queen Elena, was to remain Orthodox. Sigismund must esteem, protect and honor her, and not force her to become a Catholic.

GLINSKY REVOLTS AGAINST SIGISMUND

These negotiations took place in March, 1507. By April 29 Muscovite detachments had invaded Lithuania. Sigismund had hoped that he could attack Muscovy at a favorable moment, but circumstances had changed dramatically in Vasily's favor, and the grand prince was not slow to take advantage of them. Prince Mikhail Glinsky appeared to have won Sigismund's approval; but although the new king was not as suspicious of Glinsky as were the Lithuanian magnates, he did not trust him as much as King Alexander had done. This was enough to encourage Glinsky's enemies and disturb Glinsky, who felt that his present position, when compared with the eminence he had enjoyed during the whole of Alexander's reign, was the equivalent of royal disfavor. Glinsky was not permitted to remain isolated on his estates. Early in 1507 Sigismund assigned Glinsky's brother, Prince Ivan Lvovich, the vicegerent of Kiev, to Novgorod Litovsky. In the rescript the king gave Prince Ivan he vainly tried to claim that the assignment was not a diminution of the latter's position. He would retain his titles and receive a seat in the council next in importance to the one held by the governor of Samogitia.

This failed of its effect, for the insult was obvious. Everyone continued to suspect that the Glinsky family was trying to restore the Kievan state and believed that therefore Kiev could no longer remain under their control. His sworn foe, Jan Zaberezski, openly called Prince Mikhail a traitor. Glinsky demanded a hearing before the king. Occupied with other matters of moment, Sigismund kept putting it off, for however enticing the prospect, the evidence against Glinsky was inadequate. The king refused to sacrifice Zaberezski to Glinsky, but Prince Mikhail was understandably unwilling to wait. He went to Hungary and asked Sigismund's brother, Ladislas, the king of Hungary, to intervene. Ladislas' mediation was of no help. Finally Glinsky said to the king: "You are forcing me to perform an action both of us will later greatly regret." He withdrew to his estates and began corresponding with the grand prince of Muscovy, who promised to help him to deal with all his enemies.[5]

In writing to Moscow Glinsky stated that the present moment was highly favorable both to him and to the grand prince, because Lithuania had not yet mustered its forces and no help could be expected from elsewhere. Vasily replied that he would soon send forces into Lithuania, where Glinsky should quickly initiate operations. In response to this hint, Glinsky and 700 cavalrymen crossed the river Nieman and appeared before Zaberezski's estate near Grodno. That night Glinsky ordered the residence surrounded. Two foreigners in Glinsky's service carried out their master's sanguinary vengeance. A German named Schleinitz burst into Zaberezski's bedroom and a Turk cut off his head and brought it to his master on his sabre. Glinsky carried the head on a pole four miles before he hurled it into a lake. After killing his chief enemy Glinsky dispatched cavalry to seek out and punish other Lithuanian magnates hostile to him while he, his forces constantly growing, withdrew to Novgorod Litovsky.

Sigismund now adopted a different attitude to Moscow. Dispatching a second group of envoys to negotiate peace, he proposed that Mengli-Girey, the khan of the Crimea, should serve as mediator. At that same time he attempted to arouse Vasily's brother, Prince Yury Ivanovich of Dmitrov, against the grand prince. Lithuanian representatives asked Yury to help arrange peace between Muscovy and Lithuania, but this was merely a pretext for secret negotiations, in which Sigismund said: "Our brother, we know that with God's grace you conduct your affairs wisely and advance them intelligently, as befits the son of a mighty ruler. Rumors reach us that many princes and boyars have abandoned your brother, Grand Prince Vasily Ivanovich, and come over to you. We hear only good reports of you, and this gives us great pleasure. We desired to be at peace with your brother, Grand Prince Vasily Ivanovich, and to be allied with him against our common enemies, but he covets our ancestral towns, estates, lands and rivers along our borders and has spurned our offer. Our dear brother, we remember the true and sincere fraternity our ancestors displayed and wish to enjoy good relations with you. To this end we solemnly pledge to consider your friends as our friends and your enemies as our enemies, and stand ready to help you whenever you wish us to do so. In your behalf, our brother, we would ourselves come with all our strength and all our forces to fight for you as we would for ourselves. Should you choose and desire to become our friend, be quick to send an honorable man, a junior boyar, to us. We shall swear in his presence to be your loyal brother and true friend as long as we live."

Prince Yury's response to Sigismund's overtures has not been preserved, but the reply Grand Prince Vasily sent in June, 1507 to his sister Elena, who had intervened in the negotiations, is known. Vasily justified the policy his father had adopted towards King Alexander, and continued: "When our brother-in-law Alexander died and his brother Sigismund took his place, he sent envoys to us. We wanted peace, but he did not. King Sigismund aroused Muslims against Christians and sent a host of soldiers and officers to attack our men and our princes. We sent our officers with a large army. They resisted the king's forces and returned successfully. You mention that Prince Mikhail Glinsky has sent us a petition. It is not merely Prince Glinsky who has petitioned us. Many Russian princes and many Orthodox people say they are under great pressure because of their faith and are forced to become Catholics. They beg us to take pity on them, help, and protect them. We think that even you, our own sister, are under constraint. After our brother-in-law Alexander died, we repeatedly sent men to call upon you and ask you to let us know how you fared; envoys from King Sigismund have visited us frequently, but we have had no news from you. Whenever similar misfortunes have afflicted Russia we have arisen and defended her, and we intend (God willing) to do so in the future. Sister, think of God and of your soul, and remember the injunction we received from our father and mother. Do not become an apostate, forfeit our parents' blessing, or damage our Orthodox faith. You have written to say that we should have a close relationship with King Sigismund. If King Sigismund wants peace and understanding with us, we are willing to come to suitable terms with him."[6]

Sigismund had promised to send new envoys to Moscow, but for some reason failed to do so. In the letter to his sister Vasily mentioned that the forces he had sent into Lithuania had already returned. Lithuanian sources state that the Muscovite officers retreated as soon as they heard the king was approaching. Sigismund took the fortress of Gzykov and destroyed a few villages and estates belonging to Muscovite subjects, but lack of supplies and intense heat compelled him to return to Vilna. Whatever the accuracy of these reports, therewith ended the military activities of 1507.

In the spring of 1508 hostilities resumed with greater intensity. Glinsky caused alarm in Lithuanian Russia, ravaged the estates of the Slutsky and Kopylsky families, and took Turov and Mozyr. Vasily told Glinsky that he was sending troops under the overall command of Prince Vasily Ivanovich Shemiachich to assist him. The grand prince instructed Glinsky to employ these forces only to acquire adjacent towns. He was not to lead them far into the king's territory and should proceed slowly until a second and larger army arrived from Moscow. Glinsky hoped Shemiachich would help him acquire Slutsk, which, as he told Vasily, lay close to the towns he controlled. Some people thought Glinsky was anxious to obtain Slutsk because he wanted to marry Princess Anastasia of Slutsk so as to acquire title to Kiev, which the ancestors of the Slutsk princes had once controlled.

Prince Shemiachich thought he should be further north, the direction from which the Muscovite forces were supposed to come. He decided to move towards Minsk, while carrying out raids deep into Lithuanian territory in an effort to keep the country off balance and prevent an army muster. His troops thrust to within eight miles of Vilna and four

of Novgorod Litovsky, and went as far as Slonim. Glinsky and Shemiachich waited two weeks near Minsk hoping in vain to hear that the
Muscovite army was on its way, but finally had to retire to Borisov.
From here Glinsky sent a letter to the grand prince in which he said
that Vasily ought to respond, not merely because he (Glinsky) was
making this appeal, but in his own interest and on behalf of all oppressed Christians, who reposed their entire hopes in him and God. If
Vasily failed to order his forces to proceed to Minsk with all speed,
Glinsky's brothers and supporters, as well as all Christians, would despair; the towns and estates which had been taken with the help of the
grand prince's forces would be placed in jeopardy, and a splendid military opportunity would have been lost, for campaigns are undertaken in
the summer time.

The grand prince knew the movements of his commanders, Prince
Shchenia of Novgorod, Prince Yakov Zakharevich of Moscow, and Prince
Grigory Fedorovich of Velikie Luki, and instructed Shemiachich and
Glinsky to effect a junction with them at Orsha. The latter set out,
taking Drutsk on the way. Prince Shchenia and his Novgorod troops
reached Orsha when they did, and the combined armies undertook a
siege of the place, which proved unsuccessful. The third commander,
Yakov Zakharevich, halted near Dubrovna. Sometime after June 11,
1508 word came that Sigismund was on his way to relieve Orsha. The
officers withdrew, first to take up a position across the Dnieper, and then
further to Dubrovna, where they remained a week. The king did not
follow them beyond the Dnieper or commit his troops. Lithuanian accounts state that the king did cross the river after his forces had driven
the Russians back from the bank, but night put an end to the fighting.
Glinsky urged the Muscovite commanders to offer battle the next day,
but they refused and withdrew at midnight. The king was reluctant to
pursue them and went back to Smolensk.

Putting distance between their forces and the king on the other side
of the Dnieper by moving southeast from Dubrovna, the Muscovites proceeded towards Mstislavl, where they burned some settlements, and
from there to Krichev. While at Smolensk, Sigismund decided to take
the offensive. His forces were supposed to be under the command of
Prince Konstantin Ostrozhsky, hetman of Lithuania, a refugee from
Muscovy, but a dispute between two noblemen caused serious disturbances in Lithuania and immobilized Ostrozhsky and the main army.
Lithuanian detachments were able to do no more than set fire to Belaia,
overrun Toropets, and occupy Dorogobuzh, which the Russians had

previously burned since they knew they could not hold it. These activities ceased when Vasily advanced his forces to the threatened frontier. The commander at Smolensk, Stanislaw Kiszka, tried to establish himself in Dorogobuzh but fled when he learned a Muscovite army was approaching. The Lithuanian workmen fortifying Dorogobuzh were massacred, and the Lithuanians evacuated Toropets when Shchenia came up.

Sigismund realized he could not win the war. Avoiding pitched battles, the Muscovites had withdrawn from Lithuania, but they were certain to return at the first favorable opportunity. This required the king to maintain large forces on constant alert, a task which domestic disorders made difficult, if not impossible to do. The dispute between the two nobles had aborted Ostrozhsky's campaign; the furor Glinsky had occasioned showed no signs of subsiding, and the towns which had belonged to Muscovy remained under Russian control.

When the Muscovite forces left Lithuania, Prince Mikhail went to Moscow and entered the grand prince's service. Vasily gave him money, horses and armor, and granted him two towns, Maly Yaroslavets and Medynia, on the spot. He also gave him some villages near Moscow and assigned troops to accompany him to Lithuania, where they were to help him protect the towns he controlled there.

ETERNAL PEACE BETWEEN VASILY AND SIGISMUND

Sigismund was forced to end the war in the fall in order to prevent Glinsky from waging a winter campaign to strengthen his position. He sent a courier to Moscow from Smolensk to obtain safe-conducts for his envoys, who arrived on September 19 to conclude a permanent peace. To become free of the threat posed by the Glinsky family and to recover that family's holdings in Lithuania, the king was obliged to make the substantial concession of acknowledging Moscow's permanent control of the lands Ivan had acquired. The harsh terms Lithuania had been obliged to accept when Alexander and Ivan effected their truce became the basis for the permanent settlement negotiated by their successors.

Vasily had got what he wanted. As he intended, the peace was proof that at the moment he held no foreign territory. Both rulers bound themselves to cooperate against all their enemies, including the Tatars, with the exception of Mengli-Girey, khan of the Crimea. Members of the Glinsky family and their followers were guaranteed safe transit from Lithuania to Moscow. Prince Mikhail's premonition had been fulfilled. Both he and the king had good reason to regret his achievement, for each had lost a great deal, and Glinsky fully intended to make the king feel even sorrier in the future.

HOSTILE RELATIONS WITH THE CRIMEA

Sigismund originally had hoped to induce the Crimean Tatars to launch a major attack on Muscovy, and had spent lavishly in an effort to sunder Mengli-Girey's alliance with Moscow. The Crimean horde had degenerated into a band of robbers.[7] Fear of Ahmad and his sons and of the Turks had previously caused Mengli-Girey to value his Muscovite alliance, for if the Turks expelled him he planned to seek refuge with the prince of Muscovy. Moreover, Ivan's reputation, power and success were bound to inspire a barbarian with respect.

Now the situation was different. Mengli-Girey no longer had reason to fear the remnants of the Golden Horde and apprehended no danger from the Turks. Ivan was no longer the ruler of Moscow. His place had been taken by his young son, who was in danger both at home and abroad; the Tatars, like the Lithuanians, had expected Ivan's sons to fall out. Mengli-Girey, now old and feeble, was surrounded by a host of greedy sons, relatives and princes. This covetous group greedily craved Sigismund's gifts and promised in return to ravage Muscovite territory. The Crimeans found it even more profitable to play both sides of the street. Promising to aid the side providing the greater largesse, they accepted gifts from both Moscow and Lithuania. They made promises, took money from both sides, and then, taking advantage of the two powers' mutual antagonism, devastated the territory of each.

In their dealings with the Crimea both Moscow and Lithuania were essentially facing bandits seeking tribute, not men who would abide by formal covenants. The situation was further complicated by the involved claims to earlier power and dominion which the khans were trying to reassert, at least formally, and, most humiliating of all, King Sigismund pandered to these pretensions. He agreed to accept the following charter from Mengli-Girey: "Great Khan Mengli-Girey of the Great Horde, supreme ruler of his mighty domain, speaks to his commanders, chiliarchs, hundredmen, tenmen, nobles and princes, and to all the Russian people, boyars, metropolitans, priests, monks, and all common men. We would have you know that, when their horses were weary, the great khans, our forefathers, and the great khan, Haji-Girey, our father, used to go to the Lithuanian land, and Grand Prince Vitovt received them with great honor and favor. For this reason they granted him Kiev and gave him many other places. Grand Prince Casimir and the Lithuanian princes and magnates made the same request of us. We gave them Kiev, Vladimir, Lutsk, Smolensk, Podolia, Kamenets, Braslavl, Sokalsk, Zvenigorod, Cherkasy, and the Haji lighthouse (Odessa), all the way from Kiev to the mouth of the Dnieper . . . Putivl, Chernigov, Rylsk, Kursk, Oskol, Starodub, Briansk, Mtsensk, Liubutsk, and Tula . . . Kozelsk and Pronsk. To exalt our brother Casimir we further assigned Pskov, Great Novgorod, and Riazan to the Lithuanian throne. Now we have seen fit to grant our brother Sigismund a domain in Lithuania, together with all the above-inscribed lands."

Although it was early in his reign, Vasily had lost no time obtaining a sworn pledge from Mengli-Girey to maintain the alliance with the Crimea that had existed in Ivan III's time. During the summer of 1507 a large Tatar force was reported proceeding across the steppe. It was expected to attack the area around Belev, Odoev, and Kozelsk. The grand prince immediately sent troops to the borderlands but the Muscovites could not prevent the Tatars from acquiring immense plunder. The commanders pursued the raiders into the steppe. Overtaking them on the Oka they defeated them on August 9 and stripped them of all their booty. No further Tatar raids took place during the rest of the time Vasily was at war with Lithuania.

Glinsky went to the Crimea to seek the khan's protection and arouse him against Sigismund. Mengli-Girey agreed to make an alliance with Glinsky and promised to obtain Kiev for him, but he also promised Sigismund to send Tatar auxiliaries to Kiev and even as far as Vilna. Refusing the aid, the king wrote on June 11, 1508 that Glinsky and the Muscovites had been driven out and he required no Tatar assistance in Lithuania. As he was now standing on the borders of Muscovy, he asked the khan to send an army to attack Briansk, Starodub and Novgorod Seversk, adding: "If you are unable to send your sons, at least send a few thousand men to demonstrate our true brotherhood and faithful friendship. We have sworn and pledged our word, and we intend to fulfill our obligations as long as we live. We want no other friend save you, and to you alone we shall show every favor." Sigismund also promised to send more money to the khan.

The raiders had not forgotten the defeat they had sustained on the Oka, and the khan refused to send another army to the Muscovite borderlands. He deemed it a more prudent course to use the alliance to extract all he could from the prince of Muscovy, and from his stepson, Abdul-Letif,[8] the former ruler of Kazan, who was now a prisoner, and involve Vasily in a war with Astrakhan, which long had been at peace with Moscow. The khan was not the only one asking for gifts. Envoys regularly brought a host of demands from the khan's sons and daughters to the grand prince. All of them sent their profound respects but only token gifts, while demanding substantial presents in return, and in addition to the khan's family it was necessary to include all the Tatar nobles and princes as well. Mengli-Girey wrote to the grand prince: "My brother, besides other gifts Grand Prince Ivan used to send to Yamgurchey-Saltan a full set of sableskins, and 2,000 squirrel and 300 ermine skins. You have failed to follow his example. No presents have been received by twenty of my nobles and princes. You should send them cloth; otherwise they will say, 'we renounce our oath,' and bring intense pressure to bear upon us, something that should never happen!"

Calling for an end to customs duties on his traders, the khan wrote to the grand prince: "I am sending a merchant, but if the goods he wishes to buy are too dear, I have told him to go to Kazan as well in search of good skins. Wherever he sells my wares or to whatever town he goes, you should have an official present to guard and protect him and see that he is not taxed, robbed or attacked. My money is as good as yours. In the days of our fathers and grandfathers our merchants often traded in Moscow and other towns and never paid duty. Their money is my money. To levy duty on them is to insult me. Our traders never trade in the merchants' quarters but trade where they please without restriction." The khan also demanded the tribute from Odoev that had been paid in Ivan III's time.

The grand prince came to terms with the khan about the merchants, and issued instructions that they were not to be subject to taxation or forced to trade in the merchants' quarters, but he refused to attack Astrakhan, saying: "No ships were built on the Volga in my father's time and they cannot be built there now. It is impossible for me to transfer troops there." The grand prince also refused to allow Abdul-Letif to proceed to the Crimea, but he was willing to release him and assign him a town. Mengli-Girey's envoy insisted that Letif get Kashira, but the grand prince had no intention of acceding to this request. To ensconce Letif so near the steppe would in effect place the borderlands in pawn to the Crimeans, or at least give Letif an opportunity to flee from Muscovy. Letif was assigned Yurev, and in the process he had to sign a capitulary which illustrates the relationship existing at the time between Tatar service princes and the Muscovite state.

Calling himself a tsar and the grand prince's brother, Letif swore to have the same friends and enemies as the grand prince; not to make treaties without the grand prince's concurrence, and immediately to show the grand prince any communications he might receive from other rulers. While in the grand prince's service he and his forces were not to attack or plunder any place in Muscovy. He was not to harass Christians and must surrender anyone who did so, or who desecrated a church. No penalty attached to anyone who slew such a person at the scene of the crime. Whenever Letif's representatives went to Moscow they were to be supplied at posting-stations, but his merchants must proceed at their own expense.

Letif was not to arrest or rob Muscovite envoys and traders, or detain Russian prisoners escaping from the Horde. He agreed not to harm Yanay, the Tatar prince living in Meshchersk, Shig-Avliar, the Tatar prince established in Surozhik, or any other Tatar ruler or prince who might settle in Muscovy. He was not to enroll nobles, princes or irregulars previously in their service, even though such men had subsequently defected to the horde of Kazan, nor was he to recruit soldiers in these regions. The only Tatars in the grand prince's service he might receive were those connected with four families—Shirinov, Baarynov, Agrinov, and Kipchakov. Letif also pledged not to attack Kazan without informing the grand prince, not to leave Muscovy, and to obey the grand prince. For his part the grand prince swore to consider Letif his friend and brother, but omitted these words from his final rescript because of previous complications.

Muscovite representatives in the Crimea were constantly importuned by greedy nobles and members of the royal house. The grand prince sent a distinguished ambassador, Vasily Morozov, but told Mengli-Girey that if Morozov were exposed to the insults and violence which Zabolotsky, the previous envoy, had been obliged to endure, he would send no more senior men. Morozov was instructed to refuse all demands for money and hand over nothing besides the gifts the grand prince had sent. Morozov did so, but related how difficult it was to carry out his orders: "I reached the city, dismounted, and proceeded on foot to the gate, near which I perceived all the leading nobles to be seated. They greeted me in their customary fashion, but when Prince Kudaiar's turn came, he refused to inquire after my health and said to the interpreter: 'Tell the ambassador he is a slave!' The interpreter refused, but when the prince threatened him with a knife he told me what Kudaiar had said as I was approaching the entrance to the palace on my way to the khan with my gifts. Prince Kudaiar snatched a squirrelskin coat from my assistant. As I reached the palace door the guards lowered their staves in front of me and shouted to the interpreter: 'Hand over the tribute!' I made my way inside through the staves, saying, 'I do not understand.' Appak, a nobleman, said: 'Do not hang back; go straight in to the khan.'

The khan inquired after my sovereign's health and greeted me. His sons also greeted me and bade me welcome. Since I was chief of the delega-tion, the khan handed me a cup from which he had drunk, and his sons did likewise. Shortly afterwards the khan handed me another cup, and I returned the compliment to the khan, his sons, and the princes. When my cup reached Prince Kudaiar, I complained to the khan that the prince had called me a slave and stolen a coat. I said: 'Prince Kudaiar, I shall not allow you to drink from my cup. I am not your slave. I am the slave of my sovereign, Grand Prince Vasily Ivanovich, your brother.' The khan tried to justify Kudaiar's conduct, saying: 'We allotted him this gift.' I replied: 'My lord, this is your privilege. Give him everything if you so desire.' After this exchange the khan dismissed me and told a man to bring me mead. As I heard, he upbraided Kudaiar and banished him . . . . His son, Ahmad-Girey, sent a courtier to threaten me: 'The khan's son has ordered me to say that if you persist in your refusal to hand over the gifts I used to get from Zabolotsky, I shall have you brought before me on the end of a chain.' I answered: 'I am not afraid of your chains and I will not give you any presents. I have none with me.' "

LIVONIAN AFFAIRS

When seeking war with Muscovy, both Alexander and Sigismund had tried to stir up the master of the Livonian Order, but the answer Pletten-berg had given Alexander demonstrated that their efforts were doomed to failure. With the good offices of Emperor Maximilian, Livonia and the Hansa towns devoted their efforts solely to recovering the prisoners and merchandise they had lost during the reign of Ivan III. In the fall of 1506 Gardinger [an Imperial envoy] came to Moscow to renew Maximilian's request to free the prisoners. Vasily told him: "If Emperor Maximilian will make a friendly fraternal alliance like the one that existed in my father's time, and if the master, the archbishop, and the rest of the Livonians cease their support of our enemy in Lithuania, make overtures to our governors in Great Novgorod, and offer seasonable concessions concerning our patrimonies of Great Novgorod and Pskov, our regard for Emperor Maximilian will lead us to respond to their petition with instructions to the governors in our patrimonial lands of Great Novgorod and Pskov to conclude an appropriate peace with Livonia and free the prisoners."

No envoys from Livonia came to Moscow while the war with Lithu-ania was going on, but in March, 1509, as soon as it was over, the master entered into negotiations with the governors of Novgorod and Pskov, who successfully concluded a fourteen-year truce. Under its terms the Germans pledged not to support the grand prince of Lithuania or his successors, and received the right to trade in all commodities in the Novgorod territory except salt. Both sides agreed to provide guides and supplies for their envoys without charge. Maximilian requested that the Hansa towns be permitted to restore their trade with Novgorod and Pskov to its previous level and to have the goods returned which Ivan III had taken from them. Vasily replied that he would approve the emperor's request about trade if the Hansa towns made formal application to the governors of Novgorod and Pskov, but he refused to give back the merchandise.

THE FALL OF PSKOV

Freed of apprehension from Kazan, the Crimea, Lithuania, and Livonia, Vasily decided to deal with Pskov, where the constant clashes between the native population and his vicegerent had been brought to his attention.[9] Beginning in either 1508 or 1509, the governor of Pskov was Prince Ivan Mikhailovich Repnia-Obolensky. The people of the city called him "the Apparition" because, according to their chronicler, he had not received a formal invitation to assume office from the people, and they simply "came upon" him one day in residence in a palace outside the city. This was not normal procedure, and the priests refused to go out to greet him with crosses. The chronicler also states that Prince Ivan was cruel to the people. In the fall of 1509 the grand prince went to Novgorod, where he received a complaint from Obolensky that Pskov treated him dishonorably, as the city had never done with previous governors. The grand prince's affairs suffered neglect, and his judges and revenue collectors were forced to endure insult and violence.

Immediately following the governor's complaint, the elected leaders and some boyars of Pskov came to Novgorod bringing the grand prince a gift of 150 rubles. They submitted a petition to Vasily in which they declared that the governor and his assistants, as well as his representatives in the outlying areas and their assistants, had dealt harshly with them. The grand prince replied: "We wish our patrimony well, and desire to protect it as our father and ancestors did. I shall cite my governor before you if many complaints against him are received." Dismissing the leaders and nobles, Vasily sent a lord-in-waiting, Prince Peter Vasilievich Veliky, and a secretary, Dalmatov, to Pskov with instructions to hear both sides of the dispute between Prince Obolensky and the people of Pskov and bring them together. The mediators returned to report that the

MUSCOVY IN THE SIXTEENTH CENTURY

From *Moscovia* by Antonio Possevino

people could never be reconciled with their governor. The people of Pskov returned once more to beg the sovereign to appoint another governor, since they could no longer tolerate Repnia. The grand prince told Repnia and anyone in Pskov dissatisfied with the governor to report to him in Novgorod.

The governor came, and so did Leonty, one of the elected officials, but instead of complaining against Obolensky he attacked his fellow official, Yury Kopyl. Yury went to Novgorod to answer the charges, and lost no time in sending a letter to Pskov containing these words: "All will share the responsibility if the leaders of Pskov do not come and speak out against Prince Ivan Repnia." In great alarm the people of Pskov dispatched nine officials and elders drawn from all ranks of the merchant community. The prince held no regular court; instead he proclaimed: "Those of you with complaints are to assemble on the day of Epiphany, when I shall dispense justice to all. I do not intend to hold court now." The complainants had to go home, but they returned at the appointed time. On the day of Epiphany Vasily ordered the people from Pskov to approach the river, where he and his entourage had assembled to perform the ritual of blessing the waters. "Officials of Pskov, boyars and petitioners," the boyars informed them, "the sovereign has bidden all of you assemble at the palace. Anyone failing to appear will be punished, since our lord wishes to hear all of you."

The Pskov chronicler says that the men of Pskov went straight from the river to the palace. The leaders, nobles and merchants were escorted inside, while the lesser folk remained outside. Muscovite boyars at once appeared and said to the people from Pskov: "God and Grand Prince Vasily Ivanovich of all Russia have placed you under arrest." The leaders were interned on the spot in the palace, while the lesser officials had their names taken and were consigned randomly to the custody of inhabitants of Novgorod, who were ordered to guard and maintain them until the hearing. According to other accounts the grand prince summoned Prince Repnia, the governor, and the leaders of Pskov, listened to what all had to say, and determined that the Pskov leaders had not obeyed the governor, had opposed him in legal and financial matters, and refused to pay him the respect they had shown previous governors. In addition, the leaders had often insulted and mistreated their own people; but the most serious charge was that they had taken their sovereign's name contumaciously and in vain. The grand prince accordingly found against the leaders. He arrested them and placed them in detention centers guarded by Muscovite soldiers.

The leaders and others admitted their guilt and begged the sovereign to show favor to his patrimony of Pskov and to dispose of its affairs as God would have him do. The grand prince told his boyars to inform them: "Your crimes have merited royal displeasure and punishment, but your sovereign is prepared to be merciful if you do his bidding. You must remove the assembly bell, dissolve the assembly, and accept two governors in Pskov and a like number in the outlying areas. The sovereign desires to come in person to Pskov, pray in Holy Trinity Cathedral, and publicly proclaim his decree that governors alone possess the right to administer justice in Pskov and its area. If you fulfill the sovereign's behest, the sovereign will have pity on you and will not deprive you of your lands and estates; but if you refuse to acknowledge the sovereign's favor and fail to carry out his orders, the sovereign will feel free, with God's help, to act as he sees fit. Christian blood will be upon the heads of those who scorn their sovereign's favor and refuse to do his bidding." The leaders and the rest of the people of Pskov replied: "We beg the sovereign's favor, but the sovereign should send one of his men to Pskov to state his conditions." They solemnly swore to serve Vasily, his children, and his successors to the end of time.

The population of Pskov learned what had happened to their leaders from a merchant, Filip Popovich, who had heard about it on his way to Novgorod. Leaving his wares behind, he returned in haste to Pskov to inform his fellow citizens. The chronicler relates that the people of Pskov became alarmed, fearful, and depressed—"their throats grew dry with sorrow and their mouths fell slack." Although the Germans had attacked them many times, never had they experienced such misery as they did at this moment. The assembly was convoked, and the people debated whether to oppose the sovereign and try to keep him out of the city. They recalled the oath they had sworn forbidding them to rise against their ruler, and he held their leaders, nobles, and prominent citizens as hostages. Deciding resistance was impossible, they sent a courier, Evstafy the hundredman, to the grand prince. He made a tearful appeal: "Lord, show mercy to your ancient patrimony. We, your wards, have always been at one with you and will not oppose you. May God's will be done, and yours, among the humble folk of your ancestral domain."

An official, Tretiak Dalmatov, came to Pskov bearing the grand prince's demands. In Vasily's name he told the assembly: "If my patrimony would live as it has lived in the past, it must carry out my two behests—dissolve the assembly and remove the assembly bell. You must accept two governors, although I shall not place governors in the outskirts. If you agree, you will live as you did of old, but if you refuse to accede to these two demands, your sovereign will deal with you as God prompts him. He has ample forces at his disposal, and those who ignore their sovereign's command will be responsible for the bloodshed that occurs. Your sovereign also wishes to inform you of his desire to worship in the Holy Trinity Cathedral in Pskov." Finishing his announcement the official sat down on a bench. The people of Pskov bowed to the ground but could not speak, for the eyes of all but tiny children were filled with tears. They finally recovered and said to Dalmatov: "Sovereign envoy, please wait until tomorrow. We shall consider and give you a full answer then." Again everyone wept bitterly. The chronicler says: "Why have the torrents of our tears not made our eyes fall from their sockets? Why have our hearts not been torn away from their roots?"

There was nothing for the men of Pskov to discuss. They spent the day groaning, wailing, and sobbing. One man would throw his arms about another, and both would weep together. The leaders and nobles held in Novgorod wrote to say their lives were surety to Vasily that Pskov would fulfill its sovereign's command. It was sheer ruin to oppose the grand prince, who stood at the head of a large army. At dawn the next day the assembly bell rang; Tretiak appeared, and the men of Pskov gave him their answer: "Our chronicles tell us that we, the people of Pskov, swore to the ancestors and the father of the grand prince that we would never desert our sovereign, the grand prince of Muscovy, whoever he may be, to go over to the Lithuanians or the Germans. If we ever did so, or renounced the prince's authority in order to be independent, God's wrath, famine, fire, flood and pagan attacks were to be our lot. The sovereign grand prince is subject to the same sanctions as we are, if he fails to treat us as we were treated in the years gone by. God and our sovereign are masters in the patrimonial city of Pskov, of our persons, and of our assembly bell. We do not wish to forswear our oath and cause bloodshed, nor do we want to oppose our sovereign and be prisoners in our city. Our sovereign grand prince desires to pray in the life-giving Holy Trinity Cathedral and spend time in his ancestral domain of Pskov. We rejoice with brimming hearts that our sovereign has not utterly destroyed us." The assembly bell was removed from Holy Trinity cathedral on January 13, 1510. As they gazed upon the bell the people of Pskov wept at the passing of the old ways and the loss of their freedom. Tretiak took the bell that very night to the grand prince in Novgorod.

A week before the grand prince came to Pskov, his officers appeared in force, administered an oath to the people, and informed the leaders of the date of the grand prince's arrival. Leaders, boyars, junior and senior officials, and merchants repaired to Dubrovno to greet the ruler, who entered Pskov on January 24. Arriving earlier that day, the bishop of Kolomna told the local clergy that Vasily had ordered them not to advance to welcome him. Unaccompanied by any clergy the people of Pskov met Vasily some three versts outside the city and bowed to the ground. When the sovereign inquired after their health, they replied: "May our lord, grand prince and tsar of all Russia, enjoy long life." The bishop of Kolomna awaited him with the clergy of Pskov in the city square. In the Holy Trinity cathedral all chanted and prayed for their sovereign to enjoy long life. When giving his blessing the bishop said: "Our Lord God has blessed your taking of Pskov." On hearing his words the inhabitants of Pskov present in the cathedral burst into bitter tears, saying: "It is the will of God and our sovereign. Since olden times we have been the patrimony of his fathers, grandfathers, and ancestors."

Three days later the grand prince summoned leaders, officials, merchants and other Pskov citizens to hear his dispositions, as he had promised to do. When they assembled, Prince Peter Vasilievich Veliky read the names of some from a list and ordered them imprisoned in the barracks. Then he said to the rest of the people of Pskov: "Your sovereign is not concerned with you. He will take those with whom he is concerned with him, and he has issued a rescript defining your future status." The prominent Pskovites left the barracks under escort and dispersed to their homes, but that same night began a mass transfer of them, and their wives and children, to Moscow. Hurried away sobbing and weeping bitterly, they could take no more than a few personal belongings and had to leave the rest of their property behind. In all 300 families were relocated. The chronicler declares that the glory of Pskov had departed. As he puts it, disaster overtook Pskov because its people were arrogant and intolerant and given to slander and spitefulness. The assembly had been a scene of constant disorder. They wished to rule a city but proved incapable of managing their own affairs.

Sending the boyar, Peter Yakovlevich Zakharin-Koshkin, to inform Moscow of the occupation, Vasily remained in Pskov for four weeks in order to establish his new regime. He distributed the villages that previously had belonged to the Pskov nobles now resettled in Moscow among his boyars, and appointed new officials: Grigory Morozov and Ivan Cheliadnin as governors, Misiur-Munekhin as the chief civil official, Andrei Volosaty as the latter's principal assistant in charge of transport, twelve municipal supervisors, and twelve Muscovites and twelve men of Pskov as regional administrators. Assigning them villages, he instructed them to participate in the judicial process along with the governors and tax-gatherers, and to uphold the law. Vasily drew up a new charter for Pskov and sent his governors into the surrounding areas to summon the inhabitants to swear allegiance to it. He imported fifteen trustworthy merchants from Moscow to supervise tax collection, for the people of Pskov heretofore had paid no taxes and enjoyed free trade. He established a new mint. Government fusiliers and guards also came from Moscow. On his departure the grand prince left 1,000 military servitors and 500 Novgorod fusiliers stationed in Pskov. On Holy Trinity Day that year 300 merchant families from ten towns in Muscovy arrived to take the place of their Pskov counterparts who had been transferred. They were assigned quarters in the center of the city and the previous native owners were moved to outlying areas.

The chronicler complains of the first governors: "The governors, tax collectors and civil officials were a law unto themselves. They cared nothing for the oath they had sworn, and engaged in acts of lawlessness. They showed no mercy to the unfortunate people of Pskov, who were unfamiliar with Muscovite law. When the governors in the outlying districts traded with the inhabitants, they did not act in good faith. They made false accusations, or deliberately misdelivered goods in order to charge the declared recipient with theft. The governors' assistants charged five, seven, or ten rubles interest on bail bonds. Any man of Pskov who invoked the grand prince's charter, which specified the rate for bail bonds, was put to death. These exactions, and the general violence, caused many to leave their wives and children to seek refuge in foreign towns, and foreigners living in Pskov went home. Only natives were left, because "a man cannot burrow down into the ground or fly up into the sky."

The grand prince heard how his governors were behaving, and in the following year, 1511, he removed Morozov and Cheliadnin and replaced them with two princes, Peter Veliky and Semen Kurbsky. Peter had once been a prince in Pskov and knew the people. According to the chronicler, the new governors, who held office for four years, were well-disposed and those who had fled began to return. Governors came and went, but the chief civil administrator, Misiur-Munekhin, stayed on and apparently acquired great influence and authority. He spent seventeen years in Pskov and died in 1528. After his tenure his successors also changed frequently. In the words of the chronicler, "officials are cunning and the land is empty." The grand prince's coffers in Pskov were full, but none of his officials returned content to Moscow, for the inhabitants of the two places could not abide one another. Misiur will figure in another portion of this narrative.

II

SMOLENSK

RENEWAL OF WAR WITH LITHUANIA

The grand prince of Muscovy strongly desired to consolidate the conquests his father had made in Lithuania. Sigismund, his opponent, was anxious to free himself from a debilitating war that had taken a turn for the worse after Glinsky's defection, without making major concessions. At the same time Glinsky's plans had failed to prosper and he had been obliged to leave his home territory. An end to the war between Muscovy and Lithuania could bring no advantage to him.

Glinsky's presence in Moscow would not further the cause of peace, and it was equally obvious that this talented, energetic, knowledgeable and experienced man was bound to devote all his resources to restoring his previous position and winning back his estates. A man who had enjoyed the status of a grand prince in Lithuania and had grown accustomed to the exercise of princely power in Alexander's reign was not likely to accept the situation that existed in Muscovy, where the grand prince was bringing to fruition the measures his father had initiated to curb the power of the nobility. Glinsky closely followed events in the west and carefully observed Sigismund's actions. He was pleased when the latter encountered difficulties, and lost no opportunity of encouraging the grand prince to take advantage of the king's restricted freedom of manoeuvre and begin a new and successful war.

Sigismund knew that Glinsky would not allow him to enjoy uninterrupted peace with Moscow. Early in 1509 he tried to persuade Vasily to turn Prince Mikhail over to him. "Your sister, Queen Elena," he told him, "has informed you that the renegade Prince Mikhail forgot the kindness and favor that his suzerain, our brother Alexander, showed him. Glinsky was a person of no consequence, but our brother made him a lord. He used spells to destroy Alexander's health and drive him to his grave. The queen told us this informally, explained the details in a letter, and sent a delegation to discuss the matter with us. By fleeing when we were absent this monster acknowledged his guilt. Now he resides with you. Our brother, we should like to remind you that you are partly responsible for the misery which this criminal has caused your sister and us. You should surrender the traitor who murdered your brother-in-law, and his relatives and abettors, or put him to death in the presence of our envoys. If you agree, we shall treat any of your subjects who insult you and flee to us in the same way." Vasily refused to entertain the proposal.

Such demands inflamed Glinsky's anger with Sigismund. He wrote to Johann, the king of Denmark, in an attempt to arouse him against the Polish king. Sigismund obtained the letter from Johann and transmitted it to Vasily with the comment: "See for yourself. Is this a wise thing to do? We are at peace, but our renegade, who now serves you and resides in your land, sends a malicious letter like this to a Christian king. Our brother, you really ought to execute this criminal and stop him from doing such things in the future." Vasily made no reply.

Sigismund let the problem of Glinsky drop, and prior to 1512 relations between the two courts were confined to complaints about provocations on the frontier and demands for mediators to settle them. Then, that summer, Vasily wrote to Sigismund: "A report has reached us that your nobles, the commanders of Vilna and Trokai, have arrested our sister, Queen Elena, in Vilna, carried her to Trokai, dismissed all her attendants, and taken her money. The nobles in the towns and estates she received from her husband have refused to help her. These men held her three days in Trokai and then removed her to Birshany. We have repeatedly told you that you and your nobles must not insult our sister and must not force her to become a Catholic. I want to know why my sister was exposed to this intolerable affront and whether it was done with your approval. Brother, make sure that you and your nobles inflict no insult or despite upon our sister. You must restore her money; her attendants are to rejoin her, and your nobles are not to set foot in her towns and estates if you would avoid unpleasantness between us. I desire you to inform me why our sister, your sister-in-law, has had to suffer such gross insult, and whether you approved of these actions. We are sending junior officers to the border towns to meet with your governors of Smolensk, Polotsk and Vitebsk in an effort to resolve the problems there. They will arrive on St. Dmitry's Day (October 26, 1512); you should send your officials to our border towns for the same purpose in the autumn, on St. Nicholas' Day" (December 6, 1512).

Sigismund replied: "We are absolutely certain that our nobles, the commanders of Vilna and Trokai, never touched our sister-in-law's money, people, towns, or estates. They did not take her to Trokai and

Birshany, nor did they insult her. With our approval they merely told her on one occasion that her highness should not proceed to Braslavl but remain in her other towns, because reports were circulating that the border areas were unsafe. We are astonished that our brother has not taken the trouble to ascertain the truth, and relying on statements made by malicious persons has charged us with actions we never contemplated. From the moment we became ruler of our patrimony always we have shown our sister-in-law the greatest honor. We have not forced her to become a Catholic and have no intention of doing so. Far from depriving her of the towns and estates my brother Alexander gave her, we have assigned her additional towns, estates and dwellings, and in the future, God willing, we shall continue to esteem her highness. To convince yourself, your envoy may approach the queen, our sister-in-law, to inquire of her, and communicate whatever he learns to you, my brother. In future, my brother, you would be better advised to ignore spiteful gossip and seek to prevent disagreement between us. Our scribe will accompany your envoy to the queen, and in his presence her highness will tell your representative whether these rumors are true or not."

Vasily's statements reveal that he did not yet consider the issue of Elena's treatment sufficiently serious to break off relations with Lithuania, and he agreed to receive some Lithuanian nobles on December 6 in order to resolve border disputes. It is not clear whether a Muscovite envoy and the royal scribe visited Elena or what she told them if they did so. There is merely a subsequent Muscovite protest that Sigismund had failed to respond to Vasily's question about his sister's status. During November and December of 1512, Elena was busy on her holdings in Samogitia, hearing complaints, and instructing her bailiffs and stewards to satisfy them.

A different kind of report soon reached Moscow. In May two of Mengli-Girey's sons made a raid, attacked the frontier towns of Belev, Odoev, Vorotynsk and Aleksin in force, and made off with prisoners. The grand prince sent troops against them, but the Tatars withdrew with considerable plunder and the officers did not pursue them. In June one of these sons, Ahmad-Girey, planned a raid on Riazan, but turned back when he learned that a Muscovite army was waiting for him on the Osetr and Upa rivers. In October Ahmad's brother, Burnash-Girey, again tried to take Riazan. He failed, but he managed to inflict severe damage on the surrounding countryside before retiring with his booty. In the wake of the first attack the grand prince placed Abdul-Letif under official displeasure because of his duplicity, put him under guard, and deprived him of his appanage. The chronicles say the place was Kashira, but it will be remembered that Letif was given Yurev, not Kashira. No one can say whether an exchange subsequently took place or whether the chronicles are mistaken. The nature of Letif's duplicity is likewise unknown. He might actually have been cooperating with the Crimean leaders and displayed hostility to Moscow on hearing of their approach, or it might simply have been that his remaining at liberty was conditional upon observance of the treaty of alliance which the Crimeans had now violated.

In the fall Moscow learned that the raids conducted by the khan's sons were the result of an agreement Sigismund had made with Mengli-Girey. This was adequate grounds for breaking with Lithuania. The grand prince sent a carefully worded letter reproaching Sigismund for his insulting behavior to Elena and arousing Mengli-Girey against Moscow. Circumstances strongly favored a war policy.

When Albert, margrave of Brandenburg, Sigismund's nephew by marriage, became grand master of the Teutonic Order[1] he refused to cede Pomerania and Prussia and acknowledge himself his uncle's vassal, and prepared for war with Sigismund. Livonia's ties with the grand master obliged that country to declare war on Poland also. The emperor and other German feudatories supported Albert. Glinsky closely followed Sigismund's relations with his western neighbors, and in 1508, before Muscovy made peace with Lithuania, he had persuaded Vasily to make an alliance with Emperor Maximilian. Glinsky pointed out that Maximilian planned to place Hungary under the jurisdiction of his brother, a relative of Sigismund, and such a device would inevitably embroil Sigismund in conflict. Glinsky undertook to deliver a letter from Vasily to Maximilian, in which the Muscovite ruler proposed an alliance with the emperor against Sigismund to recover their patrimonies—Hungary for Maximilian and the West Russian lands for Vasily. It is not known whether the note was ever delivered or what form the subsequent negotiations assumed, because the records of the Imperial foreign office covering the years 1510-1515 are lost. The chronicles state that an Imperial envoy, Schnitzenpaumer, arrived in Moscow in February, 1514. The text of the alliance he concluded has survived: Austria and Muscovy agreed to wrest from Sigismund both the territory of the Teutonic Order and Kiev and adjacent towns.

Vasily renewed military operations against Lithuania before this treaty was concluded. In April of 1511 Glinsky encouraged officials of the Order to believe that peace between Moscow and Lithuania would soon come to an end. He sent Schleinitz, a German in his service, to Silesia, Bohemia and Germany to hire soldiers and send them to Moscow via Livonia. Even people in Poland secretly accepted money from Glinsky. One of them, Lada, a Czech living in Cracow, was arrested on the Muscovite frontier and sent back to Cracow where he was put to death. On December 19, 1512 the grand prince took the field in person with two of his brothers, Yury and Dmitry, his brother-in-law, a baptized Tatar prince named Peter, Mikhail Glinsky, and two Muscovite commanders, the Princes Daniel Shchenia and Repnia-Obolensky. Their target was Smolensk.

For six weeks they beleaguered the city and then tried to storm it. The grand prince gave the Pskov fusiliers three barrels of mead and three barrels of beer. They drank it up and joined fusiliers from other towns in a midnight attack on the fortress. They met with initial success; the rest of the night and all next day fighting raged on the Dnieper side and elsewhere, but after sustaining severe losses from enemy cannon they were compelled to withdraw. The grand prince returned to Moscow in March, 1513.

In the summer, on June 14, Vasily took the field again. He remained in Borovsk, but sent his commanders, Boyar Prince Repnia-Obolensky and Lord-in-waiting Andrei Saburov, on to Smolensk. The governor of the city, Yury Sologub, met them in battle before the ramparts. Defeated, he shut himself up in the fortress. Informed of the victory Vasily came himself to Smolensk, but the siege after his arrival proved unsuccessful. Whenever his cannon opened a breach during the day the besieged managed to close it up at night. The grand prince sent frequent messages containing threats and promises to the people of Smolensk, but to no avail. They refused to surrender, and Vasily had to be content with devastating the surrounding countryside. He lifted the siege and returned to Moscow in November.

CAPTURE OF SMOLENSK

The grand prince made a third attempt on June 8, 1514, supported by two of his brothers, Yury and Semen. A third, Dmitry, stayed at Serpukhov to maintain the southern frontier against the Crimea, while the fourth, Andrei, remained in Moscow. The siege of Smolensk began on July 29. The artillery was under the command of Stefan, a bombardier. During a barrage he fired a shot from his huge cannon which struck a cannon inside the fortress. It exploded, killing many of the besieged. A few hours later Stefan fired another round, this time of small lead-covered balls, which killed even more people. The inhabitants were filled with gloom. They knew they could not hold out, but they feared the king if they surrendered.

The grand prince called for a third volley, and large numbers of the
besieged again fell. The bishop, Varsonofy, came out on the bridge to
beg the grand prince for a twenty-four hour intermission. Vasily refused to grant it and ordered his cannon to open fire on all sides. With
tears in his eyes the bishop reentered the city, summoned all the clergy,
put on his robes, took a cross and the icons, and, accompanied by
Governor Sologub, the nobles and the people, came before the grand
prince. "Lord and grand prince," they said, "much Christian blood has
been shed, and our land, a part of your patrimony, stands vacant. Do
not destroy our city; instead, accept its surrender." Vasily approached
the bishop, who gave him a blessing, told him and Sologub and the
nobility to enter his camp, and ordered the rest of the clergy and the
people to return to the city, which was placed under heavy guard. The
bishop, Sologub, and the nobles spent the night in camp, also under
guard. The next day, July 30, the grand prince told his officers, Prince
Daniel Shchenia and others, and his chief civilian officials and their
associates, to enter Smolensk, register all the inhabitants and administer
an oath to them whereby they would swear no longer to support or
favor the king, but to support and favor the grand prince. This process
was completed by the next day.

A ceremony of blessing the waters took place on August 1. Vasily,
accompanied by the bishop, triumphantly entered the city behind a
procession of crosses, to be met by the whole people of Smolensk.
After praying long life for the prince in the cathedral the bishop said:
"Vasily, Orthodox tsar, grand prince of all Russia, and autocrat, with
God's grace may you know joy and good health for many years in the
city of Smolensk, your patrimony." Receiving congratulations from his
brothers, boyars and officers, Vasily attended service and proceeded to
the palace, where he took his seat. Muscovite boyars and officers and
prominent citizens of Smolensk repaired there again to offer him the
customary greeting according to their rank. The grand prince inquired
after each man's health and bade him be seated.

Vasily promulgated his dispositions in a charter, which he proclaimed
to the princes, boyars and people of Smolensk. He designated Boyar
Prince Vasily Vasilievich Shuisky as vicegerent and invited everyone to
a banquet, at the conclusion of which each man received gifts. The
grand prince said to the king's governor, Sologub, and his son: "If you
serve me I shall reward you, but if you prefer not to do so I shall not
compel you." Sologub asked permission to join the king, which was
granted. His fate was to be executed in Poland as a traitor. The same
offer was made to all the king's military servitors, many of whom

entered Muscovite service, receiving two rubles in cash and clothing. Those who refused were given a ruble and sent off to the king. The people of Smolensk were offered the same choice. Any who decided to move to Moscow obtained money for the journey, while those who wished to remain in Smolensk were allowed to keep their patrimonial and service holdings.

After settling affairs in Smolensk the grand prince, beginning his return journey, reached Dorogobuzh. He sent officers to Mstislavl, where the local prince, Mikhail Izheslavsky, made submission to the ruler of Muscovy, as did the inhabitants of Krichev and Dubrovna. To protect Smolensk in case Sigismund attacked, Vasily dispatched Prince Mikhail Glinsky to Orsha, and sent other officers, the brothers Mikhail Golitsa and Dmitry, sons of Prince Ivan Bulgakov-Patrikeev, and the master of horse, Ivan Andreevich Cheliadnin, to Borisov, Minsk, and Drutsk, respectively. The king marched from Minsk to Borisov in hope of encountering them. He scented victory, and his expectations of it derived from Mikhail Glinsky.

GLINSKY'S TREACHERY

Foreign accounts credit Glinsky with a major role in the capture of Smolensk. They say he negotiated with people inside the city, won many over to his side, and they in turn persuaded the majority of the inhabitants to surrender before the king arrived, as the commander, Sologub, had hoped he would soon do. Reports of the capture of Smolensk circulating in Livonia had Glinsky say to the grand prince: "I make you a present of Smolensk, which you have wanted for so long. How will you reward me?" The grand prince is supposed to have replied: "I shall make you a prince in Lithuania." This story contradicts Herberstein's account, which has Vasily, while still in Moscow, promising to assign Smolensk to Glinsky. However this may be, Glinsky had no promise from the grand prince concerning Smolensk, but he had hoped to be given the city. He believed that he had been the chief architect of its capture, and that he was responsible for the successful conduct of the war in general. His initiative had procured talented foreign soldiers; Stefan, the capable artilleryman, was probably one of them. Glinsky had connections in Cracow; it is reasonable to assume that he had some in Smolensk as well, which he had used to secure the city's surrender.

Extremely anxious to be an independent prince Glinsky felt he was entitled to Smolensk, but Vasily would have been very foolish to let him have the place he had coveted so long. Smolensk enjoyed a highly strategic location, and was the key to the whole Dnieper region. Even if Vasily remained suzerain, Glinsky had displayed a talent and capacity for broad strategic thinking and an ability to put his plans into execution that rendered it unlikely that the grand prince could continue to maintain effective control of his valuable acquisition.

If the testimony cited above is to be believed, Glinsky, deceived in his expectation of obtaining Smolensk, would be forced to wait until the grand prince had conquered another principality in Lithuania. This was a doubtful enterprise, for the king was on his way with an army. Glinsky opened negotiations with Sigismund after obtaining a gracious reception from the latter's brother, Ladislas, king of Hungary and Bohemia. Sigismund was delighted to entertain Glinsky's overtures, for he considered that Glinsky's advice had contributed materially to the military success Muscovy had enjoyed.

Glinsky made up his mind to desert the Muscovite detachment he was leading and flee secretly to Orsha, but one of his personal attendants hastened that night to inform Prince Mikhail Golitsa of Glinsky's intentions, and showed him the route Glinsky planned to take. Informing the other commander, Cheliadnin, Golitsa lost no time setting out with his troops, blocked the road Glinsky was following, and caught him in the darkness as he was advancing a verst or so ahead of his attendants. At dawn Cheliadnin caught up with Golitsa, and the two of them brought Glinsky before the grand prince at Dorogobuzh, who ordered him placed under escort and taken to Moscow. Correspondence with the king removed from his person constituted damning evidence against Glinsky.

THE RUSSIAN DEFEAT AT ORSHA

After dealing with Glinsky the grand prince ordered his commanders to proceed against the king. Remaining in Borisov with 4,000 soldiers, Sigismund sent the rest of his army forward under the command of Prince Konstantin Ostrozhsky to engage the Muscovites, who, according to foreign sources, numbered 80,000 men, while Ostrozhsky had no more than 30,000. A few skirmishes took place at the end of August, and then Cheliadnin crossed the Dnieper near Orsha, where he took up a position on the further bank to await the enemy. Wishing the victory to be decisive, the Lithuanians made no attempt to prevent his crossing. The battle took place on September 8, 1514. The Russians began the attack, and the fortunes of war alternated for a long time until at last the Lithuanians deliberately turned and fled. The move brought the

Russians within range of the Lithuanian artillery, and a tremendous volley shattered the Russian ranks as the soldiers ran in pursuit. This caused great confusion, which quickly spread throughout the entire Muscovite army. The Russians sustained a crushing defeat. All the commanders were captured and a great many soldiers were killed. The Kropivna river, which flows between Orsha and Dubrovna, was choked with bodies of Muscovite soldiers who had jumped into it from the high banks.

Although Sigismund informed the master of Livonia that at Orsha the Muscovites had lost 30,000 of their 80,000 men and that eight senior commanders, 30 line officers, and 1500 noblemen were taken prisoner, the official Lithuanian records list no more than 611 prisoners captured at Orsha and other places as well. The Muscovite accounts charge that Ostrozhsky first offered Cheliadnin peace terms and then suddenly attacked without warning. Prince Mikhail Golitsa immediately advanced, but Cheliadnin was jealous of him and refused to come to his assistance. When the Lithuanians attacked Cheliadnin, Golitsa refused to help him. Finally the enemy attacked Golitsa a second time and Cheliadnin again betrayed him and fled. His action decided the outcome. Both Muscovite and Lithuanian sources agree that the battle of Orsha had serious consequences.

SIGISMUND FAILS TO EXPLOIT VICTORY

The towns of Dubrovna, Mstislavl and Krichev quickly went over to the king. When Prince Mikhail Izheslavsky, the governor of Mstislavl, heard of the approach of the king's army he sent Sigismund a letter in which he promised to serve him, adding that only compulsion had made him briefly serve the grand prince of Muscovy. Varsonofy, bishop of Smolensk, soon took similar action. Like the leading citizens of the city, the princes and the magnates, he concluded that the position of his new sovereign, Vasily, was untenable, and he had a relative take a letter to Sigismund in which he said: "Come at once to Smolensk or send your commanders in force, and you will have no difficulty in taking the city." The Smolensk boyars and the people preferred Muscovite jurisdiction and informed the governor, Prince Vasily Shuisky, of the bishop's design. Shuisky arrested Varsonofy and the other conspirators and informed the grand prince at Dorogobuzh. His move coincided with the appearance of Konstantin Ostrozhsky before Smolensk. Ostrozhsky had only 6,000 men, since he counted on support from the bishop, princes and magnates. Shuisky soon showed him that he could anticipate no assistance from that quarter. On his own initiative he hanged all the conspirators, except Varsonofy, from the city walls in sight of the Lithuanian army. A man to whom the grand prince had given a coat was hanged wearing the coat, and a man who had received a silver cup or spoon was hanged with these objects tied around his neck.

Ostrozhsky wasted further time sending communications to the city urging the inhabitants to surrender to Sigismund and making futile attacks on it. The party sympathizing with the king no longer existed and the rest of the inhabitants resisted him stoutly. Ostrozhsky had to withdraw, and Muscovite soldiers and some of the people pursued him and seized much of his transport. The grand prince approved Shuisky's actions, augmented his forces, and retired from Dorogobuzh to Moscow.

When the chronicles turn to describe the desperate attempt made by Saburov, the governor of Pskov, to take Roslavl,[2] they cease for some time to record the hostilities between Lithuania and Muscovy. The latter, of course, needed to recuperate after the Orsha disaster, but Moscow's battle losses were limited to manpower. The king acquired no advantage from his victory. He failed even to recover Smolensk, control of which fully compensated Vasily for all the losses he had suffered. A letter sent by Andrei Nemirovich, commandant of Kiev, to the council of Lithuania explains why Sigismund won a brilliant victory but proved unable to capitalize on it: "Alp-Saltan, a Crimean prince and son of Mengli-Girey, informed me that he was ready with all his forces on the near side of the Tiasmin river and ordered me to join him in a raid on Muscovy. He refused to go alone. Several times I asked your majesty to tell me what to do, but I have not received any answer. You should try to send me instructions soon. I also asked the administrators and boyars of Kiev to accompany me on our sovereign's business, but all of them refused. You should certainly inform them that they must at once cooperate with me in our ruler's service." A communication like this demonstrates how the bandits of the Crimea hindered Sigismund, although he lavished money to provoke them against Moscow.

In the spring of 1515 the aged Mengli-Girey died. His son and successor, Mohammed-Girey, reproached Moscow for violations of their treaty by failing to inform the khan that the grand prince intended to lead an expedition against Smolensk: "You treated our friend the king in a hostile manner and stole from us the city (Smolensk) we had bestowed upon him. Our father, the mighty ruler, awarded Smolensk to Lithuania, while assigning other towns of our disposition to your father; namely, Briansk, Starodub, Pochap, Novgorod Seversk, Rylsk, Putivl, Karachev, and Radogoshch. If you wish to remain on terms of friendly fraternity with us you must give these towns back to us, because we have now awarded them to the king . . . and if you wish to remain on terms of friendly fraternity with us you must assist us financially and increase your gifts." Besides money the khan asked for falcons and other valuables and the dispatch of Abdul-Letif to the Crimea.

The form of address in communications to the grand prince of Muscovy was now more polite: "I bow to my brother," or "many, many bows." This may be compared with the salutation in the khan's letter to the grand prince of Riazan: "Here is the royal word of Mo-hammed-Girey, mighty khan of the Great Horde, to Ivan, prince of Riazan, our friend and supporter . . . we are your mighty ruler and lord."

Appak, a Crimean nobleman and chieftain who supported Muscovy, wrote to the grand prince: "The khan demands that you cede eight towns. If you agree you will be his friend, but if you refuse he will con-sider you his enemy. If you give him as much money as the king he will certainly leave these towns in your hands. The khan has good reason to be friendly with the king; year in, year out a stream of money flows constantly to the mighty and humble alike." Appak also told Mamonov, the grand prince's envoy: "You have just arrived to represent the grand prince before the khan. You must be adroit in your dealings. No matter what the khan demands, you must never take a hard line. You have to humor him. Unless you respond favorably the khan will send you home empty-handed, for he can take what he likes from you. Always agree with the khan, no matter what he wants; you will incur no disgrace for doing so."

Appak went on to complain to Mamonov that the grand prince had not been generous to him: "Through Abdur-Rahman Lithuania sends the khan 15,000 gold pieces as well as garments, cloth and other goods. The king also makes presents to the khan's sons and daughters, the mullahs, and individual princes and nobles. Everyone is satisfied and no one complains to the khan about the king's gifts. The king also sends Abdur-Rahman an additional 2,000 gold pieces and garments and cloth, besides a further sum for his servitors, which Abdur distributes in his own name among members of the royal family and various nobles, and this too advances the king's interests. The king's affairs naturally prosper. How often has the king said to me: 'Why do you not abandon Muscovy and enter my service? You can ask me for whatever you want and I shall see that you get it.' But talk is cheap and actions speak louder than words. The king made an arrangement with Abdur-Rahman and he must abide by it."

Mamonov reported that when he was proceeding with gifts for the khan, guards blocked his way with staves: "They held me up a long weary time, while everyone demanded the traditional tribute. I refused to listen, but when I tried to retreat they would not let me. Appak was of no help. He went twice to the khan, but as he was coming and going the rest of them kept on scolding me because I had not paid the customary tribute. I would not listen and I would not pay. Prince Appak came to me and in the khan's name demanded 30 squirrelskin coats and 30 caftans to distribute among those to whom the grand prince had reduced the number of his gifts in punishment for neglecting his affairs." Mamonov refused and two of his men were arrested. A Tatar came and demanded gifts. When Mamonov ignored him the Tatar chased the envoy on horseback, twirling a lasso, and tried to trample him beneath the horse's feet. Finally he burst into Mamonov's hut armed with a knife and robbed him of all the khan had demanded. Mohammed-Girey sent a letter to the grand prince justifying such conduct: "You failed to send gifts to many people, who strongly importuned me. Your envoy observed many such incidents. Solely for the purpose of maintaining our fraternal friendship I was reluctantly constrained to confiscate your envoy's store of goods and distribute them among my people—some got coats and others caftans." The khan appended a list of those to whom the grand prince should make presents in future.

Moscow had to put up with such explanations. Replying to the khan, Vasily overlooked the insults his envoy had been obliged to endure and merely asked for a convenant. Mamonov conveyed his request to Prince Bogatyr, Mohammed-Girey's son, and the latter replied: "Who does me greater honor, the king or the grand prince? I shall support the one who does." Mamonov repaired to Ahmad-Girey, the khan's brother, who said: "You see what kind of a sovereign my brother is. When our father ruled we obeyed him. Now our brother sits on the throne, but he lacks authority. His son and the princes lead him around by the nose." The envoy visited the khan's chief wife. She had her own views about Mohammed-Girey and said: "The khan squanders the presents he gets from the king and the grand prince with the wives he likes best."

SIGISMUND AROUSES THE CRIMEAN TATARS AGAINST RUSSIA

Prince Bogatyr promised to work on behalf of the ruler who showed him the greatest honor. The king was the obvious winner, and in 1516 Bogatyr devastated the territory around Riazan. When Mamonov complained to Prince Appak, who favored Moscow, the latter replied: "The grand prince brought this all upon himself. I have repeatedly told him to send as many gifts as the king." The khan wrote to Vasily: "My son

Bogatyr attacked Riazan without my knowledge. Prince Vasily should not encourage malicious individuals, who declare this is sufficient grounds for rupturing our relationship." Promising to attack Lithuania, the khan called on the grand prince to help him conquer Astrakhan: "Let us take Astrakhan. Three or four thousand of the grand prince's fusiliers and artillery can do the job. My brother, the grand prince, is welcome to all the city contains, including fish and salt. I shall be satisfied to know that Astrakhan belongs to me. Although I enjoy a good fraternal relationship with my brother, the grand prince, I cannot guarantee that our men will not attack Meshchera at some future time. My people are restless. They come to me from all quarters and say they will not obey me in this matter. Princes from the Golden Horde conceived the notion of attacking Meshchera without any suggestion from me. It is now held by our enemy, but it has belonged to us since ancient times. My brother, the grand prince, should convey it to my brother or my son. When our family held the place none of our people dared even to look at it."

The grand prince instructed his envoy to offer Meshchera to Mohammed's brother, Ahmad-Girey, and promised to help the khan take Astrakhan, in hope of obtaining a covenant and rupturing the alliance between the Crimea and Lithuania. The king countered by increasing his subsidy, with the result that 20,000 Tatars appeared near Tula in the summer of 1517. Princes Odoevsky and Vorotynsky dealt with them very successfully. Their infantry outflanked the Tatars and intersected their line of march in the woods, where many were killed. Cavalry pursued the bandits along the roads and overtook them at the fords. Many drowned in the rivers and many were taken prisoner. Only a very few of the original 20,000 made their way back to the Crimea. Those who succeeded were dressed in rags and came on foot. Elsewhere, below Sula, Prince Vasily Shemiachich destroyed a Tatar detachment that had come to plunder the Putivl area. The grand prince summoned his brothers and his boyars to council and put the question: "In view of what has happened should we continue to maintain relations with the khan and keep sending cossacks with communications for him?" The council convinced him to maintain relations in order to restrain the khan from an open break with Moscow.

VASILY'S ALLIANCE WITH ALBERT OF BRANDENBURG

Sigismund continued to be active in the Crimea. Mutual interests inevitably led Vasily to make an alliance with Albert of Brandenburg, grand master of the Teutonic Order. The Germans in Lithuania had strongly supported Alexander when the king was at war with Ivan III, and Sigismund was anxious to arouse them against Vasily as well. The council of Lithuania, when informing Plettenberg of the grand prince's attacks on their country, wrote: "You will find yourself in a dangerous position if he manages to acquire some of our fortresses, like Smolensk, Polotsk, Vitebsk, Mstislavl and Orsha. This is especially true because the Poles hold the view that their land runs along the Dvina all the way to the sea and your city of Riga lies within their territory."

Plettenberg needed no reminder of the perils Livonia might anticipate from Moscow or of Muscovy's pretensions. He was fully aware of these dangerous claims, and he hated Moscow. He was ready to make an alliance with Lithuania and Poland and go to war at once, but was deterred by his own weakness and the unsatisfactory relations existing between Poland and the Teutonic Order. The grand master by no means shared Plettenberg's hostility; in fact, he actively solicited Moscow's cooperation against Sigismund. Muscovite envoys returning from the emperor via Prussia informed the grand prince of a request the master had made of them: "The great sovereign should show favor to, protect, and make an alliance with me, I desire to send a legate to the great sovereign for this purpose."

The grand prince told the master that he was willing to favor and protect him. In 1517 Schönberg, Albert's representative, arrived in Moscow to conclude an alliance. Its curious articles reveal the relationship between the contracting parties: "By God's will and in accordance with our own desires, we, Grand Prince Vasily, by God's grace tsar and lord of all Russia, grand prince of Vladimir, etc. (the full list of titles follows) have given this, our rescript, to Albert, a German, grand master of Prussia. He has sent legates to beg us to show our favor to him and protect him from his enemy, the king of Poland and grand prince of Lithuania. We (the titles follow again) have agreed to cooperate with him and wish to support and protect him and his land from his enemy, the king of Poland."

Besides promising cooperation against the king the grand prince agreed to furnish the master a subsidy. Albert asked for a monthly subvention of 40,000 Rheinish gold pieces to maintain 10,000 infantry (four gold pieces per soldier), 20,000 gold pieces to maintain 2,000 cavalry (ten pieces per man with mount), and an additional sum for artillery (cannon and gunners). The grand prince promised to send the money to Prussia as soon as the master took the towns belonging to him which were under Sigismund's control, invaded Poland, and marched on

Cracow. Schönberg asked the grand prince to put his promise in writing in the event that the press of other urgent business led him to forget it, but Vasily refused. He instructed the envoy he sent to the master to say that if the latter asked him to swear that the grand prince would supply the promised money, the envoy should do everything in his power to avoid such a commitment, but if all efforts failed he might give the required pledge. With a second envoy Albert asked the grand prince to transmit 50,000 silver bars to Pskov. When the master opened hostilities the silver could be conveyed to Königsberg and minted in the presence of Russian officials. A Rheinish gold piece was the equivalent of 20 such units. Vasily replied that silver was available but that the Germans would have to begin operations first.

THE MEDIATION OF EMPEROR MAXIMILIAN

Albert had not yet begun hostilities against Sigismund when Vasily's other ally, Emperor Maximilian, halted his own preparations and offered to mediate between Moscow and Lithuania. Vasily was inclined to explore the offer. He had achieved his main goal, the capture of Smolensk, and entertained little hope of further conquest without allies. His defeat at Orsha had taught him a sanguinary lesson of the need for caution. The grand princes of Muscovy always had tried to take advantage of favorable opportunities, proceeded gradually, and avoided hasty decisions. Similar calculations motivated Vasily in his conversations with Albert's envoys. He refused to obligate himself not to make peace with Sigismund until all Russian and Prussian towns had been wrested from the latter, and he accepted the emperor's mediation.

HERBERSTEIN'S EMBASSY

The final round in these negotiations brought Sigismund von Herberstein, the emperor's ambassador, to Moscow in April, 1517. Herberstein made a speech: "The whole universe knows that for many years Christian rulers have quarreled bitterly among themselves, displayed rancor, and shed much Christian blood. Their actions have not benefited the cause of Christianity, for only unbelievers and enemies of Christ's name, such as the Turks and Tatars, have been able to profit from them in order to advance their interests more boldly. Many have fallen into captivity; many kingdoms and cities have been conquered, and the chief cause of it all has been the Christian rulers' inability to agree. Christian rulers must always remember that God conferred their offices upon them to honor Him, advance His faith, and protect all of His people, Christ's sheep.

"Emperor Maximilian has always understood this. He has fought many wars not from ambition, but to bring the whole world to Christ. God has blessed his efforts. The pope and all Italy are presently on friendly terms with him. His grandson Charles, the son of Philip, peacefully rules the twenty-six Spanish principalities. The king of Portugal is a relative, and the king of England and Ireland is an old friend. The king of Denmark, Norway and Sweden is married to his granddaughter and has entrusted his person and his possessions to his majesty. In spite of their disagreements the king of Poland has sought his support. Nothing need be said concerning your eminence; you know the fraternal love that exists between you. Finally, even the king of France, and Venice, who invariably place their own interests above those of the Christian commonwealth, have made peace with him. Wherever one looks in the world today, east and west, or north and south, one sees that all the Christian rulers are related to his Imperial majesty, on terms of fraternity, or at peace with him. Amity universally prevails.

"A state of hostility exists only between your eminence and Sigismund, the king of Poland. Once the war between you has ended, his Imperial majesty will have achieved his goal. The emperor has sent me here to remind your eminence that peace best serves the interests of the Almighty Creator, His Immaculate Mother, and all Christians. He would also remind you of the great benefits you and your people will derive from peace and the miseries you will suffer in war, and to recall to you how dubious are the risks of conflict. When I was with the Polish king in Vilna I met the Turkish ambassador. He stated that his sultan had defeated the Egyptian sultan and conquered Damascus, Jerusalem and all his lands. The Turks were powerful before they won these territories. What plans will they not formulate after achieving such great victories?"

The grand prince transmitted the following reply to Herberstein through his boyars: "The emperor, our brother, knows that we did not start the war with Sigismund. The king began it. We have always prayed that all Christians might live together in peace. The emperor, our brother, earlier asked us to make peace with the king, and we replied that if our enemy King Sigismund desired peace with us he should send envoys to us, as the custom has been. When they come our regard for our brother Maximilian will dispose us to seek suitable terms." To this Herberstein replied that the emperor had previously suggested that the grand prince should send envoys to the king of Denmark, to whom representatives from Poland and the Empire would also go in order to engage in negotiations, but the grand prince had not assented to the proposal. The emperor had charged Herberstein on his departure to bring both hostile parties to the conference table at some border point, but the ambassador had seen with his own eyes how the border towns had been burned and destroyed. Since they were unsuitable as meeting-places, he asked the grand prince to send envoys to Riga.

The grand prince replied: "On previous occasions we have frequently advised our brother that we will not send envoys to Denmark or anywhere else. If King Sigismund is anxious for peace he must send envoys here to us in Moscow. Consider the position. Is it proper for the king to refuse to send envoys to Moscow and thus establish new precedents while forgetting the traditional practices that formerly existed?" Herberstein tried to insist on a meeting at the frontier but met with no success. He then sought permission to dispatch a relative to the king with a request for him to send envoys to Moscow. The relative was dispatched, and returned with the answer that the king was ready to make peace but denied that he was invariably obligated to send envoys to Moscow to conduct the discussions.

When communicating this answer to the boyars the loquacious Herberstein made another long speech, in which he said that men, as intelligent beings, must learn to live on good terms with one another. He cited the moderation displayed by Philip of Macedon, who made peace with the Athenians after defeating them, and contrasted it favorably with the behavior of Philip's son, Alexander the Great, an insatiable conqueror. He praised the restraint and high principles of his sovereign, Maximilian, an example of which was the emperor's restoration of Verona to Venice.[3] He also mentioned Themistocles' defeat of Xerxes, and Pyrrhus, who in the space of an hour lost the fruits of all his victories.

Herberstein's long speech did much to persuade the grand prince to send his envoys to the frontier, but the only answer the Imperial envoy received was the one he had heard before: "We do not choose to send envoys to the frontier or anywhere else. If King Sigismund wants peace he must send envoys to us. We will not set aside the customs we inherited from our ancestors. The practices of our father's time are the practices we follow now. We shall not diminish the legacy God has bestowed upon us. God willing, we shall increase it, insofar as merciful God aids us. We do not care to send envoys to the frontier or anywhere else. The Polish king has conducted a levy and stands on the alert with his army. We too stand on the alert against our enemy and are ready to fight him with God as our Helper." Long fruitless discussions ensued. Herberstein declared his understanding of the king's answer to be that Sigismund was prepared to send envoys to Moscow and merely denied

The
City of Moscow
in the
Sixteenth Century

Колуски

10.
Серпуховьском

Moſkua fluvius

9.
ИВСКИ

ШБЛЦКН

НИКНЦКН

ТБЕСКН

ОСНРЕТЕСКН

КРОСКН

From *Tabula Russioe
ex autographo, quod
delineandum curavit
Feodor filius Tzaris
Boris desumta* (1613)
after a drawing attri-
buted to Fedor Boris-
ovich Godunov

that the grand prince possessed the right to insist that he do so. Herberstein also said that he wanted to dispatch his relative to the king with another request to send envoys to Moscow. This time he planned to tell a white lie, which was that Maximilian had sent three couriers in the interim to demand that matters be brought quickly to a conclusion.

Herberstein sensed the awkwardness of his position. Maximilian had made an alliance with the grand prince against the Polish king and had sworn to cooperate against the common enemy, but now his representative was functioning merely as a mediator and he was providing no military support. Seeking to justify his ruler's actions Herberstein told the boyars that Schnitzenpaumer, the previous Imperial envoy, had grossly exceeded his instructions when he concluded the alliance between the grand prince and the emperor directed against the king. He had committed his sovereign to an unseemly course. A Christian ruler must do everything in his power to find peaceful solutions and prevent the outbreak of war.

Herberstein argued further that the fraternal regard the emperor entertained for the grand prince was the sole inducement that had led Maximilian to agree to implement the agreement since he was recorded as opposing transgression of this basic Christian principle, particularly as he was the leading Christian sovereign. But if the Polish king rejected a peaceful course the emperor was prepared to join the grand prince in an attack on him. Herberstein concluded his remarks by saying: "If your tsarist eminence concurs, I shall designate a period of time within which the king must dispatch envoys. If he ignores the date that is set I shall consider my business here completed, for his refusal will mean that peace cannot be achieved."

The boyars replied that Schnitzenpaumer had acted fully in accordance with the accepted practices followed by accredited envoys obeying their rulers' instructions. The grand prince had adhered to the treaty and would continue to do so. He was convinced that Maximilian had done all in his power to induce Sigismund to make a satisfactory settlement without recourse to war, and if the emperor hesitated to cooperate with the grand prince against their enemies he would be well advised to remember the oath he had sworn when he made the treaty. The grand prince was pleased to respond to the emperor's request to seek peace with King Sigismund, and if such peace were achieved the grand prince expected Maximilian to cooperate with him against the rest of their enemies. If peace eluded them the emperor was duty bound to declare war on the king. After this exchange Herberstein transmitted safe-conducts for the king's envoys.

The king's envoys, the hetmen Jan Szczit and Bogusz, arrived in September, 1517. Three years had elapsed since the battle of Orsha. Sigismund decided the time had come to undertake military probes into Muscovy, even though his envoys were in Moscow to discuss peace terms. Remaining in Polotsk the king sent the hetman, Prince Konstantin Ostrozhsky, with a large force to attack Opochka, a town on the outskirts of Pskov. The governor of Pskov, Vasily Mikháilovich Saltykov-Morozov, beat back their fierce onset with considerable loss to the attackers. Undeterred, Ostrozhsky remained before Opochka twelve days, October 6-18, sending detachments to harass the other outlying towns of Pskov, Voronach, Bele and Krasny. Additional Muscovite forces raced to Opochka and scored three victories over the enemy. Commander Ivan Liatsky destroyed a Lithuanian detachment on its way to join Ostrozhsky and seized its cannon and muskets. The commander was forced to lift the siege of Opochka and withdraw from Muscovite territory.

News of the envoys' approach and Ostrozhsky's offensive reached Moscow simultaneously. Refusing to receive the envoys the grand prince made them wait in Dorogomilov and told Herberstein: "King Sigismund has sent envoys to us but has again practised the deceit typical of him. While his envoys were on their way he sent his senior commander, Konstantin Ostrozhsky, into our borderlands. Our officers have engaged the enemy, but we shall not receive Sigismund's envoys until they have defeated him. We issued safe-conducts to the envoys and we shall respect, maintain and refrain from insulting them."

Herberstein was upset by this decision and worked hard to secure an immediate audience for the envoys. On October 18 he declared he could wait no longer and would leave Moscow at the end of the month. He received the same answer as before. The sovereign would not receive the Lithuanian envoys until his officers had defeated the king's forces. That very day, October 18, on which Herberstein sent his communication, Ostrozhsky retired from Opochka. The grand prince learned of it October 25 and at once told Herberstein: "Our officers have defeated the Lithuanian forces with the aid of All-Merciful God. The Just Lord and Righteous Judge has ruled justly and we have instructed the Lithuanian delegates to appear in our presence on October 29. You must decide whether you wish to join them." The grand prince received the envoys on the appointed day. Herberstein indicated that he was most anxious to participate in the discussions, which began November 1.

Ivan III had proclaimed Kiev and all the West Russian towns to be part of his patrimony. His son's boyars now initiated negotiations by placing Sigismund on notice that he must yield their sovereign's ancestral patrimony, which included Kiev, Polotsk, Vitebsk, and other towns the king illegally held. This claim became institutionalized and constituted an invariable ritual in all later negotiations with Lithuania. This demand is of fundamental historical significance and underscores the nature of the struggle waged by the two rulers, one calling himself grand prince of Lithuania and Russia, the other, grand prince of all Russia. Regardless of the outcome of negotiations in each instance, or the form a particular truce or peace treaty might assume, Moscow deemed it essential in future to assert the right of its grand prince, or tsar, the descendant of St. Vladimir, to hold all the Russian lands which had belonged to the latter. The rulers of Muscovy were convinced that the failure to advance this right would cause others to think they had forgotten or renounced it.

This attitude tells a good deal about the character of the rulers of Muscovy. Once they set themselves a goal they never lost sight of it, and they continually reminded themselves and others of their aims. They were uncommonly dedicated to the maintenance of ancestral tradition, and this dedication became the strongest force propelling the Muscovite state along the road to achievement of an all-Russian empire. The son would never give up what the father had acquired. The custom had been for Lithuanian envoys during Ivan III's reign to conduct their negotiations in Moscow; no matter how hard he tried, Herberstein could not persuade Vasily to send his envoys abroad.

In the negotiations the Muscovite boyars demanded, besides the cities, punishment for the magnates who had treated Grand Princess Elena dishonorably, restoration of all the towns and estates she owned in Lithuania, and the return of all her moveable property and money. The Lithuanian envoys countered with a demand for half of Great Novgorod, Tver, Viazma, Dorogobuzh, Putivl, and the whole Northern Territory.[4] After these preliminaries Herberstein was summoned alone to the palace. The boyars told him: "Schnitzenpaumer agreed that the emperor and the grand prince should cooperate against King Sigismund. This meant that the grand prince was to recover his patrimony, the Russian towns of Kiev, Polotsk, Vitebsk, etc., while the emperor would get his Prussian towns. Consider whether the Lithuanian envoys speak properly when they charge that the grand prince controls the king's towns but claim the king holds none of our sovereign's patrimony."

To avoid answering this awkward question Herberstein simply resorted to the device he had employed previously. He told the boyars that Schnitzenpaumer had exceeded the emperor's instructions. Schnitzenpaumer was merely to discuss the possibilities of an alliance, not to conclude one, although if an alliance existed the emperor would abide by its terms. Concerning his own role Herberstein said: "I would be glad to act but I cannot. I can discover no room for compromise. You advance non-negotiable demands and the Lithuanian envoys do likewise; I can find no basis for compromise. Could I discover any way to reconcile the interests of the rulers, I would gladly spend more time here. They do not trust each other. The best thing to do is have your sovereign send me home."

The Lithuanian envoys told Herberstein they had made wild demands only to show themselves a match for the boyars. Were the boyars to abandon their position, they would take up the real issues they had been sent to negotiate. Discussions resumed after this exchange. The Lithuanian envoys stated that the king reposed full confidence in the emperor. Assuming the office of mediator Herberstein went back and forth between the boyars and the envoys, conveying the demands each group served upon the other. The envoys declared that the king was willing to accept peace on the same terms Ivan III and King Alexander had arranged. The boyars replied that another truce made by those contracting parties, and a peace between Vasily and Sigismund involving new conditions, had intervened in the meantime. They enumerated the wrongful acts perpetrated by the Lithuanian government. Savva Karpov and other members of the king's forces had guided Ahmad when he advanced to the Ugra river. Alexander had provoked Shig-Ahmad against Moscow and Khaletsky, a Lithuanian nobleman, had been one of his guides. Sigismund had similarly aroused Mohammed-Girey, for whom Yakub Ivashentsov, one of the king's courtiers, had served as guide. After peace was made Sigismund once again had stirred up the Crimeans by promising them an annual subsidy of 30,000 gold pieces.

Further, the boyars rehearsed the affair of Elena in detail as it was understood in Moscow. When she was conveyed to Birshany certain magnates, including Nicholas Radziwill, commandant of Vilna, Grigory Ostikov, Klochko, and Butrim, the regional administrator of Vilna, together with Avram, the local treasurer, contrived a plot against her, the like of which no Christian society had ever known. They assigned one of the king's men, Gitovt, a Volynian, to her service. Calling him to Vilna, they gave him poison and sent him back to the queen with instructions for her personal attendants, Dimitry Fedorov, and Dimitry Ivanov, the keeper of the keys, to trust Gitovt implicitly and carry out the magnates' instructions just as he told them. These three villains, Gitovt, Dimitry Fedorov and Dimitry Ivanov, prepared a potent poison, which they introduced into the queen's mead. She died the same day.

Dimitry Ivanov rushed to Vilna to tell the magnates of their success and was rewarded with an estate.

All the extraneous issues were finally reduced to the single question of Smolensk. The envoys insisted on its return, which the boyars categorically refused to consider. Herberstein supported the Lithuanians. In a long elaborate speech he sought to persuade the grand prince to return Smolensk to the king. Once again he alluded to the magnanimity of Pyrrhus, who gave the Romans back their prisoners, and to Maximilian's restoration of Verona to Venice. His speech revealed traces of his long sojourn in Moscow. He was now both familiar with the contemporary scene and had learned something of Russia's history, as can be seen in his famous *Commentary*. Herberstein associated Ivan III with Pyrrhus and Maximilian. Ivan had taken Kazan but restored it to its native rulers. Herberstein wrote Vasily: "If you restore Smolensk to the king your magnanimous generosity will exceed that of your father. He returned Kazan to Tatar unbelievers, but you will display generosity to Christians, not pagans, and to all Christendom, not just your enemy the king. Everyone without exception will extol your advance of the Christian cause and your generosity will demonstrate the love you entertain for his Imperial majesty."

Vasily replied: "You say that our brother Maximilian restored Verona to Venice. Our brother knows very well how this restoration was accomplished. We will not now nor will we in future surrender any portion of our patrimony." The negotiations were broken off. The Lithuanians and Herberstein took their departure. Herberstein promised to use his influence to induce Sigismund to agree to a truce for at least three years, during which the emperor's envoys would strive to achieve a permanent peace between Muscovy and Lithuania. Shortly before his departure Herberstein raised the question of the release of Prince Mikhail Glinsky. The emepror had employed him at his court, and Glinsky had faithfully served Maximilian's relative, Albert, duke of Saxony. Herberstein argued that even were Glinsky guilty, his incarceration constituted a sufficient punishment. Should the grand prince consent to free him and allow him to enter the emperor's service, Maximilian would bind Glinsky with an oath never to plot against Muscovy.

Vasily answered: "Glinsky's actions merited most severe punishment, and we ordered his execution. Then he remembered that his parents were Orthodox but that when he was a young student in Italy he forsook the Orthodox faith and became a Catholic. He asked the metropolitan to receive him back into Orthodoxy. The metropolitan persuaded us not to execute him and conducted a close scrutiny in order to determine whether Glinsky had ulterior motives. He convinced the metropolitan of his sincerity. We would do anything in the world for our brother, but we cannot release Glinsky to him." To this Herberstein observed: "In that case my sovereign has requested that Glinsky serve neither the king nor the grand prince. He wished to enroll him in the service of his grandson, Charles. Although you refuse to grant this boon, you should at least free Glinsky and arrange for me to interview him after his release." Vasily made no response to this request.

The grand prince sent a state secretary, Plemiannikov, to accompany Herberstein as an envoy to the emperor. When the envoy returned he escorted Maximilian's "new" envoys, Francesco da Collo and Antonio di Conti. Like Herberstein, Francesco da Collo tried, in an eloquent speech, to persuade the grand prince to make peace. He dilated upon the danger posed by the Turks to all Europe, but particularly to Russia, because of their proximity to the Tatars, who shared a common faith and customs with the Turks. When these envoys entered into concrete negotiations they encountered the same difficulties as their predecessors. Once more the Imperial representatives insisted that the grand prince restore Smolensk to the king; once again the boyars declared that Vasily would never do so. Failing to achieve a permanent peace, the envoys declared that the grand prince would be well advised to follow the emperor's example of concluding a five-year truce with all kings and princes directed against the Turks, the enemies of Christianity, by making a five-year truce with the Polish king. To this the grand prince agreed, provided that each side kept what it then possessed, and freed its prisoners. Since he held many nobles captured at Orsha, the king unequivocally rejected the second condition. This Imperial mission also left Moscow empty-handed. The grand prince sent an envoy, secretary Borisov, to the emperor, with a proposal to suspend hostilities for a year, from Christmas 1518 to Christmas 1519, while negotiations continued. Maximilian's death put an end to further contacts.

Vasily's arrangements with Austria proved to be as useless as the alliance Ivan III had made. Maximilian had failed to carry out the main stipulation of the agreement, which was to cooperate with Vasily against Sigismund. The emperor pretended to be impartial, but he strongly supported Poland. He summed up his position in a letter he wrote to Grand Master Albert: "It is undesirable to weaken the king and strengthen the Russian tsar."

ATTACK ON POLAND

Albert had exercised restraint in the hope that the emperor would resolve the Order's quarrel with Poland peacefully, but at last he decided
to have recourse to arms. He informed Maximilian that he would no
longer endure further postponement and, sending Schönberg to Moscow
again, he asked the grand prince to transmit money so that he might
begin operations immediately. Vasily conferred with his brothers and
the boyars and decided to render the master financial assistance. He
sent money to maintain 1,000 infantry to Pskov, but stipulated that the
master might not have it until he had actually declared war.

The master asked the grand prince to inform the king of France that
Moscow was allied with Prussia. Vasily assented, and drew up the first
communication Moscow had ever sent to France: "To the most eminent
and illustrious Gallic king. Albert, margrave of Brandenburg, grand
master and prince of Prussia, has appealed to us to inform you that
we hold him in esteem. We desire to inform you by this, our rescript,
that we esteem the master. We shall defend him and his country and we
shall assist him in future. We shall support him and protect him from
his enemy Sigismund, the king of Poland. May God grant that our support and assistance will aid the Prussian master to recover the lands and
towns belonging to the masters of old which our enemy Sigismund now
wrongfully holds. The Prussian grand master has told us that your ancestors showed great favor to the Order. Be mindful of the favor your
ancestors displayed; support the master, and join us in protecting him
and his country from our enemy, King Sigismund." These exchanges
took place in spring, 1518.

Elizar Sergeev, the Muscovite envoy, informed Königsberg of the
grand prince's decision to help the Order as soon as war was declared.
Albert urged the grand prince to furnish full rather than partial support.
Returning to Pskov from Prussia, Elizar recommended against sending
money to the master because he had not commenced military operations. The next development occurred in November, 1518. The master
wrote to the grand prince that the Christian rulers had begun peace
negotiations preliminary to forming a general alliance against the unbelievers, but that he had no intention of becoming a party to them
unless the ruler of Muscovy approved. Dietrich Schönberg arrived in
Moscow a third time in March, 1519, to say that the pope recently had
assumed the role of chief peacemaker. The papal legate, Nicholas Schönberg, was attempting to persuade all the Christian rulers to join an
alliance against the Turks, and the pope had proposed that Albert should

be commander of a united Christian army designed to operate in Hungary against the unbelievers. This development rendered it highly advantageous for Albert to make peace with Poland, but he intended to undertake no move without the grand prince's concurrence. Until he heard from Moscow he would make no commitments of any kind to the pope, although he had indicated that he would send envoys to Rome.

Albert now preferred to have the grand prince conclude a five-year truce with the king, but if Vasily was determined on war, the master would honor his commitment. To start operations against Poland Schönberg needed the money which Vasily had promised, and an agreement on joint strategy. The envoy requested that another letter be sent to the king of France, couched in more diplomatic language, and produced a draft copy. He also asked for a circular to the dukes and princes of the Empire, calling upon them to insist that the new emperor, whom they were in the process of electing to succeed Maximilian, should observe the treaty his predecessor had made with the ruler of Muscovy, and protect the Teutonic Order, which had been founded to defend the German people. The master's final request was for permission to send one of his subjects to Novgorod or Pskov to learn to speak and write Russian from a local priest.

Envoy Zamytsky brought the master Moscow's response to Schönberg's third mission. The grand prince told Albert he was prepared to make a truce upon satisfactory terms, but the master must never forget the oath he had sworn. Here is Zamytsky's description of his reception: "The master received me most honorably. He came in person to hear what I had to say and personally escorted me to table. He assigned me his own place and sat to my left at the banquet." Albert informed the envoy that the general mobilization against the Turks had failed to materialize and nothing now prevented the initiation of hostilities with Sigismund. He intended to begin them without fail in July or August with an attack on Danzig and renewed his request for prompt transmittal of the subsidy.

After repeated requests of this sort the grand prince at last decided, in September of 1519, to send the money. When the grand master asked the master of the Livonian Order to escort a Muscovite courier with the money, Plettenberg replied: "I live closer to the ruler of Muscovy than the Prussian master and I know Russian habits. They are long on talk but short on action." When he was told that a courier had actually arrived in Riga with the money, Plettenberg stood up, raised his hands to the heavens, and cried: "Thank you, Lord, that the mighty sovereign

and tsar of all Russia has shown such great favor to the grand master.
We must be prepared to lay down our lives in recompense for such kindness."

Albert attacked Poland, and as soon as Vasily was satisfied that he
had done so, he sent a further sum to hire 1,000 infantry. Moscow's
support was limited. Lacking other assistance the enfeebled Order was
powerless to resist Sigismund. Hard pressed, Albert had to sue for peace.
Under the terms of the agreement the master was granted hereditary
title to the Order's lands, but had to acknowledge himself a vassal of
Poland. Such was the ignominious end of the illustrious Teutonic Order,
whose involvement with Lithuania made it loom so large in the history
of Russia.

Muscovy obtained at least one advantage from the alliance with
Albert. It served to divert the enemy's strength. After the descent on
Opochka the Lithuanians no longer attacked Russia, whereas the Russians managed several times to invade Lithuania. In 1518 Prince Vasily
Shuisky with a force from Novgorod and heavy artillery, and his brother, Ivan Shuisky, with a force from Pskov, attacked Polotsk. After
reaching the city they set towers in place and fired volleys against the
walls. The army was augmented by another Muscovite detachment under
the command of Prince Mikhail Kislitsa. The inhabitants ably and
vigorously beat back the besiegers and soon famine broke out in the
attackers' camp. A crust of bread cost three kopecks or more, and fodder became expensive. A further misfortune occurred when the enemy
seized the boats a group of young officers had used to cross the Dvina in
search of forage. Pursued by Volynets, a Lithuanian officer, the young
men hastily retreated to the bank but were unable to cross the river,
and many of them drowned. The Shuisky brothers had to lift their
unsuccessful siege of Polotsk.

The next year Prince Mikhail Kislitsa with men from Novgorod and
Pskov again invaded Lithuania near Molodechno and other fortresses.
"God brought them back to Smolensk," as the chronicler puts it.
Another and more significant campaign took place the same year. Prince
Vasily Vasilievich Shuisky started from Smolensk, Prince Mikhail Gor-
baty proceeded from the Novgorod-Pskov region, and Prince Semen
Kurbsky advanced from the Northern Territory. Making descents on
Orsha, Mogilev and Minsk they fought and took prisoners as far as Vilna.
Five Lithuanian magnates prepared to engage them, but when they
heard that their advance units had been destroyed, they withdrew far
into the interior, where the Muscovite detachments did not follow. The
commanders returned to the frontier well satisfied with the severe

devastation they had inflicted on the enemy's territory. Other officers attacked Vitebsk and Polotsk.

The purpose of these raids was to induce Sigismund to make peace, of which Moscow stood sorely in need. The country had suffered severely during six years of war, given the straitened condition of its miltiary and financial resources. After the capture of Smolensk and the battle of Orsha no substantial military activity had taken place for several years, but it was always necessary to maintain strong forces on the frontiers. After these raids, late in 1519 the grand prince summoned his brothers and boyars to council and said: "We have rendered good account of ourselves against the Lithuanians. We have raided their territory almost as far as Vilna. Much Christian blood has been shed, but the king will not come to terms with us. What can we do to make him seek peace?" The grand prince hit on the idea of sending an individual boyar to his Lithuanian counterpart to make private representations.

In pursuit of this goal a boyar, Grigory Fedorovich, sent an attendant in January 1520 to Nicholas Radziwill, commandant of Vilna, with a message that if the king wanted peace he should send envoys to Moscow. In March Radziwill replied that the grand prince should issue safe-conducts for envoys. One of Radziwill's men took the document with him, and in August the envoys, Janusz Kostewicz and Bogusz Bogowitinowicz, arrived to begin negotiations. The boyars advanced the same demands they had made earlier, including compensation for the insults done to Queen Elena. The Lithuanian envoys replied: "These events you mention never occurred. Slanderers told your ruler such a tale, but it is our ruler, his brother King Sigismund, he should believe, and not listen to spiteful persons." Answers like this naturally failed to give satisfaction and were considered nothing better than no answers at all. The peace negotiations foundered on the same rock. Smolensk was the insoluble problem. The envoys proposed a truce, by the terms of which Smolensk would remain under Muscovite control but no exchange of prisoners would take place. The grand prince insisted on a prisoner exchange, but the envoys refused. Finally it was agreed that the king should send ambassadors at Easter, 1521, or six months later, and hostilities should cease in the meantime. Sigismund did not send his envoys within the prescribed period, for the situation had changed to his advantage. He had defeated the grand master and now the position in the east had become what he had been impatiently awaiting since the beginning of his reign: the two Tatar hordes, Kazan and the Crimea, were now allied against Moscow.

KAZAN AND CRIMEA AGAINST MOSCOW

Although Khan Mohammed-Amin had defeated the grand prince's forces, in 1506 Kazan made peace with Moscow on the same terms that had obtained in Ivan III's time. The khan renewed his oath in 1512 and went so far as to ask the grand prince to send a trustworthy man, the boyar Ivan Andreevich Cheliadnin, in whose presence he desired to make formal repentance of his crimes. Cheliadnin went and the khan, as the chronicler tells it, made a full confession in secret before him, repeating his vow to maintain peace, friendship and amity with the grand prince. In 1516 a new embassy from Kazan arrived with news that Mohammed-Amin was dangerously ill. In the name of the sick khan and the people the envoys begged the grand prince to pardon Abdul-Letif, who was again under arrest as a result of the Crimean raids, and allow him to become khan of Kazan in the event Mohammed-Amin died. Vasily assented to the proposal and dispatched a lord-in-waiting, Tuchkov, to Kazan to make the khan and the people swear not to receive anyone as ruler of Kazan without the grand prince's approval. After they took the oath Vasily released Letif and gave him the safe town of Kashira, preliminary to his going to Kazan.

Mohammed-Amin died in December, 1518, but Letif had died a year earlier. The question of who was to be khan of Kazan arose again. The issue had important and serious implications for the Crimea. Mohammed-Girey had made strenuous efforts to unite all the Tatar enclaves under the control of his own house, a policy which Vasily was naturally obliged to combat as vigorously as he could. Needing the grand prince's assistance to acquire Astrakhan and Kazan, Mohammed-Girey sent Vasily a solemn rescript in which he pledged his cooperation against Lithuania in return for Vasily's support against the sons of Ahmad. He swore to stop all raiding and plundering operations and to cease demanding tribute and harassing and insulting Muscovite envoys. The rescript was brought by Prince Appak, who arrived in Moscow before the death of Mohammed-Amin. As Amin's successor the grand prince designated Shig-Aley, Ahmad's grandson, an inveterate foe of the Girey house, who had been assigned the fortress of Meshchersk when he came to Russia from Astrakhan with his father. Appak expressed strong disapproval of the action, but was told that the people of Kazan greatly desired it and if this arrangement were not made they might choose a ruler even more hostile to the house of Girey.

The khan voiced no further objections, since at the moment he lacked the strength to wrest Kazan from Shig-Aley and Moscow. He was forced to try another tack. Shig-Aley soon found himself involved in serious difficulties with the people of Kazan because he invariably set the interest of Moscow above theirs and had constant recourse to the Muscovite commander in his entourage. Representations from the Crimea thus fell on fertile soil. The nobles formed a conspiracy and when in spring, 1521, Sahib, Mohammed-Girey's brother, appeared with an army before Kazan, the city came over to him without firing a shot. Shig-Aley and the grand prince's commander were allowed to depart for Moscow, but the Muscovite ambassador and some merchants were stripped of their belongings and interned.

The grand prince had sympathizers in Azov, including the Cadi, who kept him informed of the khan's activities. For doing so they were of course handsomely rewarded. On May 10 he learned from them that Mohammed-Girey intended to launch an all-out attack on Moscow and that Tatars from Kazan had passed Azov on their way to ask the khan to give them a ruler. The khan had obliged by sending his brother with an escort of 300 men.

The next report from Azov related that a Crimean envoy had told the khan of Astrakhan in Mohammed-Girey's name: "We are brothers. I was on good terms with Moscow, but its prince betrayed me. Kazan belongs to us, but he has installed his own man there as sultan, against the wishes of all the people of Kazan except the chief mullah. The people have sent an envoy to me to ask for a sultan. I have named one and sent him to Kazan, and I intend to make an all-out attack on Moscow. If you want to remain on friendly fraternal terms with me you will join my expedition in person or send your officers." The khan, the princes, and the chief men of Astrakhan were reluctant, for they hesitated to be on bad terms with the ruler of Moscow.

MOHAMMED-GIREY STRIKES MUSCOVY

These warnings arrived too late. Mohammed-Girey had reached the Oka defense line. A Muscovite force under the command of Prince Dmitry Belsky and Andrei Ivanovich, the grand prince's brother, was overwhelmed by the enemy's massive strength. Bypassing towns the Tatars fanned out to plunder the open countryside from Kolomna all the way to Moscow, while to the east Sahib-Girey, the new khan of Kazan, devastated the regions around Nizhegorod and Vladimir and effected a juncture with his brother. Moscow had not beheld an enemy at the gates for a long time; during Vasily's reign the Crimean raiders had been confined to the borderlands and even there they were regularly and successfully repulsed. Mohammed-Girey's attack was all the more unexpected because

Appak has just concluded a solemn covenant with Moscow in the khan's name. Kazan also had not been considered a threat while Shig-Aley was on the throne.

Vasily now found himself in exactly the same situation as Dmitry Donskoy had been when Tokhtamysh attacked,[5] or Vasily Dmitrievich at the onslaught of Edigey.[6] His response was similar. Leaving Moscow he went to Volok to raise troops. The khan halted on the Severka river but his units, coming close to Moscow, ravaged such villages as Ostrov and Vorobevo, as well as a monastery on the Ugra river. Refugees streamed in from everywhere and struggled with one another at the Kremlin gates. In the terrible press plague broke out. If conditions had not altered after three or four days the plague would have attained epidemic proportions, especially as the weather was extremely hot, it being the end of July. When the defenders manned the artillery they found there was not enough powder. Under the circumstances Peter, the baptized Tatar in charge of the defense of Moscow, and the boyars decided to negotiate with the khan. Although the khan had neither the means nor the desire to storm Moscow and intended to withdraw as soon as he heard the grand prince's forces were on their way, Moscow could not long survive so perilous a position.

Mohammed-Girey agreed to leave Moscow as soon as he received a written undertaking from the grand prince to pay tribute. A commitment was made and the khan retired to Riazan, which was under the command of the lord-in-waiting, Khabar Simsky. Evstafy Dashkovich accompanied Mohammed-Girey on his foray to Moscow. He had fled from Lithuania to Moscow during Ivan III's reign, returned to Lithuania in Vasily's time, and now was one of the Dnieper cossacks supporting the khan. Dashkovich planned to capture Riazan by a ruse. He proposed that the inhabitants should ransom their prisoners, as this would give him an opportunity to meet those paying ransom at the city gates. To further the enterprise the khan was to trick Commander Khabar. Calling him a slave and a tributary he summoned Simsky to appear before him in his camp. Khabar replied that he did not believe the grand prince had actually agreed to become the khan's tributary and demanded proof. The khan let him see the letter the grand prince had signed. Meanwhile Dashkovich, following his plan, edged closer to Riazan. He deliberately allowed a few prisoners to escape and run to the city. Bands of Tatars pursued them, insisting they be returned. The people of Riazan gave up the prisoners, but the Tatar bands at the city walls kept growing larger. The defenders' cannon, under the control of a German, Johann Jordan, suddenly fired a volley and the Tatars scattered in terror. The khan demanded Jordan be surrendered to him, but Khabar refused. Moham-med-Girey had not planned to assault cities. Failing to take Riazan by guile, and disturbed by reports of hostile movements on the part of the forces of Astrakhan, he withdrew, leaving a copy of the grand prince's agreement to pay tribute with Simsky.

Mohammed-Girey's raid had very serious consequences. Rumor ex-aggerated the number of prisoners the Crimeans and the people of Kazan took in Muscovy (numbers ran as high as 800,000), but this ex-aggerated testimony shows the extent of the devastation. The Crimeans sold their prisoners in Kaffa and the people of Kazan sold theirs in Astrakhan. The size of the booty whetted Mohammed-Girey's appetite. On his return he made three proclamations, in Perekop, Crimeagrad and Kaffa, ordering princes, nobles, and all Tatars to ready themselves and their mounts for an autumn raid on Muscovy. The raid never took place, and in spring, 1522, the grand prince, seizing the initiative, advanced to the Oka with numerous troops and artillery to encounter the khan. Although Mohammed-Girey failed to appear on that occasion either, Vasily had to maintain a continuous alert. Constant raids had also to be expected from Kazan; thus, it was essential to remove Mohammed-Girey's brother from power there as quickly as possible.

TRUCE WITH LITHUANIA

These developments required the conclusion of a speedy truce with Lithuania. Negotiations with Sigismund were resumed in August, 1521, directly after Mohammed-Girey's departure. In March, 1522, Stanislaw Dolgirdow (or Dovkirdovich) came from Lithuania to say that the king refused to send ambassadors to Moscow until the grand prince had indicated whether he desired permanent peace or a truce without a prisoner exchange. Vasily Polikarpov was entrusted with the reply. He was to tell the king to send council members as ambassadors, because the grand prince wished either peace or a truce, and a prisoner exchange. If Lithuania rejected these terms and dismissed him, Polikarpov was instructed to say: "Our sovereign desires permanent peace with King Sigismund, but he is willing to accept a truce without a prisoner ex-change." He had to fall back on the second position, but it succeeded in bringing Lithuanian ambassadors to Moscow in August, the commandant of Polotsk, Peter Stanislawowicz, and the treasurer, Bogusz Bogowitino-wicz. They concluded a five-year truce with no prisoner exchange. Smolensk remained under Muscovite control. Provision was made to continue negotiations for a permanent peace during the five-year period.

Helped by the good offices of envoys from the emperor, Charles V, serious discussions took place in 1526, but proved unproductive. The truce was extended to 1533, and then again for one more year. Smolensk continued to be the bone of contention which prevented achievement of a permanent peace. The king was absolutely determined never to acknowledge Moscow's right to the city, while the grand prince was equally adamant in his refusal to yield a single bit of his patrimony. The recovery of Smolensk was the glory of his reign. Measures Vasily took to integrate Smolensk into the grand duchy of Muscovy emerge from the instructions he gave his envoy, Zagriazsky, when he was sent to Lithuania: "If the Lithuanians ask why the grand prince has transferred people from Smolensk to Moscow, you are to reply that those he desired to have go to Moscow went to Moscow, and those he chose to leave in Smolensk stayed in Smolensk. Those the grand prince has summoned to Moscow enjoy his favor and have obtained homes, shops and estates there." Smolensk remained under Muscovite control, but the prisoners taken in the "Great Battle" (as the battle of Orsha was known in Lithuania) remained in Sigismund's hands. By 1525 many had died, and those who survived were in wretched condition. A list compiled for the king shows that the prisoners, who had previously been given food, now received none. They complained that they were dying of starvation, and of some it was said: "They have no food. They eat only what they can beg in Christ's name. They are closely confined under heavy guard."

STRUGGLES AGAINST KAZAN

The truce with Lithuania enabled the grand prince to devote his entire attention to the situation in the east. When he made his brother ruler of Kazan, Mohammed-Girey alarmed Moscow, and he lost no time carrying out a policy he had long desired, the conquest of Astrakhan. He succeeded in his undertaking. Forming an alliance with Mamay, khan of the Nogays, he managed to seize Astrakhan while its ruler, Hussein, strove to make a closer alliance with the prince of Muscovy. Mohammed-Girey's triumph was short-lived. His allies, the Nogay princes, feeling seriously threatened by his success, suddenly attacked the Crimean camp, killed the khan, and slew many of his men. In pursuit of Mohammed-Girey's sons the Nogays burst into the Crimea and ravaged it at the same time as the khan's other ally, Evstafy Dashkovich, and his cossacks were also engaged in devastating it. The dead khan's place was assumed by his brother, Saidat-Girey, whose first move was an appeal to the grand prince to send 200 rubles and make peace with Sahib-Girey of Kazan. In return he promised to become the prince's ally.

The grand prince had no intention of subsidizing the Crimea, which now constituted no danger in its devastated condition, nor of easing his pressure on Sahib-Girey in Kazan, especially because when Sahib-Girey heard that his brother had taken Astrakhan he ordered the Muscovite envoy and the merchants, taken prisoner when Shig-Aley was expelled, to be put to death. The Muscovite envoy to the Crimea received these instructions: "You are not to pay tribute under any circumstances whatsoever. The only exception is the presents to the khan, and anything you may choose to distribute on your own behalf in order to obtain advantage, but not as tribute. You are forbidden to make payments to members of the royal family and the Tatar nobility. If they brandish whips before you when demanding gifts you are to brush them aside and go straight to the khan. If palace attendants demand payment you are not to give it to them. It is better for an envoy to endure personal humiliation than to pay tribute.

"If the khan neglects to call the grand prince his brother in his covenant you are not to accept the document. You need not state that the grand prince will cooperate with the khan against Astrakhan and the Nogays; it is enough to declare that the grand prince will cooperate with the khan against his enemies. If the khan asks the grand prince to come to terms with Sahib, the ruler of Kazan, you are to say: 'An accommodation is out of the question. Sahib became ruler without the grand prince's approval and has put a Muscovite envoy and merchants to death. This is utterly uncivilized behavior; hostilities between rulers are no excuse for murdering envoys and traders.' "

In the summer of 1523 the grand prince journeyed to Nizhny Novgorod, from which he sent Khan Shig-Aley with ground and naval forces up the Volga to attack Kazan. He also dispatched other officers with cavalry detachments, instructing them to take strategic places as they proceeded overland to Kazan. After a series of successful operations the officers returned with numerous Cheremis prisoners, but the campaign had wider implications. The town of Vasilsursk was built at the mouth of the Sura river not far from Kazan. In Moscow Metropolitan Daniel, praising the grand prince for taking this action, declared that the new town would serve as a base from which to conquer Kazan. The town was indeed intended to become a Muscovite advance post inside the territory of Kazan, the first step in the final conquest of the khanate. Twice the rulers and people of Kazan had sworn to maintain friendly relations, but their oaths had proved unsatisfactory guarantees. By building Vasilsursk Vasily took the first step towards the final subjugation of Kazan. His son Ivan took the second when he built Sviiazhsk. The third was the capture of Kazan itself.

In summer, 1524 a substantial force, numbering more than 150,000 men, under the principal command of Prince Ivan Belsky, again appeared before the walls of Kazan. Taking fright, Sahib-Girey left his thirteen-year old nephew, Safa-Girey, in Kazan while he sought refuge in the Crimea, although he promised to return with a Turkish army. Proclaiming young Safa-Girey ruler, the people of Kazan prepared for a siege. Prince Belsky sailed up the Volga from Nizhny Novgorod, while Khabar Simsky led the cavalry overland. Prince Paletsky was to follow the main detachment up the Volga with supplies and artillery. Belsky disembarked his forces July 7 and pitched camp near the fortress of Gostiny in sight of Kazan, where he waited twenty days for the cavalry to come up. It failed to arrive, but in the meantime the wooden walls of the citadel in Kazan caught fire. The Muscovite units failed to take advantage of the blaze in order to storm the citadel, nor did they subsequently interfere with the attempts of the people of Kazan to put up a new wall.

On July 28 Belsky transferred his camp to the bank of the Kazanka river. Taking up position nearby, Safa-Girey several times tried and failed to demolish the Russian camp with charges by Cheremis infantry. Time passed, but neither the cavalry nor the supply boats arrived. The army ran short of food, for the Cheremis had devastated the entire area, barred all the roads, and prevented detachments from foraging. They also severed the lines of communication, and Moscow was not informed of the army's plight.

After hunger had seriously undermined the morale of Belsky's troops a rumor spread that the Tatars had defeated the cavalry. Alarmed, the commanders considered withdrawing, until they learned the rumor was false. A small unit had sustained a defeat, but the main detachment, proceeding under Simsky's command, had beaten the Tatars in two engagements at Sviiag. The cavalry successfully surmounted all dangers, but the same could not be said of Paletsky's convoy. Blocking a narrow strait between two forts with heaps of wood and stone, the Cheremis assailed the Russian ships from the banks with showers of arrows and logs. The commander managed to bring no more than a handful of ships through to join the main force.

Undeterred by this disaster Belsky invested Kazan on August 15, after the cavalry arrived. Siege engines advanced to the walls under the protection of mounted units. The people of Kazan fought back, but they soon lost their chief artilleryman (there was only one in the city), sued for peace, and promised to send envoys to Moscow for negotiations. Belsky was delighted to lift the siege because famine had seriously impaired the army's effectiveness. Envoys went to Moscow, admitted the guilt of the people of Kazan, and begged the grand prince to confirm Safa-Girey as their ruler. Vasily hesitated, but finally approved their request. He had not committed such a large force against Kazan just to exchange one member of the Girey house for another, but the unsuccessful campaign had failed to justify expectations.

As often happened in such cases, charges were made against Belsky, the senior commander. He was accused of inexperience, timidity, and outright treachery. It was alleged that the people of Kazan had bribed him to pull back from the walls. The most serious charge apparently was that Belsky had wasted time at Gostiny instead of taking advantage of the fire in the citadel and preventing the inhabitants from rebuilding the walls. The final report on operations exonerated Belsky. He could not assume the initiative without cavalry to protect his main force from attacks by the Kazan cavalry and the Cheremis, who were everywhere, keeping him immobilized. Subsequent developments also justified Belsky's actions; during the final siege of Kazan Ivan the Terrible found himself in exactly the same position. The Tatar cavalry led by Prince Yapanchi harassed him incessantly and never allowed his army, which was suffering from hunger, time to recoup. Ivan was at last obliged to divide his forces. One part remained with him while the other operated against Yapanchi.

During the next four years the sources make no reference to Kazan. Then in 1529 Safa-Girey sent men to Moscow stating that their ruler was anxious to reach a full understanding with the grand prince, swear an oath of fealty, and exchange envoys. The grand prince sent Andrei Pilemov to Kazan to receive Safa-Girey's oath, and Prince Ivan Paletsky followed soon afterwards to enforce its provisions.

In Nizhny Novgorod Paletsky learned that Safa-Girey had broken his oath and seriously affronted Pilemov. Again recourse to arms was had, and a large river and cavalry force proceeded to Kazan in the summer of 1530. As before, the fleet was under the command of Prince Ivan Belsky, but the cavalry was led by Prince Mikhail Glinsky, now released from confinement. Repulsing several enemy attacks Glinsky crossed the Volga and effected a juncture with the fleet. The Russians won a fierce battle on July 10. Next they occupied the redoubts and made an attempt on the fortress. Three Kazan noblemen approached the commanders, begged them to lift the siege, and promised to obey the grand prince. The commanders administered an oath to the people of Kazan which bound them to be loyal to the grand prince and place no ruler on the throne without his approval. They withdrew and returned to Moscow, accompanied by envoys from Kazan.

A few chronicles add that the commanders who took the redoubts almost captured the fortress as well. It was left undefended for three hours, during which time everyone fled the city, leaving all the gates open. At that moment Belsky, the infantry commander, was locked in a dispute with Glinsky, the cavalry commander, over precedence and who should be first to enter the city. While they argued a fierce storm arose and rain poured down in buckets. This frightened the cannoneers and fusiliers transporting the cannon. They abandoned the guns, which the people of Kazan promptly appropriated. Although this story should not be rejected out of hand, its details are unconvincing.[8]

In Moscow the envoys approved a binding covenant, to which Safa-Girey and the people of Kazan were supposed to swear before Ivan Polev, the grand prince's representative. By its terms Kazan was to hand over to Polev all the prisoners and arms it had taken in the recent wars. The envoys were to remain in Moscow until he returned. Polev soon informed the grand prince that Safa-Girey was procrastinating in the matter of taking the oath and restoring the arms. The khan forwarded a note demanding that the grand prince release the Kazan envoys and send them home escorted by envoys of his own. The grand prince was also to restore all the cannon, muskets and prisoners he had taken. The khan would not swear to observe the treaty and free Ivan Polev until he had done so.

When the grand prince received the note he said to the Kazan envoys: "You swore that the khan and the people of Kazan would obey us; here is an example of their obedience!" The envoys replied: "According to the khan's courier the people believed Moscow had sent troops to attack Kazan. The report was false but, as you know, few honest men are left in Kazan. People are petty and no one thinks of the common defense. Everyone is terrified and it is a case of each man for himself. The grand prince is fully sovereign in his country; God and he are free to work their will there. The same is true of Kazan. The ruler's will is law, and we are slaves of God and the khan. We were sent to petition the grand prince on behalf of the khan and the people of Kazan. We spoke sincerely and with no intent to deceive, but the khan has not kept his part of the bargain. He is surrounded by Crimeans and Nogays and malicious advisers. The rest of the people has no sympathy with them and awaits the grand prince's decision whether he will permit Safa-Girey to remain khan of Kazan or send us another ruler."

The grand prince replied: "If Safa-Girey will obey me and behave honorably I shall be happy to let him be khan of Kazan, but, as you can see, he is acting dishonorably." The envoys responded: "We do indeed see that he is behaving wrongfully. He has violated his oath, neglected his responsibilities, and forsaken us. He is not an honorable man. God and the grand prince know what dispositions to make in Kazan. We are wholly in the grand prince's power, and whatever khan he chooses to set over us is the ruler we desire." They followed this statement by asking Vasily to restore Shig-Aley, who had never raided Kazan and would not tolerate ill-intentioned people. They suggested that Vasily send Shig-Aley to Kazan after instructing him how to attend to his duties and treat the inhabitants. They also suggested the grand prince should send them, Shig-Aley, and the prisoners to Vasilsursk. While there they promised to get in touch with people in Kazan, the Cheremis of the hills and plain, and other local princes, and tell them the grand prince was anxious to help and protect them.

The grand prince inquired: "What was your intent when you came to us? Did the princes and people instruct you to request Shig-Aley?" The envoys replied: "We received no instructions. We have told you why we were sent. Now we ask the sovereign to show us his favor and let us serve him. We do not wish to serve Safa-Girey. He has ruined us, but the sovereign has restored us. Safa-Girey sent us on important business, but he has scorned our best efforts and abandoned us. He does not need us, and we do not need him. We have families, brothers and friends in Kazan, and our people captured by the grand prince also have fathers, brothers, relatives and friends there. As soon as we reach Vasilsursk and communicate with them they will support us."

The grand prince took counsel with his boyars and sent a courier, Posnik Golovin, to Kazan, ostensibly to carry a reply to Safa-Girey. He was instructed to talk with two Kazan noblemen and seek out their views. The courier must have brought back a favorable report, because the grand prince conferred again with his boyars, and sent Shig-Aley and the envoys, not to Vasilsursk, but to Nizhny Novgorod, which was safer because it was closer to Moscow. When Safa-Girey learned of these activities he decided to kill Polev, the Muscovite envoy, and resume open warfare with the grand prince. But as soon as messages from the envoys in Nizhny Novgorod reached Kazan the nobles and the people expelled Safa-Girey, murdered his Crimean and Nogay advisors, and packed his wife off to her father, the Nogay prince Mamay. They feared Shig-Aley and asked the grand prince not to appoint him, but to name his younger brother, Enaley, who held the fortress of Meshchersk.

Assenting to their proposal the grand prince dispatched Enaley to Kazan and assigned Kashira and Serpukhov to Shig-Aley. The latter was dissatisfied and entered into correspondence with Kazan and other places without the grand prince's approval. This was in violation of his oath and led to his removal from Kashira and Serpukhov and confinement in Beloozero. Moscow was delighted with Enaley. When he and the people of Kazan asked the grand prince to leave a few cannon in their city because a few enemies were still to be found in the otherwise friendly country, Vasily granted the request, calling Enaley brother and son in the process. When Enaley decided to marry the daughter of a Kazan nobleman he first asked the grand prince's permission. By 1531 all such issues as these touching Kazan were decided in Moscow.

TROUBLES WITH THE CRIMEA

Kazan was pacified but the Crimea remained turbulent. In the fall of 1527, Islam-Girey, a kinsman of Saidat-Girey, whose envoys were then in Moscow, appeared on the banks of the Oka. The Muscovite commanders on the scene prevented the Tatars from crossing the river. Islam lost many men, killed by the junior officers pursuing them, and beat a hasty retreat. When news of Islam's raid spread, the grand prince ordered Saidat-Girey's envoys drowned.[9]

Saidat-Girey was expelled and his place was taken by Sahib-Girey, the former ruler of Kazan. In August, 1533 the grand prince learned that two of the khan's relatives, Islam-Girey and Safa-Girey, were on their way to the Muscovite borderlands. Vasily lost no time equipping a force, summoned his brothers, Yury and Andrei, and dispatched officers to Kolomna and the Oka region, while he proceeded in person on August 15 to the village of Kolomenskoe, after attending mass in the cathedral of the Assumption. He ordered cannon and muskets placed around the Kremlin while he was away and told the inhabitants of the suburbs to bring their possessions into the city. That same day the Tatars appeared before Riazan, set fire to its outskirts, and fanned out to ravage, plunder and take prisoners in the surrounding countryside.

The grand prince ordered his commanders to cross the Oka and intercept the pagans. Prince Dmitry Paletsky, commander of one detachment, destroyed a host of Tatars some six miles from Nikola Zarazsky, and Prince Ivan Ovchina-Telepnev-Obolensky attacked another band. While pursuing it he came upon the main Tatar force. The enemy defeated Obolensky and captured some of his men, but advanced no further and withdrew from Muscovite territory in fear of encountering the grand prince's main army. The officers set out in pursuit but could not over-take the khan's forces.

Such raids did not impair normal relations with the Crimea. Moscow tried to make alliances and obtain covenants, but the bandits were inter-ested only in gifts and complained that Moscow sent very few presents. They declared it was more profitable for them to fight the grand prince than to be at peace with him. Vasily had no intention of subsidizing them to no purpose and conveyed his views in this answer to the khan when the latter complained: "If you manifest your friendship tangibly we shall respond in kind, and seek to cooperate in every way possible, but we have never sent gifts to anyone under duress. If you wish to be friends with us you must inscribe a solemn covenant." The khan refused to budge from his position: "You made me nine gifts. We sent you earlier a list containing the names of 120 persons, but your gifts were only enough for fifteen people. You know very well what our people are like; they live by war." Sahib asked for more than falcons and furs; he demanded that the grand prince send him a good baker and a cook. Vasily refused further to indulge such greediness. He abandoned the fulsome style he had used in his correspondence with the khan. Instead of expressions of humility his communications now began with a trans-lation of the Tatar term, "many, many bows." He no longer treated the khan's envoys with the deference he had shown them before. This moved the khan to write to the grand prince: "Our couriers report that you no longer show them the honor they used to receive in the old days. You should continue to do so. He who would honor the master must throw his dog a bone."

Sigismund of Lithuania continued his annual subsidy of more than 20,000 rubles and a like value of cloth to the Crimea, but stipulated he would send it only in years when the Crimeans refrained from attacking Lithuania. Khan Sahib-Girey was displeased with this arrangement and wrote the king: "Your actions show that you do not wish permanent peace with me. If you did, you would send me 50,000 rubles, as you used to send my brother, Mohammed-Girey." The khan also complained to the king about the Ukrainian cossacks, who constantly took advantage of the Tatars and, like the Muscovite and Putivl irregulars, gave advance warning of Tatar raids on Moscow. Lithuanian towns still paid a tribute, commonly known as Horde Pence, for the support of the Crimeans.

RELATIONS WITH OTHER STATES

Vasily's reign was absorbed in the problems of Lithuania and the Tatar hordes. Relations with other countries in Europe and Asia were not of

comparable significance. The sixty-year peace with Sweden concluded in
1508 was reaffirmed twice, in 1513 and 1524. Truces with Livonia were
negotiated in 1509, 1521, and 1531. A truce was made with the seventy
Hansa towns stretching "from sea to sea" in 1514. Reciprocal free trade
between the Hansa towns and Novgorod was reestablished on its former
basis. German merchants regained their church and their original trading
depots there. They agreed to restore and not to desecrate Russian
churches or harass Russian communities in their towns, and not to aid
Lithuania. A treaty of alliance was made with Johann, king of Denmark,
in 1511, and again in 1517 with Christian. The latter's request to allow
Danish merchants to build depots with churches in Novgorod and Ivangorod was granted.

Pope Leo X sought the help of Grand Master Albert to establish ties
with Moscow. On behalf of the pope, Schönberg, Albert's envoy, told
the grand prince: "The pope longs to unite the grand prince and the
Russian people with the Catholic church. No diminution of or change in
their good customs and laws will occur. His sole desire is to strengthen
these customs and laws, and he will confirm and bless them with an
apostolic decree. The Greek church has no leader, for the patriarch of
Constantinople is under the thumb of the Turks. The pope is aware that
Moscow possesses a most spiritual metropolitan. He wishes to honor the
metropolitan by making him a patriarch, comparable in rank to his
predecessor in Constantinople. He also wishes to crown the most eminent tsar of all Russia as a Christian monarch. The pope seeks no personal advantage; he craves only the glory of God and the unity of
Christendom. The grand prince need not attack Lithuania. Time is on
his side. King Sigismund has no successor. When he dies the Lithuanians
will never accept a Pole as their ruler, nor will the Poles accept a Lithuanian, and the two countries will fall out. Should the grand prince
seek his patrimony in Constantinople, the road lies open and assistance
is at hand." The pope meant the league of Christian rulers against the
Turks which he was inviting the grand prince to join. Peace with King
Sigismund was an essential prerequisite to such a move.

The Muscovite envoys replied to Albert: "Our sovereign desires
friendly relations with the pope, but by God's grace our sovereign adheres firmly to the Greek faith he inherited from his ancestors, as he
ever has, and he desires to maintain his faith unsullied." An exchange of
envoys between Rome and Moscow ensued, but produced no significant
results. The grand prince unequivocally rejected the pope's proposal to
unite the churches, and to the offer to join the anti-Turkish alliance
he replied: "God willing, we shall always champion Christianity against

unbelievers. We wish to enjoy close friendship with you and the other Christian rulers, and a free exchange of envoys."

Muscovy set greater store on its relations with Turkey, although in spite of Moscow's best efforts they remained approximately what they had been in Ivan III's time. The simple facts of geography rendered sustained conflict between them impossible. They were separated by the steppe, and the Turks had no interest in seeking conquests in the cold northern part of Europe. At the same time they had no mutual interests to bring them together. Moscow enjoyed constantly growing success in its struggle with the Islamic Tatar kingdoms, and sooner or later the sultan was bound to become involved. In the meantime minor communities of interest in such matters as trade existed. The sultan was satisfied to maintain relations on that level, but the grand prince set his sights higher.

In 1513 he sent an envoy, Alexeev, to Constantinople to assure the sultan that relations between Vasily and Selim would remain as friendly as they had been in their fathers' time. Alexeev was told: "Press your hands tight against your body above your girdle and bow to the sultan, as is their custom, but do not fall on your knees before him or strike the ground with your forehead." The sultan, replying in a letter written in Serbian, called for unrestricted official and commercial intercourse between the two countries. In another letter he sought to have Khan Letif released and transferred to the Crimea. In a third he asked the grand prince to assist Kamal, the sultan's envoy, in a quest for rare merchandise. Kamal declared: "My sovereign sent me to inform the grand prince that he desires fraternal friendship with him and to ascertain whether the grand prince reciprocates his sentiments, but my sovnever authorized me to put anything in writing."

In 1515 the grand prince sent another envoy, Korobov, to Constantinople to concert an alliance with the sultan against Lithuania and the Crimea. He was also to try and outlaw the Turkish officials' habit of appropriating the goods and possessions left by Russian merchants who died in Turkey. Korobov returned with a letter in which the sultan agreed to ban the practice but ignored the alliance. He promised to send a new ambassador to Moscow, but this too failed to materialize. In 1517 the grand prince informed his boyars he had heard nothing from the sultan since Korobov's return and felt he should make further overtures. Vasily sent a courtier, Golokhvastov, but all he brought back from the sultan was a promise of free trade. One beneficial result of all this was that although the sultan declined alliance with Vasily he forbade the Crimean khan to raid Muscovy. The khan's displeasure with this edict may readily be imagined.

Muscovy's supporters in Azov supplied the gist of the sultan's message to the khan: "I have heard that you intend to attack Muscovy. Consider your well-being and do not venture to attack the grand prince, because he is my good friend. If you attack him, I shall attack you." This communication made the khan furious because all his forces were in readiness. To avoid such occurrences in the future the khan tried to incite the sultan to anger with the grand prince, while the latter tried to maintain friendly relations with the sultan as a check on the Crimeans. In 1521, when the grand prince learned of Selim's death, he sent an envoy, Gubin, to Constantinople to hail the accession of Suleiman, the new sultan, complain about Mohammed-Girey, and attempt to negotiate an alliance. One of the main problems in doing so had always been the difficulty of communicating across the steppe. Gubin was charged with persuading the Turkish government to accept a site in the steppe near the river Don where armed escorts from Moscow and Turkey could meet and arrange for an exchange of envoys. Since it was thought necessary to designate the meeting place somewhere on the Don, inquiries were conducted among the Riazan cossacks. They declared that the point half way between Azov and the Muscovite border where the land narrows between the Don and the Volga served as the chief crossing-point for the people of Astrakhan, so that guides could not meet there. Medveditsa, close to the Muscovite border, might be adequate, but the best site was Khopor.

Provided with this information, Gubin was to do all in his power to persuade Turks to come to Khopor, with Medveditsa as a second choice. To dispose of the khan's charges, Gubin was to state in Constantinople: "Rumors in Moscow say that Mohammed-Girey has written to the sultan that Kazan belongs to the Crimea, and that our sovereign has ordered the mosques there destroyed and Christian churches with bells be put up in their place. As is customary, the wicked, scheming Crimeans have uttered unjust words and are telling lies." Gubin was also instructed to narrate the sequence of events in Kazan as it had occurred and assure the sultan that no destruction of the mosques was contemplated. Muscovy's supporters informed the grand prince of further charges the khan had made. According to them the khan had informed the sultan that Vasily had concluded an alliance with the shah of Persia and sent him arms, including 30,000 muskets. When the sultan again forbade the khan to fight with Muscovy the khan said to him: "You tell me not to attack either Muscovy or Wallachia. Where do you think I shall get food and clothing? The prince of Muscovy is cooperating with Kizylbash, the shah of Persia, against you."

On his return Gubin escorted a Turkish envoy, Iskander, prince of Mankup, who declared that if the grand prince desired friendly fraternal relations with the sultan he should send a "trustworthy man" to conclude a binding agreement. Ivan Semenovich Morozov was accordingly dispatched to Turkey, but this "trustworthy man" was unable to execute his commission, conclude a treaty, or even persuade the sultan to send an official to Moscow empowered to make an alliance. He returned with some strange stories: for example, a Greek, Hadrian, a representative of Absalom, the sultan's treasurer, approached him and said: "Absalom has asked me to tell you that we have a system of contributions and that you, sir, should not forget us. Previous envoys paid us tribute, and you, sir, ought not to neglect us. It is fitting for you to honor Absalom, because he stands close to the sultan and holds an office of great responsibility. Your affairs will suffer neglect if you fail to honor him." The envoy replied: "My mission has nothing to do with tribute. Officials of government carry out the business of state without hope of gain. I have no objection to showing Absalom a few tokens of my personal affection in order to establish good relations with him, but I am categorically opposed to offering bribes to anyone in return for official favors." Hadrian said: "This is Absalom speaking: 'I shall select splendid gifts for the envoy in the sultan's name if he honors me, but if he does not, the presents he receives will be paltry.' " The envoy replied: "I am here on matters of state. I seek no gifts and I shall not offer bribes to get them." After Hadrian departed an attendant arrived to say: "This is the sultan's word: 'Absalom enjoys my confidence. He is my secretary, treasurer, and son-in-law. For my sake you must honor him and see that he receives some presents.' " This time the envoy answered: "If the sovereign so says, we shall make him a present, for the sovereign's sake. This is the way we do things at home." Morozov sent a squirrelskin coat to the treasurer.

Relations continued but were limited as before to commerce, although already it was possible to foresee the hostile confrontations between the two states that lay not far in the future. On a second mission Iskander stated that Sahib-Girey of Kazan had asked for the sultan's protection, and his act of submission meant that Kazan now formed part of the sultan's domain. He was told that Moscow had always controlled the destinies of Kazan. Iskander journied home via Putivl and the Crimea. He wanted to return along the Don, but the grand prince would not allow it. Reports came back from those in his company and others that Iskander had been sent to spy out a suitable spot on the Don to build a Turkish fortress.

Iskander came to Moscow a third time, now on a trade mission. He displayed considerable hostility and threatened to embroil the grand prince in a quarrel with the sultan. He died in Moscow, and dispatches for the sultan he had already prepared were found among his papers. He had written that when a prisoner from Azov came to Moscow and announced that the king of Hungary had defeated the Turks, Vasily was supposed to have been filled with joy and ordered the church bells rung. The well-known figure, Maxim the Greek,[10] was accused of having dealings with Iskander. Moscow maintained relations with the Nogay princes and the Indian king, Babur, in the interests of trade. Relations with Moldavia and Astrakhan were minimal.

MOSCOW GAINS RIAZAN, SEVERSK AND VOLOTSK

Although the chroniclers describe the wars with Lithuania and the Crimea and the capture of Smolensk and Pskov in detail, they virtually ignore the incorporation of the grand duchy of Riazan and the Seversk duchies into Muscovy. Dying without issue, Fedor, the appanage prince of Riazan, bequeathed his realm to Ivan III; thus, parts of Riazan proper, as well as the area known as Old Riazan, already belonged to Moscow by Ivan's time. Vasily called himself grand prince of Riazan before the process was fully completed. Ivan III administered Riazan during the minority of its own prince, Ivan Ivanovich, and his son continued this policy. When the grand prince of Riazan attained his majority he realized that he was merely the grand prince's lieutenant. He was faced with the choice of voluntarily becoming a tributary of Moscow or having recourse to arms in order to reassert his former sovereignty. He chose the second alternative.

In 1517 the grand prince learned that the grand prince of Riazan had made personal contact with Mohammed-Girey and actually contemplated marrying his daughter. Vasily summoned him to Moscow. At first he refused to go, as he anticipated the fate awaiting him, but he was caught in the same trap that had ensnared the princes of Nizhegorod and Tver before him. One of his chief boyars, Semen Krubin (or Korobin), went over to Vasily and persuaded his master to go to Moscow, where he was arrested and imprisoned. His mother was shut up in a nunnery.

Later in 1521, the prince of Riazan took advantage of Mohammed-Girey's raid to escape from Moscow and seek refuge in Lithuania.

Mohammed-Girey dispatched envoys to Sigismund and asked the king to send the prince of Riazan to the Crimea. Sigismund replied: "The grand prince of Riazan came to us under a safe-conduct we issued him. We pledged that he was free to come to us or go from us without constraint. We strongly urged him to go to you and solemnly promised that you would restore him as grand prince of Riazan, but he absolutely refused. We summoned him a second time and told him you would regain his patrimony, that we had your promise to that effect in writing, and that he had no chance of regaining his throne without your aid. We told him that you would receive the credit for restoring him to Riazan. When his subjects learn that he is dependant upon you they will voluntarily submit to you without a struggle. He will serve you and his resources will assist you in reducing the grand prince of Muscovy, our common enemy, to the same state of dependence upon you in which his predecessors were to your ancestors. We brought pressure to bear on the prince of Riazan and at last he agreed to the proposal, but only on condition that you promise in writing to free him if you fail to restore him to his throne. When you free him he will return your agreement. Consider the matter and let us know your decision as soon as possible." The people of Riazan were distinguished for their bold and stubborn nature. Moscow applied the same technique on them as it had employed with the peoples of Novgorod and Pskov—to resettle large groups of them in other areas.

The Seversk duchy, another principality which had once belonged to the house of Sviatoslav, was next to fall. It no longer contained any members of the house of Oleg, whose estates were now held by two descendants of Ivan Kalita of Moscow, both named Vasily. One was Vasily Semenovich, grandson of Mozhaisky, prince of Starodub, and the other was Vasily Ivanovich, grandson of Shemiaka, prince of Novgorod Seversk. These princes had long hated each other intensely, but fearing to engage in open hostilities they were content to slander one another before the grand prince of Muscovy. According to some accounts Shemiachich had ruined several princes with his calumnies, and Semen, father of the prince of Starodub, had slandered Shemiachich to Ivan III. Vasily Semenovich continued his father's feud. His hatred of Shemiachich was so fierce that he said: "Only one thing can happen. Either I shall kill Prince Vasily Ivanovich or he will kill me." He and Prince Pronsky made charges against Shemiachich in Moscow.

When the latter heard what they had done he sent a representative to Moscow to ask the grand prince for permission to defend himself at court. The style of the communication, which Shemiachich's representative was to follow when reading it to the grand prince, is very strange. After calling attention to the low level to which the proprietary princes had sunk in comparison with the grand prince, ruler of all Russia, Shemiachich wrote: "Show mercy and favor to me, your slave, and allow me to come to you; suffer me to beg you to allow me to stand before you, my sovereign, and confront the man whom my cousin, Prince Vasily Semenovich, sent to you, sovereign, to lay charges against me. Sovereign, sift my guilt; you and God are my judges, my lord. I place my life in your hands and God's. If, my lord, you find me not guilty and are disposed to show mercy and favor to me, as God guides your majestic heart, protect me from my cousin, Prince Vasily Semenovich, because my cousin has often slandered me before you, my lord, and made serious charges against me. He wants to destroy your confidence in me, my lord, and prevent me from serving you."

The Muscovite government had to pay close attention to the activities of the Seversk princes because Lithuania might try to take advantage of the situation, as can be seen from Shemiachich's next words: "My lord, you are aware that Lithuania has made frequent overtures to me, but I have never in any way faltered in my support of your father, the grand prince, and of you, my lord." The grand prince instructed the courier bearing Shemiachich's safe-conduct to Moscow: "On your way stop and visit Prince Vasily Semenovich. Caution him in our name, but also give him a word of praise."

Shemiachich made his defense in Moscow. The grand prince told him: "We have not heard our servant, Prince Vasily, make speeches attacking you. We have never been influenced by slander and we are not influenced by it now. We have shown our favor to you, our servant; we are doing so now, and we intend to do so in the future. We have determined that the attacks made against you are malicious and we do not believe them." One of the men who had made these charges was subjected to investigation, but when Shemiachich asked that the other, a man in the service of the prince of Starodub, be surrendered to him, the grand prince said: "This man was a prisoner in Lithuania. He heard people talking about you there and saw fit to report to us. We will not surrender him to you."

Shemiachich was honorably dismissed from Moscow and returned to his principality. These events occurred in 1517. In 1523 he was again summoned to Moscow and this time imprisoned. It was rumored that he was incarcerated because he had sent a letter to the governor of Kiev offering his services to King Sigismund. There is a story that while Shemiachich was in prison a holy fool wandered about Moscow with a broom in his hands. When passers-by asked him what he was doing with it, he answered: "The realm has not been fully cleansed. Now is a good time to sweep away the remaining offal." Earlier Shemiachich had expelled his cousin from their ancestral domain of Starodub and incorporated it into Muscovy. Vasily also acquired the Volok appanage when its prince, Fedor Borisovich, died in 1513 without issue.

III

DOMESTIC AFFAIRS

VASILY AND HIS BROTHERS

Moscow's enemies had eagerly awaited Ivan III's death. They expected that it would mark the beginning of a conflict between Vasily and his nephew, Dmitry, who would be liberated by his numerous partisans. They were disappointed in their hopes. Dmitry's supporters made no move and he died a prisoner in 1509. Sigismund of Lithuania had also lodged vain hopes in Dmitry. Failing results in that quarter he tried to arouse Vasily's natural brother against the grand prince, but this undertaking likewise proved abortive. The appanage princes intensely desired their extrication from the position of inferiority in which the new order of affairs instituted by their elder brother, the grand prince, had placed them, but they were powerless to achieve their goal.

In 1511 the grand prince learned that his brother, Semen of Kaluga, intended to flee to Lithuania. Vasily summoned him to Moscow. Realizing his plan had been discovered, Semen foresaw the fate awaiting him. He begged the metropolitan, the bishops, and his other brothers to intervene on his behalf. The grand prince forgave Semen, but transferred all of his senior and junior boyars. Semen died in 1518.

An interesting document has survived to shed light on the nature of the relationship between Vasily and another of his brothers, Dmitry. It is the instructions Vasily gave Ivan Shigona on how the latter was to speak to Dmitry in private in the name of the grand prince: "Brother, consider whether you are behaving properly. Have you forgotten that our father adjured us to live in harmony? I have repeatedly told you to carry out our instructions in the matter of Kozelsk and in reference to

Ushaty.[1] You failed to do so and again sent men into Ushaty's domain to sack his villages. The answer you directed our junior officers to bring us was unseemly, and you ignored the letter we sent you by Fedor Borisov. Now you have done even worse. You have entrusted a letter concerning important affairs to an irresponsible person, the sort of individual who should never be sent to us. We are at a loss to understand the way in which we have offended or affronted you, although you have implied that we did so in both the note you sent with our junior officers and in the letter you wrote to us. Surely it is wrong thus to respond to a father and thus to write to him." The grand prince resisted claims based on the traditional prerogatives of appanage princes, but in this instance he took refuge in the ancient precedent of requiring a younger brother to acknowledge his older brother as a father. Dmitry died in 1521.

A petition composed by Ivan Yaganov, assigned to Dmitrov to keep an eye on the activities of Grand Prince Vasily's brother Yury, provides insight into their relationship. The petition reveals that junior members of Yury's court supplied the grand prince with information through Yaganov concerning his brother's activities. Early in the reign of Ivan the Terrible Yaganov was imprisoned for supplying false information; hence his supplication: "My lord, previously I served your father, Grand Prince Vasily, and reported everything I heard, whether good or bad, to my sovereign. I transmitted to my sovereign all information, whether it was important, dangerous, or deadly, which junior men in Yury's service communicated to me. Your father rewarded me and never punished or imprisoned me for what I did. He told me always to look out for his interests. In pursuit of my sovereign's and my country's concerns I fell in with some men from Dmitrov, one of whom had lost his small holding. When Yakov and I attended a carouse with these men we overheard threats. Yakov and I reported their substance to your boyars. I cannot say whether the men were drunk or crazy when they said what they did. In those days whatever I heard stuck to my ears like pitch. I reported whatever I heard, as I used to do when I served your father. If I had failed to pass on hostile remarks someone else would have done so and I would have been punished. Bashmak Litomin and Guba Dedkov overlooked reporting threats against Yakov of Dmitrov to your father and he punished them. Your writ of instruction told me to report anything, whether good or bad, to you, my lord, or to your boyars. Can a man who heard and failed to report something be considered trustworthy? Had I not entered your service, my lord, I should now have retired from Prince Yury's court. Whenever information was laid before your father he decided whether it was worthy of credence. If it was he would take action, but if it was not he ignored it. He never punished informants or consigned them to trial for trying to help him. My lord, I have saved you and your mother, the pious Grand Princess Elena, from many grave dangers, yet here I am to die of torture because I served you."

The *Life of St. Joseph of Volok*[2] relates that the grand prince was once informed that Prince Yury intended to flee to Lithuania. Yury asked Joseph to intervene, and he sent Kassian and Iona, two monks in his monastery, to Moscow to intercede for Yury with the grand prince. Their intervention was successful.

VASILY'S DIVORCE AND REMARRIAGE

Yury was heir to the throne in the event the grand prince died without issue, and Grand Princess Solomonia had produced no children. The unhappy woman had resorted to every device the best sorcerers of the time could recommend, but to no avail; she was unable to conceive.[3] Her husband had ceased to love her. The chronicler narrates that on one occasion the grand prince was riding out of town when he noticed a bird's nest in a tree. Bursting into tears he complained bitterly of his lot: "Alas, I resemble no other creature. I am not like the birds of the air, because they are fruitful. I am not like the beasts of the land, because they are fruitful. I am not like the waters, because they too are fruitful. Waves sooth them and fish grow happy." Looking down at the ground he cried: "Lord, I am not even like the earth, because the earth brings forth its fruits in season and its fruits bless You, O Lord."

Soon afterwards he conferred with his boyars, wept, and said to them: "Who will rule the Russian land and all my towns and realms when I am gone? Must I consign them to my brothers? They cannot even manage their own appanages." The boyars replied: "Sovereign grand prince, when a fig tree is barren it is cut down and removed from the vineyard." The boyars felt this way because they had good reason to be apprehensive should the state fall into the hands of a prince unable to manage a tiny appanage. Vasily's supporters, who were identified with the system he had established, felt the same way. These powerful members of Vasily's court had hoped to preserve their positions if he had a son. They feared reprisal if Vasily were succeeded by his brother, who was bound to extend the distaste he entertained for his older brother to the latter's faithful servitors. The metropolitan naturally had the greatest influence in this affair. Metropolitan Varlaam,

VASILY III

Engraving from *Portraits and Lives of Illustrious Men* by Andre Thevet (Paris, 1584)

who followed Simon, had quarrelled with the grand prince, was deprived of his office, and imprisoned in one of the northern monasteries. Daniel, abbot of the Joseph of Volok monastery, was chosen to take his place. He was devoted to the traditions of this monastery, which had never wavered in its support of Grand Prince Vasily. Daniel approved the divorce.

Others regarded the question differently. Some considered the issue to be purely ecclesiastical; religious scruples made them fear that such a concession to secular interests violated church ordinance. Others, descendants of Lithuanian and West Russian princes, had their own reasons for opposing a divorce. Their experience with the power amassed by the rulers of Moscow was unpleasant, for they had been reduced to the condition of any other servitary. The influence exerted by Sophia Paleologue, to whom they attributed the institution of the new norms and procedures which they found so galling had aroused their resentment. They had opposed Sophia and sought to deny the succession to her son. Yet Sophia had prevailed, and her son, Vasily, who had successfully completed his father's work, had become a monarch of extraordinary power. These persons were delighted at the thought that the throne might pass from Vasily, a man firmly devoted to the principles espoused by his father, the source of their antagonism, to a weak prince unable to handle his own affairs. Were that to happen obviously they would acquire greater opportunity to reassert the traditional prerogatives once belonging to the princes and their entourages.

The monk Vassian was the most determined opponent of a divorce. His was an unusual history. When Sophia and her son Vasily triumphed over the group arrayed against them, its leaders, Princes Patrikeev and Riapolovsky, fell under official displeasure. The Riapolovsky princes were executed. Ivan Yurevich Patrikeev and his son, Vasily Kosoy, were tonsured. The grand prince ordered Prince Vasily (known as Vassian in monastic life) transferred from the Kirillo-Belozersk monastery to the Simonov monastery in Moscow. The grand prince greatly respected him for his intellect and education and granted him considerable authority in church affairs. When the vital question of a divorce arose, Vassian exercised his entire newly-found influence as an seasoned elder of the church to oppose it. He was joined by Prince Semen Kurbsky, whose grandson, Andrei Kurbsky,[4] later was to become a similarly passionate advocate of the traditional rights once possessed by princes and their entourages, and was equally harsh in his condemnation of Sophia and her son. Maxim the Greek[5] shared the views held by Vassian and Kurbsky.

Notwithstanding this opposition the grand prince divorced Solomonia in November, 1525. Tonsured under the name of Sophia, she was first immured in the Rozhdestvensky nunnery and eventually removed to the Intercession convent in Suzdal. Many opinions were held at the time concerning this matter and conflicting versions have survived. Some have it that Solomonia both consented to divorce and tonsure and demanded and insisted upon it. Other accounts imply that she was forcibly tonsured. It was even rumored that Solomonia bore a son, Georgy, shortly after the grand prince married again.[6]

The next year, in January, 1526, Vasily married Elena, daughter of the late Prince Vasily Lvovich Glinsky and niece of Prince Mikhail Glinsky. It was an unexpected choice. Elena had not been brought up in the manner customary for a Muscovite woman of boyar rank. She gave great cause for satisfaction when, three years later, on August 25, 1530, she bore her first son, Ivan, and, a little more than a year after that, a second son, Georgy.[7]

VASILY'S ILLNESS AND DEATH

His elder son, Ivan, was barely three years old when Grand Prince Vasily was stricken with a fatal illness. In September, 1533, after the withdrawal of the Crimeans, Vasily took his wife and children to the Trinity monastery in order to celebrate the festival of Sergius the Miracle-Worker[8] on September 25. He next proceeded from the monastery to Volokolamsk to hunt, his favorite pastime, but fell ill enroute at the village of Ozeretsk. A crimson sore containing a tiny pimple appeared on his lower left thigh. Early in October the grand prince reached Volokolamsk, but he was very weak. On the day he arrived he managed to attend a banquet given by one of his favorites, Ivan Yurevich Shigona Podzhogin, a courtier from Tver, but the next day he experienced great difficulty bathing and taking his seat at table in the palace. The day after that was a splendid one for hunting. The grand prince could not resist; he sent for his huntsmen and rode to Kolp, a village on one of his estates. They found no game as they rode along and Vasily complained constantly of pain.

In Kolp Vasily took his place at table, although with difficulty. Undeterred, he summoned his brother, Andrei, to join the hunt. When Andrei arrived Vasily took the field with his dogs, but went no more than a mile or so from the village. After the hunt he dined in Kolp with his brother. This was the last time he was able to appear at table; afterwards he took what little food he could eat in bed.

Realizing the illness was serious the grand prince sent for Prince Mikhail Glinsky and his two physicians, the foreigners Nicholas and Theophilus. After conferring with Glinsky, a man of vast experience, the doctors applied a poultice made of meal, honey and boiled onion to the sore. This made it fester and suppurate. After spending two weeks in Kolp the grand prince decided to return to Volok. He could no longer ride; junior officers and princes walked carrying him in their arms. In Volok Vasily told them to apply an ointment. A great deal of pus oozed out; the pain intensified, and he felt tightness in his chest. The doctors administered a purgative. It was of no help, and his appetite failed.

Secretly the grand prince sent a crown agent and a secretary, Mansurov and Menshoy Putiatin, to Moscow to obtain his father's will and the one he had drawn up before he went to Novgorod and Pskov. He ordered them to tell no one in Moscow, not even the metropolitan or the boyars, of their mission. When the testaments were brought in Vasily had them read to him, unbeknown to his brothers, the boyars, or Prince Glinsky, and ordered his [new] will destroyed. Then he ordered Putiatin again to bring him the [original] documents, summoned Shigona, and conferred with both men concerning which boyars he should place on a regency council, or "to whom to entrust the royal command." Boyars attending the grand prince in Volok included Prince Dmitry Fedorovich Belsky, Prince Ivan Vasilievich Shuisky, Prince Mikhail Glinsky, and two courtiers, Prince Kubensky and Shigona. Vasily's brother Yury was present, but the grand prince concealed his illness from him and was anxious for him to leave, although Yury wanted very much to stay. His younger brother, Prince Andrei, remained at the patient's side.

The sore filled a basin with pus and part of the core, more than an inch and a half in diameter, came out. The grand prince rejoiced, believing he had secured remission. Ordinary ointment was applied to the sore, and the swelling abated. After the arrival of the boyar Mikhail Yurevich Zakharin, who had been summoned from Moscow, the grand prince conferred with his boyars and officials about ways to return to the capital. He indicated his intention to leave Volok for his beloved Josephan monastery. He was transported in a litter on which a bed had been placed. Princes Shkurliatev and Paletsky sat in the litter with him and turned him from side to side as he could no longer move. When they reached the monastery Shkurliatev and Paletsky lifted the grand prince by his arms and carried him into the church. The deacon began reciting the prayer known as the *ektenia* for the sovereign but tears prevented his finishing it. The abbot and the monks all wept bitterly and prayed, while the grand princess, her children, the boyars and the people sobbed. When mass began the grand prince came out to listen to the service, lying on a couch in the church porch.

After spending the night in the monastery Vasily proceeded towards Moscow. He dismissed his brother Andrei to his appanage. It was decided to convey the sick man into Moscow secretly, because many foreigners and envoys were present in the city at that moment. On November 21 the grand prince reached his village of Vorobevo, a little south of Moscow, where he spent two days in intense pain. The metropolitan, the clergy, boyars and junior officials frequently visited him. Vasily ordered a bridge thrown across the Moscow river below Vorobevo opposite the New Virgin [Novodevichy] convent, where the water was still low, and two days later he left Vorobevo in his litter, drawn by two horses specially trained to pull sleds. The minute the horses set foot on the bridge it collapsed and the attendants barely managed to save the litter by cutting the traces. The sick man had to go back. He was furious with the local officials who had constructed the bridge, but did not place them under official displeasure. Shortly afterwards he was brought into Moscow on the ferry raft that crossed the river below Dorogomilov. His brother Andrei arrived the same day.

Once settled in his palace the grand prince summoned the boyars Prince Vasily Vasilievich Shuisky, Mikhail Yurevich Zakharin, and Mikhail Semenovich Vorontsov, the treasurer, Peter Ivanovich Golovin, and the courtier Shigona. He ordered his secretaries, Menshoy Putiatin and Fedor Mishurin, to draw up a will in their presence. In addition to the boyars already appointed to the regency council he added the names of Prince Ivan Vasilievich Shuisky, Mikhail Vasilievich Tuchkov, and Prince Mikhail Glinsky. He included Glinsky, after a discussion with the boyars, because he was the uncle of Grand Princess Elena. At this time his brother Yury arrived in Moscow.

While composing his testament Vasily conferred with Metropolitan Daniel, Vassian, bishop of Kolomna,[9] and Archpriest Alexis, his confessor, to determine whether he might be tonsured, as he had long desired. While still in Volok he had told his confessor and the elder, Misail Sukin: "I shall not let you lay me out in a white garment.[10] Even should I recover I shall not change my mind. I am absolutely determined to become a monk." He had robes prepared in Volok and kept them in readiness. As they travelled he also insisted to Shigona and Putiatin that he was not to be laid out in white. The grand prince secretly received the last rites and was annointed with oil. The Saturday before

St. Nicholas' Day [November 25] he had publicly received Extreme Unction. The following Sunday he asked that donatives be prepared. When he learned that they were at hand he arose from his bed, and leaning on the boyar, Mikhail Zakharin, moved to a chair.

When his confessor brought the donatives Vasily stood up, greeted the priest tearfully, and took to his bed. Then he summoned the metropolitan, his brothers Yury and Andrei, and all the boyars, and said: "I commend my son, Grand Prince Ivan, to God, the Holy Virgin Mary, the saintly miracle-workers, and to you, Father Daniel, metropolitan of all Russia. I grant him the kingdom with which my father blessed me. My brothers, Prince Yury and Prince Andrei, never violate the oath you swore to me. Stand together and keep order in the realm. Defend my son against his enemies and yours and hold the banner of Orthodoxy on high against the forces of Mohammed. My boyars, senior and junior, and my princes, serve my son Ivan as you have served me. Stand united against the foe; protect Christians from their enemies, and serve my son steadfastly and firmly."

Dismissing his brothers and the metropolitan the dying man said to his boyars: "You know that our power descends directly from Grand Prince Vladimir of Kiev.[11] We are your natural ruler and you have always been our boyars. Stay strong, my brothers; help my son be a real ruler in his realm; aid the cause of justice in this land, and tolerate no dissension in your ranks. I commend Mikhail Lvovich Glinsky to you. Although he was an adult when he came to us, you must not call him a sojourner. You must regard him as though he were born here among us, because he is my close attendant. Remain united and cooperate in guarding this land and my son. Prince Glinsky, you must be ready to shed your blood or be cut to pieces in order to protect my son Ivan, my wife, and my son Georgy."

Although the grand prince was filled with grief and exhausted he felt no pain. The wound grew no larger, but it gave off an unpleasant odor. Summoning Glinsky and the two physicians, Nicholas and Theophilus, he asked whether they could dress the sore or introduce something into it in order to eliminate the stench. Trying to calm him, the boyar Mikhail Zakharin said: "Lord and grand prince, in a day or two, when you are feeling better, we shall pour vodka on the sore." The sick man asked Nicholas, the doctor: "Brother Nicholas, you are aware of the great favor I have shown you. Can you do anything, apply salve or some other medicament, to improve my condition?" Nicholas replied: "My lord, I know the great favor you have shown me. I would cut myself to pieces to help you, but I am afraid that only God can help you now." After that the grand prince said to those attending him: "Brothers, Nicholas has diagnosed my illness as incurable. I must take care that my soul does not perish in eternity." His various attendants burst into tears. They wept quietly in his presence, but outside the sickroom they sobbed loudly and seemed like men dead.

The sick man dozed and dreamed. Suddenly he chanted: "Halleluia, Halleluia, Glory, God, to Thee." He awoke and murmured: "It is the Lord's will. Blessed be the name of the Lord, for ever and ever, Amen." On December 3, late Tuesday night and early Wednesday morning, he told his confessor to have extra donatives in readiness. At this time Abbot Ioasaf of the Trinity monastery came to see him and the grand prince said: "Father, pray for good order in the land, my son Ivan, and forgiveness for my sins. Your prayers and intercession disposed God and Sergius, the mighty miracle-worker, to grant me a son, Ivan. I baptized him in the miracle-worker's abode; I entrusted him to the miracle-worker; I laid him on the shrine containing the miracle-worker's relics, and I placed my son in the arms of all your brethren. Have all your brethren intercede with God, the Holy Virgin Mary, and the mighty miracle-workers on behalf of my son Ivan and my unfortunate wife. Abbot, do not go away. Stay by my side." He received the sacraments again on Wednesday. He could no longer get out of bed, but he was raised and supported beneath his shoulders. After receiving communion he managed to take a little nourishment.

Vasily summoned the boyars, Princes Vasily and Ivan Shuisky, Vorontsov, Mikhail Yurevich, Tuchkov, Prince Mikhail Glinsky, Shigona and Golovkin, and the secretaries, Putiatin and Mishurin, with whom he spent four hours discussing his son, the structure of the state, and the way the country should be administered. When the rest of the boyars departed, three—Mikhail Yurevich, Glinsky, and Shigona—remained with him until evening. The grand prince talked about what Grand Princess Elena would do and how the boyars should treat her, and issued further instructions about the administration of the grand duchy after he was gone.

His brothers, Yury and Andrei, urged him to take some food. Vasily asked for crushed almonds but could do no more than raise them to his lips. His brothers went out, but the grand prince called Andrei back and said to him, Yurevich, Glinsky, and Shigona: "I know that my time is short. I would like to see my son Ivan and bless him with the cross of Peter the Miracle-Worker.[12] I would also like to see my wife and tell her what to do when I am gone. No, wait a minute. I do not wish to

behold my son. He is young and I am so ill. He will be frightened."
Prince Andrei and the boyars tried to persuade him: "Lord and grand
prince, send for your son and give him your blessing, and send for the
grand princess."

The sick man assented and Prince Ivan Glinsky, the brother of the
grand princess, brought in the child in his arms, followed by the nurse,
Agrafena Vasilieva. The grand prince blessed his son and said to the
nurse: "Agrafena, never leave my son, Ivan, not even for a minute!"
After the child the grand princess was escorted into the chamber. Andrei,
the grand prince's brother, and the boyar Cheliadnin had all they could
do to restrain her. She struck herself and wept bitterly. To comfort
her the grand prince said: "Cease, wife, and do not cry. I feel better
and have no pain, thank God." In fact, by then he no longer experienced
any pain.

When Elena grew somewhat calmer she said: "My lord and grand
prince, in whose hands have you left me? To whom do you remand our
children?" Vasily replied: "I have blessed my son Ivan with the governance of the grand duchy. I have made proper provision for you in my
will, just as my fathers and grandfathers did for previous grand princesses
in theirs." Elena asked the grand prince to bless Georgy, their younger
son, as well. Vasily assented and blessed him with the cross of Paisy.[13]
He mentioned estates, saying, "I have made suitable provision for him
in my will." He was anxious to say a few words to his wife about her
situation after his death but she screamed so loudly he could not make
himself heard. She refused to leave the room, but her crying at last
constrained Vasily to have her removed bodily, after bidding her fare-
well for the last time.

The grand prince summoned Vassian, bishop of Kolomna, and Misail,
the elder. He asked to see the abbot of the Kirillov monastery, where he
had hoped to be tonsured, but was told the abbot was not in Moscow.
He sent for Ioasaf, abbot of the Trinity monastery. At that moment
Metropolitan Daniel, his brothers, and all the boyars, both senior and
junior, approached the sick man. The metropolitan and Bishop Vassian
urged the grand prince to send for the icons of the Virgin of Vladimir
and St. Nicholas Gostunsky. When the icons were brought in the grand
prince sent Shigona to the confessor with orders for the latter to bring
the donatives from the church and to ask whether the confessor had
often been in attendance when a soul was separated from its body. The
archpriest replied that he had rarely been present on such occasions.

The grand prince told the confessor to enter the room and stand
before him and he asked an attendant, Fedor Kuchetsky, who had

witnessed the death of his father, Grand Prince Ivan, to take a position next to the archpriest. He told the deacon, Danilo, to sing the canon in honor of St. Catherine the Martyr[14] and the canon for the departure of the soul, and asked that a requiem mass be sung for him. As Danilo sang the canon the sick man dozed momentarily, then awoke and said, apparently beholding a vision: "Catherine, mighty Christian martyr, thy will be done, mistress, it is time!" Recovering full consciousness he grasped St. Catherine's icon and kissed it, and kissed her relics, which had just been brought to him. He summoned the boyar, Mikhail Semenovich Vorontsov, kissed him and forgave him.

He lay still for some time. The confessor approached and started to give him communion, but Vasily said: "You see how ill I am, but I am still in possession of my faculties. When my soul actually leaves my body I want you to give me the donatives. Watch carefully and do not allow the moment to slip by." In a few minutes he called his brother Yury and said: "Brother, do you remember how our father, Grand Prince Ivan, died on a Monday, the day after St. Dmitry's Day [October 26, 1505], after his illness had ravaged him day and night? Brother, the final hour of death draws nigh for me as well." Soon after that he summoned Metropolitan Daniel, Vassian, bishop of Kolomna, his brothers and the boyars, and said: "You see how faint I am and that my end is near. I have long craved to become a monk. I should like you to tonsure me now."

The metropolitan and the boyar, Mikhail Yurevich, praised his choice, but Prince Andrei, Mikhail Semenovich Vorontsov, and Shigona expressed a different view: "Grand Prince Vladimir of Kiev did not become a monk before he died and surely went to the rest he deserved. Other grand princes died without becoming monks and they surely found righteous peace." A great quarrel ensued. The grand prince called the metropolitan to him and said: "Father, I have confessed my innermost secret to you. I want to become a monk. Why delay? If you find me worthy of that station, make haste and tonsure me at once." A few minutes later he said: "Lord metropolitan, am I to be left lying here?" He crossed himself and intoned: "Halleluia, Halleluia, Glory, God, to Thee." He spoke in a chanting voice, choosing his words. The end was close; he could no longer speak clearly, but the dying man kept asking for tonsure. He grasped his coverings and kissed them. He could no longer raise his right hand, and the boyar, Mikhail Yurevich, lifted it for him. Vasily never stopped making the sign of the cross on his face and he stared up to the right, where an icon of the Virgin Mary hung before him.

Metropolitan Daniel called the elder, Misail, and told him to fetch a monastic robe. When earlier, on the Sunday, the grand prince had received the sacraments and pronounced his renunciation to the metropolitan, he had said: "If I cannot become a monk, at least array me in a monk's robe after I am dead, to fulfill my longstanding desire." The grand prince was on the point of expiring when Elder Misail brought the robe. The metropolitan and Ioasaf of the Trinity monastery fastened a collar around the grand prince's neck, but Prince Andrei and the boyar, Vorontsov, immediately opposed further action. The metropolitan turned on Andrei: "You will forfeit our blessing in this world and the next. A silver vessel is good, but a gold one is better." The grand prince was expiring and they hastened to complete the tonsure. Shigona, who stood near the dying man, later described how his spirit left his body in the form of a fine cloud.

Such was the death of Grand Prince Vasily, the monk Varlaam, at midnight, Wednesday, December 3, 1533. People sobbed and wept unconsolably. The metropolitan and the boyars tried to dissuade them, but they could not make themselves heard. The grand princess had not learned of her husband's death; therefore, the boyars admonished the people not to cry loudly so that they could not be heard in Elena's quarters. The metropolitan conducted the grand prince's brothers, Yury and Andrei, to their residence in the forecourt and administered an oath to them. They swore to serve Grand Prince Ivan Vasilievich of all Russia and his mother, Grand Princess Elena, remain on their appanages, and behave righteously, as they had pledged Grand Prince Vasily they would do. They were not to seize the government from Grand Prince Ivan nor alienate the people from him, and they must stand firmly together against their enemies, the Catholics and the Mohammedans. The senior and junior boyars and lesser princes took a similar oath. Having performed this duty the metropolitan set out with the appanage princes and the boyars to comfort the grand princess. When Elena caught sight of them she fainted and lay senseless for three hours.

Ioasaf, abbot of Trinity, and the elder, Misail Sukin, remained behind to guard Vasily's body. Monks from the Josephan monastery attired the corpse in a monk's habit, wrapped it in a dark taffeta cloth and placed it on a bier, which had been brought from the Miracles (Chudov) monastery. After the grand prince's death deacons and the archpriest chanted matins, hours, and canons, as they had done when he was alive. When they had recited these offices the junior attendants, lesser princes, merchants and everyone else were admitted to pay their last respects. Everyone wept uncontrollably.

Next morning, on the Thursday, the metropolitan ordered the great bell tolled. The boyars had a grave dug for the deceased next to his father, and brought in a stone coffin. After everything was in readiness the Trinity and Josephan monks carried out the body on their heads, chanting, "Hallowed be Thy Name, O God." When they appeared in the square the people's groans were louder than the sound of the bells. Grand Princess Elena rode alone in a sled, escorted by junior officials. At her side walked Ivan and Vasily, the two Shuisky brothers, the boyar, Vorontsov, Prince Mikhail Glinsky, and Boyar Princess Mstislavsky.

The grand prince destroyed the original will he had made before his divorce from his first wife, and the new one he drew up just before he died has not been preserved. The sole document to survive is Vasily's undertaking with his brother Yury, composed in the very old-fashioned language which had been used in the agreement made between them during the lifetime of their father, Ivan III. As he had before, Yury swore to regard his nephew Ivan as his older brother and sovereign. The present account of Vasily's death reveals the distrust the grand prince felt for Yury, which elicited and explains Yaganov's petition. The grand prince's relations with his other brother, Andrei, were far more amicable. Andrei's temperament was undoubtedly a contributing factor, but the main reason was that he was younger and in no position to seek his own advantage by plotting against the grand prince or his son while Yury was alive. This freed him from the suspicion which Vasily harbored against Yury, since it would prove no easy task to repudiate the recent laws which provided that an uncle should succeed in preference to a nephew. Hostile encounters took place between the grand prince and his brothers Yury, Dmitry and Semen, but there is no record of altercations with Andrei.

VASILY'S ROLE AND CHARACTER

Vasily's reign is generally termed a continuation of his father's administration. The comparison is apt insofar as Ivan III's rule may be considered a continuation of that of *his* predecessors. A single tradition and identical aims and goals invariably motivated the princes of Muscovy, in fact virtually every prince in northern Russia. In addition to having the same purposes these princes usually employed the same methods to attain them. This circumstance has tended to make each prince remarkably like another and to blur individual distinctions; thus, they seem like a single person to the historian. Was this actually the case? Were they really all so much like one another?

It is possible to assume an inherent similarity of temperament, since they were descended of the same blood line. Their similarity in attitude and outlook was powerfully influenced by the fact that they found themselves in identical situations. Their choice of means was similar. The same forces were constantly at work upon them as they grew and matured. From early youth each one faced certain major problems of general concern and interest, to deal with which invariably required similar responses. Acquiring these responses was the chief lesson they learned in their youth, imparted to them by their predecessors, who embodied their experience in their testaments.

Families display a strong innate similarity when their members are conscious of the important position they occupy in a society, are determined to maintain their prominence, and hold well-defined moral and political views and principles, which inform their actions. This factor explains why all the princes of Muscovy manifested a similarity of temperament, although this is not to imply that there were no differences among them. In spite of the common views and aims they shared, one prince might display greater perception and resolution in realizing them, and another display less, but the available sources are not concerned to portray differences or elucidate the characters of principal rulers. They seldom depict individual personages reacting intellectually or emotionally, speaking down through the ages, or, to put it briefly, acting like men of flesh and blood. Almost all these rulers moved silently, and those close to them, who knew them well, have remained mute.

The great importance of Ivan III's reign must be acknowledged, but it is wrong to separate his activity from that of his predecessors or to deprecate the services of many others in order to exalt one prince. Eighteenth-century historians, the first to investigate the early history of Russia, were fascinated by a few exceptional events and confused causes and results. These historians came to the conclusion that Ivan III threw off the Tatar yoke and created a unified Russia out of fragments that had existed prior to his time. It is now known that the first steps to unify northern Russia coincided with the rise of Muscovy, which began during the reign of Ivan Kalita, or, more precisely, in the time of his brother, Yury Danilovich.[15] This process had been practically completed when Vasily the Dark came to the throne and a final internecine struggle for power took place.[16] Ivan III experienced little subsequent difficulty in conquering Novgorod because the city could not obtain assistance from a single prince in northeastern Russia. In view of these considerations it is impossible to assert that Ivan III unified a fragmented Russia.

Dmitry Donskoy defeated Mamay but had to pay a heavy tribute to Tokhtamysh. Ivan III was unable to defeat Ahmad, but on Ahmad's death the Volga Tatars ceased demanding tribute from Moscow. Such developments inevitably lead to the conclusion that the Tatars with whom Dmitry Donskoy had to contend constituted a force still possessing, in spite of vicissitudes, great residual strength, whereas the Tatars by Ivan III's time had grown very feeble. The fact is that Ivan III managed to put an end to Tatar domination once and for all, but again cause must not be confused with effect. The broad moves Ivan initiated clearly flowed from the policies of his predecessors, who had increased Russia's strength before he came to the throne. His skill lay in his ability to adapt his predecessors' policies to altered circumstances.

It is unfair to exalt the role of Ivan III at the expense of his predecessors, and his reign similarly should not be used as a yardstick to measure the accomplishments of his son Vasily. The two were much alike in heredity and temperament, but there is universal agreement that Vasily was less fortunate than Ivan. This is no reason to deny the son's capacities; the greater the difficulties, the greater the effort needed to overcome them. Vasily's dominant characteristics were his consistency, firmness in achieving goals he had set, and the patience he displayed when using all means to pursue an end he deemed important. He displayed such qualities in the wars with Kazan, his stubborn efforts to acquire Smolensk, and his unremitting pursuit of alliances with the Crimea and Turkey. The best example of his determined adherence to fixed principle is that no matter how badly he needed the friendship of the Crimean khan he absolutely refused to send a regular sum of money to the Crimea, for this would look like tribute.

VASILY'S PRIVATE LIFE

The one source that scrutinizes Vasily and portrays him as an individual has been extensively excerpted above. Unfortunately, this valuable document treats only Vasily's final days and hours on earth. The last actions of a man who is fully aware that he is dying understandably cannot serve as reliable indicators of his previous behavior, but one must use whatever comes to hand.

Vasily had made a pilgrimage to the Trinity monastery and was on his way to hunt at Volokolamsk when he fell ill. His passion for these two activities constantly drew the grand prince away from the capital. Vasily seems more vivacious and more inclined to movement and change of scene than his father Ivan, who, according to a contemporary, Stefan of Moldavia, preferred to remain quietly at home while his dominions increased.[17] Besides Trinity, Vasily undertook regular pilgrimages to Pereiaslavl, Yurev, Vladimir, Rostov, Nikola on the Ugra, Tikhvin, Yaroslavl, Vologda, the Kirillov monastery, and Nikola Zarazsky. Hunting, of which Vasily was extraordinarily fond, was the other purpose for his journeys. Even when seriously ill he refused to stay quiet in good hunting weather and took the field with his dogs. His favorite ground was Volokolamsk, which he began visiting in 1515, two years after Fedor Borisovich, the last appanage prince of Volok, died. He was there in 1519 from September 14 to October 26. He also used to go to Mozhaisk for relaxation. Vasily liked to spend summers out of town. Ostrog, Vorobevo and Vorontsovo were his favorite places near Moscow. In May, 1519 he left Moscow for Nikola on the Ugra; went from there to Ostrog, where he remained to St. Peter's Day [June 29], and then spent the whole summer in Vorontsovo.

A vivid story [related above] demonstrates Vasily's relationship to the Josephan monastery. The deacon who prayed for the grand prince burst into tears in the middle of his prayer and the abbot and brethren followed his example. Prince Kurbsky supplies further details, although he is hostile both to Vasily and the monks of the Josephan monastery, who, he claims, were very much alike. Religion, the predominant concern of the times, played a very large part in Vasily's life. He was strongly drawn to the monastic life, which exercised an irresistible attraction upon the upper classes. They believed that monasteries constituted the finest and most exclusive element in contemporary society, places where men could pursue the fundamental questions of life. Alert, intelligent persons who felt impelled to reflect upon the problems life presented would frequent monasteries in search of solutions and intellectual conversation. They were not disappointed. The monasteries, with their libraries, were the sole centers of learning; they were capable of providing men the spiritual and mental strength they required to cope with serious crises, the need for which they well understood even then.

Vasily displayed exceptional favor to three monasteries. His association with its founder[18] predisposed him to the Josephan monastery. He took it under his special protection, which the monastery reciprocated by manifesting an unusual devotion to him. Close as he felt to the Josephan monastery, which had but recently come to prominence, the grand prince showed greater honor to the Kirillo-Belozersk and Holy Trinity-St. Sergius monasteries. He was so powerfully impressed by the regimen followed by the monks in the former institution that he expressed a desire to receive tonsure there. The sanctity and political importance of its founder[19] had won universal reverence for the latter. Vasily told the abbot of Trinity: "Your prayers disposed God to grant me a son. I baptized him in the presence of the miracle-worker. I commended him to the miracle-worker. I laid the child on the shrine containing the holy man's relics, and, father, I have consigned my son to the care of all of you." On a previous occasion the grand prince had said to the metropolitan, his brothers, and the boyars: "I commend my son to God, the Virgin Mary, the holy miracle-workers, and to you, Father Daniel, metropolitan of all Russia." He did not add that he was entrusting his son to his brothers. He merely reminded them of their obligations to their nephew and of the oath they had sworn. Concern over his son's tender years and the disturbances to which this might lead tormented Vasily in his final hours. "Father, pray for good order in the land," he told the Trinity abbot.

His wife and son spent little time at the sick bed. The reason is clear. Vasily was afraid that his emaciated visage would terrify his wife and frighten his son. While there was still chance for recovery he hesitated to see them until he could cheer his wife with an improvement in his appearance. Before he fell ill he had tried to please his young wife and had gone so far as to shave off his beard. When all hope of recovery was gone the sick man decided to bless his son with the cross of St. Peter the Miracle-Worker and endow the occasion with all the solemnity of the investment of an heir, but in spite of the importance of the occasion he changed his mind to avoid frightening the child by his appearance. The sick man's thoughts and concern for the future were entirely concentrated on his older son, now grand prince and successor to the throne. Although the father could think only of the new young sovereign, the mother could not forget her second child and made the father bless him too.

Vasily's relations with his family are further revealed in a few surviving letters he wrote to Elena. One makes concerned inquiry after his wife's health: "Grand Prince Vasily Ivanovich of all Russia to my wife Elena. At God's gift and by God's grace, and with the help of the Virgin Mary and Nicholas the Miracle-Worker,[20] I am alive, at God's pleasure, and in good health. I suffer no pain, thank God. You should have written earlier and informed me concerning your health. You should have let me know that you were ill, may God have mercy upon you, and kept me informed on that score. I have sent Yury Shein to the metropolitan and to you with an icon of the Transfiguration of our Lord, Jesus Christ. I have enclosed a note in my own hand with this letter. Read it and keep it by you. God grant that with His help I shall be in Moscow by Epiphany. Trufanets, my scribe, wrote this letter, which I have sealed with my signet." The note the grand prince wrote in his own hand has unfortunately not survived.

The grand prince's second letter was a reply to one from Elena informing him that a boil had appeared on young Ivan's neck: "Why did you not tell me sooner? You must write me at once of God's visitation upon my son Ivan, what has appeared on his neck, how it appeared, what his condition has been, and what it is now. Have a word with the wives of the princes and boyars to discover the nature of the malady that has afflicted my son Ivan and whether it is common among young children. If it is, ascertain its cause. Is it hereditary or is there some other explanation? Discuss these questions with your ladies-in-waiting; inquire among them, do not shrink from telling me what you have learned, and keep me fully informed. In fact, give me your opinion without waiting to learn what others think. Tell me of God's mercy to you and my son Ivan."

Elena wrote that the boil had burst. Vasily immediately replied: "Tell me whether my son's wound still flows or has the flow stopped? Is a mark still there? Has the swelling subsided? How is it now? Tell me too of God's mercy to you and my son Ivan. Have you a headache, an earache, or a pain in your side? Tell me that God has mercifully stopped your headache, your earache, or the pain in your side and not allowed them to reoccur. Write me full honest details." Vasily sent a fourth letter when Elena told him that his second son, Georgy, was ill: "Henceforth you must not withhold from me news of your health and that of our son Ivan. Give me details about God's future mercy to my son Georgy." The fifth letter contained the words: "In the future write and tell me about my son Ivan's appetite and what he likes to eat, so that I will be informed."

PRINCE AND NOBILITY

Herberstein noted that after Vasily completed the tasks his father had begun his power over his subjects was greater than all other monarchs in the entire world. He enjoyed unlimited authority over the persons and possessions of his subjects, whether clergy or laymen. None of his councillors, the boyars, dared to contradict or oppose his mandate. Herberstein also observed that Russians proudly proclaimed that their sovereign's will was God's will and that their sovereign executed the will of God. If they did not know something they said: "God and the grand prince know."

Herberstein once asked an elderly man, who had been the grand prince's envoy to Spain, why he appeared nervous at a reception for envoys. The latter replied: "Sigismund, we serve our sovereign in a different way from yours." When the boyar, Bersen-Beklemishev,[21] ventured to criticize Vasily's opinions on Smolensk the grand prince said to him: "Get out of my sight, you dog; I have no need of you!" There are indications that the grand prince discussed major affairs in council with his brothers and boyars, but there are also indications that Vasily decided important matters in private with two favorites who were close to him.

The valuable document describing Vasily's death sheds some light on these conflicting reports. It shows the man standing closest to the grand prince to be Shigona Podzhogin, the courtier from Tver, followed by the secretaries Mansurov, Putiatin, Tsypliatev, Kuritsyn, Rakov, and Mishurin, all of whom enjoyed Vasily's confidence. His son Ivan was subsequently to display a like trust in his secretaries when he became Ivan IV. Mansurov and Putiatin were secretly dispatched to fetch Vasily's wills. In similar secrecy, without the knowledge of his brothers or boyars, the grand prince communicated his instructions to destroy his extant wills solely to Shigona and Putiatin.

The account continues that when Vasily was preparing to draw up a new will he conferred only with Shigona and Putiatin and asked these close confidants which other persons he should consult on testamentary matters. It is logical to conclude that he followed the same practice in other affairs. The grand prince heard the advice offered by some or all of his brothers and boyars during the preliminary stage of the discussion. When Vasily returned to Moscow and decided to make a final disposition before he died, he summoned the boyars Prince Vasily Vasilievich Shuisky, Mikhail Yurevich, and Mikhail Semenovich Vorontsov, the treasurer, Peter Golovin, Shigona, and the secretaries Putiatin and Mishurin. He subsequently enlarged the council to include the boyars Prince Ivan Vasilievich Shuisky and Mikhail Vasilievich Tuchkov. Finally, after conferring with them, he called in Prince Mikhail Glinsky because he was related to the grand princess.

These were all the court nobles who the grand prince believed should be invited to deliberate on the future of the government. It is clear that pedigree determined position. Prince Shuisky was in first place. Members of the house of Patrikeev, which was descended from Gedimin,[22] had exercised a long sway during the reigns of Vasily's predecessors, but the original house fell into disfavor during Ivan III's reign, leaving the junior branch. After the fall of Prince Ivan Yurevich Patrikeev, the grand prince's brother-in-law, Prince Vasily Danilovich Kholmsky, commandant of Moscow, assumed first place. Prince Danilo Vasilievich Shchenia-Patrikeev occupied second place. The misfortunes that plagued the Patrikeev house soon overtook Kholmsky; the chronicler notes that in the summer of 1508 Prince Vasily Danilovich undertook a campaign against the Lithuanians around Briansk but was imprisoned and died in the fall. The reasons are unknown, but clearly the position of first place, the office of commandant of Moscow, was then fraught with considerable danger. Prince Danilo Vasilievich Shchenia assumed Kholmsky's position, since he was next in line, but he is not mentioned after 1515. Prince Dmitry Vladimirovich Rostovsky moved into Shchenia's place; Prince Vasily Vasilievich Shuisky came next, and after him came Prince Mikhail Danilovich Shcheniatev, a son of the elder Shchenia. There is no precise information as to who was commandant of Moscow after the death of the elder Shchenia.

At the end of Vasily's reign the group of boyars surrounding him was different. Prince Vasily Vasilievich Shuisky, who had previously been third, now occupied first place. He was probably commandant of Moscow. The princes of the house of Shuisky, descended from the princes of Suzdal and Nizhegorod, had long resisted submission to the princes of Moscow. One of them, Prince Vasily Grebenek, had been the last commander of independent Novgorod. Entering the service of the Muscovite princes later than other branches of the house of Rurik, they were in eclipse during the reign of Ivan III and did not come to prominence until his son's administration.

The place next to the members of the Shuisky house was held by Mikhail Yurevich Koshkin, a descendant of one of the oldest untitled boyar families of Moscow. The Koshkin family had enjoyed more success than other native boyar families in maintaining its position against the large influx into the Muscovite court of members from titled houses tracing their lineage back to Rurik and Gedimin. They always remained close to the center of power and were representative of the old Moscow boyar families, whose efforts had greatly contributed to the success of the process known as the gathering of the Russian lands. Yakov Zakharevich Koshkin had been the third man, after Princes Kholmsky and Shchenia, in Ivan III's council; now his nephew, Mikhail Yurevich, son of Yury Zakharevich, who had refused to yield precedence to Prince Shchenia-Patrikeev, had become the second most important person in Grand Prince Vasily's inner council. The account of the grand prince's death clearly shows that Mikhail Yurevich was one of the most trusted men in Vasily's immediate entourage. While still in Volokolamsk Vasily had sent for Mikhail, who carefully tended the sick man and comforted him with the hope that he would be better in a few days. Mikhail and Shigona were present when Vasily blessed his sons and took leave of his wife. He joined the metropolitan in supporting the grand prince's desire to become a monk before he died, and he helped the dying man's faltering hand make the sign of the cross.

A scion of another ancient distinguished boyar family, Mikhail Semenovich Vorontsov, occupied third place after Mikhail Koshkin. He was a descendant of Fedor Vorontsov-Veliaminov, the brother of the chiliarch.[23] The account of Vasily's death relates that the grand prince, summoning Vorontsov, kissed and forgave him. This means that their relationship had not always been untroubled. The treasurer, Peter Ivanovich Golovin, held the same position as his father, Ivan Vladimirovich Golova-Khovrin, a boyar in Ivan III's time. Last came Mikhail Vasilievich Tuchkov, a descendant of the Morozov family.

These men constituted the inner council and enjoyed a high degree of trust. Members of other equally distinguished princely and boyar houses were not part of the inner circle. After conferring with these close confidants the grand prince summoned the remaining boyars, including Prince Dmitry Belsky and his brothers, members of the Shuisky-Gorbaty family (Shuisky relatives who lived in Suzdal), and representatives of the Poplevin house, a connection of the Morozov family.

Ivan III had made Prince Kholmsky sign a pledge not to flee. A number of such undertakings has come down from Vasily's time. They indicate that, as the new order became firmly established, those who clung to the old ways were determined to preserve the time-honored right of removal. Since there were no more Russian princes with whom they could take service they felt they were entitled to go to Lithuania. Prince Vasily Vasilievich Shuisky had to promise in writing: "For the rest of my life I guarantee not to desert the land of my sovereign and his children in order to go to Lithuania, or to serve my ruler's brothers, or to go to any other place." Similar undertakings were required from Princes Dmitry and Ivan, sons of Fedor Belsky, and Prince Vorotynsky.

The number of princes descended from Gedimin serving at Vasily's court was augmented by a noble immigrant, Prince Fedor Mikhailovich Mstislavsky, who fled from Lithuania in 1526. His sworn statement shows how Mstislavsky intended to behave in his adopted country: "I, Prince Fedor Mikhailovich Mstislavsky, while still in Lithuania communicated with Grand Prince Vasily, sovereign of all Russia, to beg the sovereign to show me his favor and allow me to enter his service. The mighty sovereign showed favor to me, his slave, and sent officers

to tell me I might come to him. When I arrived the sovereign showed
me his favor, told me I might serve him, and assigned me an estate.
Certain people later told the sovereign that I intended to flee to King
Sigismund, but the sovereign continued to trust me and did not place
me under his official displeasure. I delivered a guarantee signed by
Metropolitan Daniel and all his clergy to the sovereign, kissed the cross
at the grave of St. Peter the Miracle-Worker, and signed a pledge, stamped with Metropolitan Daniel's signet, not to go over to King Sigismund,
or to the grand prince's brothers and their children, or to any other
person, but to serve and support my sovereign, Grand Prince Vasily.
My sovereign displayed great favor to me and gave his niece, Princess
Nastasia, to me in marriage.

"Now I, Prince Fedor, transgressed my oath, forgot the guarantee
Metropolitan Daniel had given on my behalf, and was unmindful of the
generosity my sovereign had displayed towards me. I planned to go over
to his enemy, King Sigismund. I was guilty, and my sovereign laid me
under his official displeasure. A guilty man, I begged Metropolitan
Daniel and the bishops to intercede with the sovereign. The metropolitan, archbishops, bishops, and the entire clergy intervened. My sovereign
showed mercy to me, his slave, and absolved my guilt." Mstislavsky
had to give a new pledge, in which he bound himself ". . . not to inform
anyone of the plans of my sovereign and his son, Prince Ivan, to render
just judgments, and to uphold the cause of my sovereigns wholeheartedly and without reservation."

The metropolitan also interceded to win pardon for M.A. Pleshcheev,
but the promise he had to make to the grand prince read as follows: "I
am to have nothing to do with evildoers seeking to harm my sovereign,
people who slander the sovereign, Grand Princess Elena, and their
children, and urge me to administer foul poison to them or desire me
to perform other wicked actions. I must hold no converse with such
persons; I am not to concert with them, nor am I to perform such deeds
myself." There were other undertakings of the same nature. Vasily
imitated his father's example by refusing to be satisfied with a simple
guarantee from the clergy; he demanded financial surety as well. As an
illustration, three noblemen had to go surety for Prince Glinsky in the
amount of 5,000 rubles, and another forty-seven persons had to guarantee the noblemen's bond. The Shuisky princes also had to provide two
kinds of guarantee.

These measures were adopted to prevent defection. Severe sanctions
were also applied to those who placed their own interpretation on the
right to offer advice, another ancient custom. Bersen-Beklemishev had

incurred official displeasure when he ventured to remonstrate with the grand prince. The dissatisfied boyar complained of the changes introduced by Sophia and her son. These complaints eventually cost Bersen his life. A secretary, Fedor Zhareny, who also dared to complain, was flogged and his tongue cut out. Failure to perform one's duty was likewise severely punished. Another secretary, Tretiak Dalmatov, was instructed to undertake a mission to Emperor Maximilian. When he declared that his means were inadequate to undertake the journey he was arrested, confined permanently in Beloozero, and his estate was confiscated.

TITLES AND REVENUES OF THE GRAND PRINCES OF MUSCOVY AND LITHUANIA

Vasily's title ran as follows: "The great sovereign, Vasily, by the grace of God lord of all Russia; grand prince of Vladimir, Moscow, Novgorod, Pskov, Smolensk, Tver, Yugorsk, Perm, Viatka, Bulgaria and other places, and lord and grand prince of Nizhny Novgorod, Chernigov, Riazan, Volok, Rzhev, Belaia, Rostov, Yaroslavl, Beloozero, Udorsk, Obdorsk, Kondinsk and other places." The title *tsar* was used as it had been in Ivan III's time. Vasily's reign marks the first appearance of a self-demeaning or derogatory nomenclature in communications to the grand prince from persons of humble station. To illustrate, the grand prince once arranged for a commoner to accompany boyars on a mission to the Crimea. Ilia Chelishchev was chosen. He signed his dispatches to the grand prince "your slave, *Ileika* Chelishchev." On another occasion an envoy, the junior boyar Shadrin, signed his communications with the diminutive *Vasiuk*. The grand prince's instructions to both men contained such salutations as "to our junior boyar Vasily Ivanov Shadrin, and Ileika Chelishchev, a man close to us."[24]

Ivan III had decreed that coins could be minted only within his dominions, at Moscow and Tver, and not in appanages. No change occurred in the sources of revenue available to the treasury; a tax on the sale of cattle is the only new impost mentioned. In 1507 King Sigismund decreed a military assessment in Lithuanian Russia. He wrote that the pressing needs of the government and the country had forced the diet meeting in Grodno to request a special assessment from everyone, laymen and clergy alike. A man cultivating 800 acres would pay 1 ruble 60 kopecks, and a man possessing 400 acres would pay 80 kopecks. Men holding smaller allotments would pay 50 kopecks, while tillers of family plots would pay 25 kopecks.

Charters King Sigismund granted the towns of Mogilev and Grodno furnish information about the sources of royal revenue in West Russia. The king derived a revenue of 150 rubles from the region, including four rubles from beaver hunters, four rubles from cowherds, three rubles from wax gatherers, seven rubles from silversmiths, and five rubles from beekeepers. A cattle tax of ten rubles was collected every three years; local officials paid forty rubles, and revenue from taverns in Mogilev amounted to some fifty rubles. A military assessment might be ordered every third year in an amount determined by the king, but his prefect collected taxes each year, including 25 rubles for the use of common lands, and a head tax in the same amount, which was transmitted directly. Local officials kept half the revenues they collected for the king.

A section in the Grodno charter reads: "When the spring crop is harvested on our estates in the Grodno district our steward must first assign the slaves their monthly allotments for a year. We take two thirds of the harvested grain and our steward takes one third. The two thirds we take are to be stored in our granaries and may not be used without our permission. All lakes in the Grodno district and the seines in the rivers belong to us. The Grodno superintendent has the duty of collecting our share of the flax grown throughout the district, as he has in the past."

A charter issued in 1529 to prefects and officials on the king's estates near Vilna and Trokai contains information on their economic life and the revenue they produced. As soon as the harvest was in a tithe had to be paid to each local church. A reserve for next year's planting must be set aside. Slaves must receive monthly allotments. Two thirds of the remainder went to the king and one third to his local prefect. Prefects kept a quarter of the spring crop themselves, while the other three parts were reserved respectively for the king, future planting, and public distribution. Any surplus remaining in the royal granaries the following spring was to be sold. When the king did not visit his estates prefects might keep vegetables grown there in the gardens, but when the king came on a visit he had to be supplied with vegetables.

Flax was to be planted in sufficient amounts to enable each slave woman to spin at least 100 inches of cloth per year. Tax-paying subjects were distinguished from unfree servants and were liable for labor from the time the spring crop was planted to St. Jude's Day [January 4]. In fall prefects kept certain peasants to work on the estates and put the rest out to work on quitrent, which consisted of a barrel of wheat or a wild boar. Members of the local petty gentry, who had long been obliged to render military service and mow hay, as well as fishermen, bee-keepers, blacksmiths and other such persons on the royal estates did not pay regular taxes, but had to work in the fields twelve days each summer.

Prefects were supposed to rent out unoccupied lands in return for cash payments and to sell fish caught in the lakes on the estates. Two thirds of the proceeds went to the royal treasury and the prefects kept the balance. Revenue from forest products such as pitch and ash belonged to the royal treasury, and the king also gained revenue from bridge and transport tolls, tavern excise, milling dues, a tax on transactions and on brewing, while prefects received the monies obtained from taxes on trade and various products and for local defense needs. Prefects were responsible for the protection of herds and had to make good any loss incurred through negligence. They also had the duty of recruiting loyal honest men to serve as supervisors, administrators, tax collectors, watchmen, husbandmen and threshers.

A charter of 1529 established a basic annual tax rate of one ruble for the inhabitants of Samogitia, of which the prefects and officials who collected the tax were to remit four kopecks from each ruble to the treasury. In addition the holder of an 800 acre unit had to send the treasury an annual sum of approximately 3 rubles 50 kopecks; the holder of a 400 acre unit had to send 2 rubles 25 kopecks, and those who held smaller allotments had to remit 80 kopecks for each service unit on their land. There were other taxes, such as 50 kopecks on a barrel of oats, and 20 kopecks per cart of hay. During a royal visit the inhabitants must supply the king with poultry, oats, hay, mead and beer.

MUSCOVITE COURT CUSTOMS

A description of a reception and official banquet for envoys gives a picture of certain customs followed at the Muscovite court in Vasily's time. On the day of the reception all stores and workshops were closed and the inhabitants lined the streets along which the envoys would pass. The crowds were swelled by servants from the boyars' city residences and military servitors brought in especially from adjacent estates to help create a strong impression in the envoys' minds that the grand prince disposed of a huge population and enormous resources. Envoys had to dismount before reaching the balustrade; only the grand prince might dismount directly at its foot. Starting from a point halfway down the balustrade courtiers, the most distinguished to the rear, descended to greet the arrivals. They extended their hands and kissed the envoys, who next entered the part of the palace where the grand prince was seated in company with his most eminent boyars. The grand prince's brothers, when present, did not rise and remained seated with bare heads, but the boyars, wearing hats, arose, and one of them announced the arrival of the envoys to the grand prince with the words: "So-and-so and so-and-so (he recited the envoys' names) beg audience with you." The grand prince sat bareheaded on a high platform. A richly decorated icon hung on the wall; his cap lay on a bench to his right, and a staff adorned with a cross lay to his left.

An interpreter translated the envoys' remarks. The grand prince stood up whenever he heard the name of the ruler to whom the envoys were accredited. When the envoys finished speaking he inquired after their health and bade them approach his person. He asked them whether they had made a good journey and told them to sit down on benches placed in front of him. The envoys bowed to the grand prince and the boyars, who had remained standing during the ceremony, and took their seats. If the envoys and their suite had brought gifts, after the introductory ritual a boyar representing the envoys cried out that envoy so-and-so saluted the grand prince with such-and-such a gift. Meanwhile a scribe made a list of the gifts and the names of the givers.

The grand prince soon invited the envoys to a banquet, and this action completed the ceremony of introduction. On entering the banquet chamber the envoys found the grand prince and his boyars already seated at table. When they came in the boyars arose; the envoys bowed on all sides and took the seats which the grand prince personally indicated to them with a movement of his hand. The tables were set in a circle. A cupboard with shelves full of gold and silver goblets stood in the center of the room. The width of his arms separated the grand prince on both sides from anyone else seated at his table. When his brothers attended a banquet the elder sat on the grand prince's right, the younger on his left. Service princes and boyars sat below appanage princes and a greater interval separated them than the space between the grand prince and his brothers. The envoys sat opposite the grand prince at a special table and the members of their suite ranged some distance below them. The officials who would escort the envoys to their quarters sat further back, and last of all came commoners whom the grand prince had been generous enough to invite.

Tables were set with cruets, salt shakers and pepper grinders. When the banquet commenced the grand prince sent bread to the envoys. Whenever he did so the envoys and everyone else, except the grand prince's brothers, stood up. The envoys bowed to the grand prince and to all sides. Salt was the highest mark of favor the grand prince could show a person attending the banquet, for bread betokened esteem, but salt meant love. The grand prince chose other items on his table besides bread as tokens of his favor. Whenever he sent them to the envoys they had to rise and bow in all directions. These ceremonies were very time-consuming and exhausting for those who were unfamiliar with them. Dishes included roast swan, served with salt, pepper, vinegar, sour cream and pickled cucumbers. Malmsey and Greek wines and various kinds of mead were provided. The plates, both large and small, were of pure gold. During the meal the grand prince conversed with the envoys in a most friendly manner, entertained them splendidly, and asked them various questions. He occasionally drank a toast to the health of the ruler to whom the envoys were accredited to show his exceptional regard for him. These banquets lasted for three or four hours, and the grand prince never undertook major business at their conclusion.

On August 15, the day of the Virgin Mary, Herberstein observed the grand prince in the cathedral. Standing near the wall by the door on the right side, the prince was leaning on his staff and held his cap in his right hand.

A description of Grand Prince Vasily's marriage has survived. Two chairs were placed in the center of the palace and covered with purple brocade. Embroidered cushions were placed on them, covered with some forty sableskins. The bride and groom were cooled with fans made from other skins. A table stood nearby, covered with a cloth and containing bread and salt. The bride entered from her chambers, accompanied by the wife of the chiliarch,[25] two intermediaries, and her ladies-in-waiting. The princess was preceded by boyars, after whom came men carrying two candles and a round loaf of bread with coins placed on top of it. When the procession reached the center of the palace Princess Elena took her seat at her place and her younger sister sat down in the place reserved for the grand prince. The escorts then took their seats. The groom was informed that everything was in readiness. Vasily's brother, Prince Yury, came first to make sure that both the senior and junior boyars were properly seated. When he was satisfied Yury sent men to tell the groom: "Sire, it is time for you to come to your wedding." The grand prince entered the palace accompanied by the chiliarch and his entire train, bowed to the icons, lifted the bride's sister from his place, sat down, and a few minutes later told the priest to pray. While the priest prayed the chiliarch's wife combed the bride's and groom's hair; Epiphany candles were simultaneously used to light candles in honor of the bride and groom, and hoops were set around them and covered with sableskins. After combing the bride's and groom's hair and placing a tall headdress with a veil on the bride's head, the chiliarch's wife scattered hops on the couple and fanned them with sableskins. The best man, intoning a blessing, cut a consecrated loaf and some cheese into portions while the bride, the groom and the guests were watching and handed everyone a piece. The maid of honor distributed little kerchiefs. The bride and groom proceeded to the cathedral of the Assumption for the ceremony, with loaves and candles borne before their conveyance. The metropolitan recited the marriage vows and handed the couple a glass of wine. The grand prince drank his, hurled his glass to the ground, and stamped on it. The pieces were collected and thrown into the river, following a traditional custom.

After the ceremony the couple sat on a portico to receive congratulations from the metropolitan, the grand prince's brothers and the boyars, both senior and junior, while choristers in two appointed stations chanted long life for the newlyweds. Returning from the cathedral the grand prince visited monasteries and churches and a feast was held in the palace. The newlyweds were served roast chicken, which the best man brought to their couch. Guests were forbidden to dispute precedence during the meal. When the couple withdrew to their bedchamber the chiliarch's wife donned two coats, one properly and the other inside out, and scattered the grand prince and princess with hops, while the intermediaries, the best man and the maid of honor offered them chicken. The nuptial bed rested on some thirty sheaves of wheat. Near its head stood a vessel containing ground wheat, candles, and ceremonial loaves. During the banquet and throughout the night the master of horse patrolled outside their chamber with a drawn sword. The next day the couple bathed and ate porridge in bed.

The grand prince's younger brother, Prince Andrei, who married the daughter of Prince Andrei Khovansky, celebrated his wedding with the same ceremonies, save that his older brother, the grand prince, took the father's role and blessed the ceremony. Prince Andrei asked the grand prince for permission to marry, which Vasily granted. A week before the wedding he attended mass in the cathedral and visited the metropolitan, whom he told of his brother's intention, and asked his blessing. He sent men to tell Prince Yury: "Brother, we approve our brother Andrei's wish to marry. We invite you to accompany us to his wedding." When bestowing the young bride on his brother, the grand prince said: "Brother Andrei, by God's will and with our approval, God has ordained your marriage to Princess Evfrosinia. Brother

Andrei, cherish your wife, Princess Evfrosinia, in accordance with God's commandments."

Successful consolidation of the new system of autocratic power made finding husbands for grand princesses more difficult. Vasily's sister Evdokia was not married when their father died. An opportunity to arrange a marriage for her occurred in 1506, but her fiancé was not of boyar rank. A junior Tatar prince, Kudaikul, son of Ibrahim and brother of Ilgam, had been captured and expressed a desire to adopt Christianity. He was solemnly baptized in the river Moscow, given the name of Peter, and he married Evdokia less than a month later. Their daughter, the grand prince's niece, married Prince Mstislavsky when he fled to Moscow. Peter swore faithfully to serve the grand prince and his children. Since he was directly related to the royal house he occupied a more prominent position than other princes and boyars.

COMPOSITION OF THE COURT

During Vasily's reign the court was composed, as it had been before, of boyars and lords-in-waiting. The term denoting a *lord-in-waiting* was originally an adjective modifying the noun *boyar*. Another form existed: *boyar,* and *lord-in-waiting so-and-so.* A description of negotiations with the Emperor's envoys contains an interesting substitution of the word *boyar* by the word *councillor,* followed directly by the term *lord-in-waiting:* "You may make any public pronouncements with which Maximilian has charged you at your reception and in the presence of our sovereign, but to hear secret communications our sovereign will send his *councillors* and *lords-in-waiting,* and you will relate your secret communications to our sovereign's *councillors* and *lords-in-waiting.*"

Herberstein defined a lord-in-waiting thus: "A lord-in-waiting performs the duties of a praetor or judge. Appointed by the grand prince, he serves as a privy councillor in constant attendance upon the grand prince." This definition is not entirely accurate; Russian sources do not endow a lord-in-waiting with the authority of a privy councillor. Nevertheless, it is understandable why Herberstein attributed great importance to a lord-in-waiting if in fact this official was in constant attendance upon the grand prince and responsible for prompt execution of his behests, or if the grand prince invariably appeared in the company of one or more lords-in-waiting, who might precede him on campaign to prepare his field headquarters. Nowadays a *lord-in-waiting* would be considered a member of the grand prince's retinue. On his deathbed Vasily appealed to his courtiers with this formula: "Senior and junior boyars and princes, serve my son now and in future as you have served me."

Vasily's court included armorers, huntsmen, cupbearers, jurists, his personal military lieutenants and sublieutenants, and equerries. Moscow had several municipal supervisors, one of whose tasks was, as has been seen, to build the bridge to carry the grand prince over the river Moscow during his illness.

Boyars assembled for a campaign from their estates attended by their servitors. The military registers record quarrels over precedence, which, unfortunately, omit details and give no reasons why one nobleman refused to serve with another. For example, in 1519 the lord-in-waiting, Andrei Nikitich Buturlin, filed a complaint against Andrei Yarovich Mikulin at Volokolamsk. The grand prince heard the case, exonerated Buturlin, found Andrei Yarovich guilty and ordered a writ against him. Prince Mikhail Vasilievich Gorbaty wrote that he would not serve with Prince Fedor Obolensky-Lopata or the boyar Ivan Buturlin. Prince Mikhail was told that he was on active service, at which time the rules of precedence were suspended. Prince Mikhail Kurbsky received an identical answer when he wrote to complain about the same individuals, as did Andrei Buturlin when he complained about Kurbsky.

THE MILITARY FORCES

Some foreign sources state that during Vasily's reign the Muscovite army numbered 400,000 men, mostly cavalry. Others say it had at least 150,000 men. Every two or three years the government carried out a census of its military servitors by district in order to determine their numbers and how many men and horses each could provide. The horses were small geldings. A few cavalrymen used spurs, but the majority used whips. They were generally equipped with bows, arrows, axes, and clusters of spiked iron balls; only noblemen and the rich carried swords. They also used long daggers resembling knives. They had to hold reins, bow, arrows, sword and whip all at once, but they managed to make dexterous use of them, as well as of a mace.

Great noblemen wore armor, chain-mail breastplates and helmets. The army's movements were executed at great speed and therefore foot soldiers and cannon did not enter battle. Grand Prince Vasily employed them for the first time to prevent a second Tatar crossing of the Oka after Mohammed-Girey's attack. Prior to this the Muscovite infantry numbered no more than 1,500 men, consisting of Lithuanians and other foreigners. Since the Muscovite army was composed mainly of cavalry it inevitably resembled the forces of eastern countries. It would attack boldly but lacked staying power. As Herberstein put it, the army seemed to say to an enemy, "flee before we flee."

Towns seldom fell to assault or siege warfare, but were reduced by protracted investiture. Herberstein observed that when a Tatar fell from his horse, lost his weapons, and was seriously wounded he punched, kicked, bit, or did anything else he could to defend himself until his last breath. When a Turk realized his situation was hopeless he meekly begged his enemy to spare him, but a Muscovite soldier neither defended himself nor asked for mercy. The army camped in the open. Nobles pitched tents while the rest of the men built little huts of branches which they covered with felt. Camps had no moats or other protective devices. The army relied on natural features of the terrain such as woods, rivers and swamps. Herberstein was astonished how little equipment a Muscovite soldier required.

A man who possessed six or more horses could put all the food he needed, which consisted of a little flour, ham, and salt, on one horse. Rich men had pepper, but master and man subsisted on the same basic diet. Soldiers sometimes went without food for two or three days when they were unable to forage. Herberstein says that Muscovite units relied more on numbers than skill in battle. They did their best to surround the enemy and attack him in the rear. The army included many musicians. When they blew their trumpets in the traditional style they produced a strange sound. They also had bagpipes. The grand prince's banner carried a representation of Joshua, son of Nun, making the sun stand still.[26]

Among Russian military narratives the Pskov chronicler tells an interesting story of his countrymen during the second Smolensk campaign. The grand prince arrived at Smolensk with his forces, which included fusiliers from all the towns under his control. Pskov's quota was 1,000 men. The city had made great sacrifices in order to meet this unusually high levy. The Pskov fusiliers and infantry, who had never served away from home before, reached Smolensk, where the grand prince put them under the command of their former city officials, who had been transferred elsewhere. The fusiliers from Pskov and other cities attacked and were supported by their artillery pieces. This account indicates that the urban population still served as fusiliers during campaigns, while the rural population supplied recruits for the artillery. The latter was important and was used to set up barrages for cover whenever the fusiliers and infantry launched an attack. The account also shows that long after their city's subjugation the inhabitants of Pskov remained subject to removal from their holdings, which were undoubtedly assigned to military servitors from other parts of Muscovy.

Foreign and native sources agree that foreigners were in charge of the artillery. Three foreign bombardiers served on the Kazan campaigns. One, the Italian Bartolomeo, converted to Orthodoxy and enjoyed substantial influence at court. The German bombardiers Nicholas and Jordan distinguished themselves during Mohammed-Girey's assault on Moscow and Riazan. The country from which came Stefan, the bombardier active during the siege of Smolensk, is unknown.

STATE CHANCELLERIES

During Vasily's reign chancelleries are first mentioned in the charter granted in 1512 to the Dormition (Uspensky) monastery of Vladimir. The monastery received confirmation of its traditional privilege of drawing its maintenance from the estates and towns under its control and its right to govern and judge the inhabitants. This right of sustenance might not carry with it a right of jurisdiction. Villages and hamlets might be assigned to a military landowner, who was allowed to judge all but capital and aggrieved assault cases. When a case involved a person living on his estate and one who did not, the landowner or his designate had to cooperate with the grand prince's vicegerents and local land and tax officials. The grand prince or a boyar assigned to the task heard cases involving landowners and their stewards.

CHARTERS

Landowners might hold villages and hamlets on permanent or hereditary tenure. This meant that they could leave them to their children, or sell, alienate, mortgage, or assign them. A grant of uncultivated woodland might carry the right to build homesteads and attract settlers with a fifteen-year remission of taxes. A charter issued by the grand prince's brother, Yury of Dmitrov, has survived. It includes an authorization for his agent Veliaminov to buy villages to which the latter would acquire the right of sale, gift or alienation. The disparate relationships existing among princes, their servitors and their local officials explain the need for such authorizations, which are reminiscent of the earlier instructions that were given to local officials to purchase villages in order to convert them into outposts of the princes' authority. In 1524 Naum Kobel and his associates asked permission to work salt pans they had discovered in an uninhabited forest in the Dvina region. No farms or pastures had ever existed there and uncultivated land lay for some fifteen miles on each side of the site. The grand prince granted them authority to clear the site of the pans, fell trees, build houses, till fields, and mow meadows. They were also permitted to enroll peasants not registered elsewhere, providing they were of good character, not robbers, thieves or law-breakers expelled from towns or other estates. Foreigners were awarded similar estates on taking service with the grand prince.[27]

Grand Prince Vasily issued an interesting charter to the inhabitants of Smolensk in 1514 which illuminates the composition of the service ranks in West Russia. Previous customs that had obtained when Lithuania ruled the city were not changed because, as the charter states, the bishop, local officials, lords-in-waiting, princes, boyars, artisans and the urban poor had all submitted a petition to preserve them. The charter assigned to lords-in-waiting functions second in importance only to the governor: "Our governors and lords-in-waiting and their assistants are forbidden to demand maintenance from craftsmen and the city poor, no matter where their duties might take them or their deputies. It is the responsibility of our governor and lords-in-waiting to protect artisans and the urban poor from bandits. Lords-in-waiting may not interfere with a man who judges his own indentured servant."

THE NOBILITY IN WEST RUSSIA

The term *boyar* no longer denoted a powerful personage at the court of the grand prince of Lithuania. Its place had been taken by the titles lord (pan) and lord *councillor*. Boyars in the original Russian duchies subjugated by Lithuanian princes retained their title and remained on their hereditary estates, but they had been reduced to the status of local military servitors. At the same time the term lord-in-waiting took on a connotation of responsible government office. This is the reason why officials called lords-in-waiting occupied higher positions than boyars. Since boyars in Smolensk and Polotsk had sunk to such a low level, the depressed condition of boyars serving in petty principalities can easily be imagined. They formed the entourages of petty princes, who had themselves lost almost all of their power and resources. In such circumstances it is not surprising to find boyars serving as bailiffs in royal outposts or on estates belonging to princes, lords (magnates) and members of the gentry.

In his statute, based on the privileges granted by his predecessors, Alexander and Casimir, King Sigismund vowed to guard both the grand duchy of Lithuania and lord councillors from loss. He agreed to compensate them for unjust exactions, not to assign their lands and offices to foreigners, nor to remove them from office without a hearing, and not to tamper with the rights traditionally possessed by gentry and townsmen. Minor princes, nobles, gentry and boyars might leave the grand duchy to serve any country not hostile to Lithuania, providing their departure did not adversely affect the king's interest. When fathers died their sons and daughters were not to be deprived of the estates their fathers and grandfathers had possessed. The king pledged not to raise commoners to higher positions than those occupied by members of the gentry. Should a member of the gentry assault another member the guilty party must pay a fine of twelve rubles, but if the man perpetrating the assault was of lower rank he had his hand cut off.

THE ARMY IN WEST RUSSIA

The dispositions made by a diet meeting in Vilna in 1507 afford insights into the nature of military service in West Russia. Nobles, princes, landowners, widows, and all members of the gentry were required to list the people living on their estates and attest these lists to the king in order to enable him to make an estimate of the service resources each person could provide from his estate. Anyone failing to appear for service at the appointed time in the proper place forfeited one hundred rubles to the king. A man who believed his wealth would protect him and failed to appear within the stipulated period without an excellent excuse was put to death.

A widow was fined one hundred rubles if her men were late arriving. If she neglected to send them within the stipulated period her estates were confiscated and assigned to her children, or relatives if she had no children. Anyone leaving the field of battle without the king's or the hetman's permission was executed. But what earlier had been negligence had now become chronic indifference, and no more than half the troops responded to the call. The diet realized it would be an act of savagery to execute all who failed to muster, and highly unjust to kill two or three while pardoning the rest. In this situation the diet stipulated that anyone failing to appear at the appointed time would be fined one hundred rubles and anyone failing to appear a week after the time had expired would be put to death.

In 1507 the king circulated a rescript defining the powers and authority of the hetman, the army commander, during a campaign. His was the right to execute soldiers who looted, committed assault, stole goods worth more than 25 kopecks, destroyed apiaries, or deserted. The diet meeting in Vilna in 1528 enacted that each owner of a populated estate must provide one well-mounted and fully-equipped soldier supported by eight attendants from each service measure into which his estate was divided. The following year the Vilna diet promulgated a highly detailed set of regulations. By its terms an estate comprising 700 service units must furnish 100 properly mounted and accoutred soldiers and an estate of 400 service units must provide fifty soldiers. The proprietor of an estate comprising eight service measures had to appear in person, and the owner of an estate consisting of less than eight service units likewise needed to appear in person, but his equipment and mount need not meet the standards specified in the regulations.

Men who maintained roads or paid quitrent, drovers and carters, and all peasants were liable for service, although exemptions were issued to those serving on the estates of princes, lords and gentry, as well as to their boyars and gentry, household servants, and gardners. Impoverished members of the gentry who possessed no attendants of their own had to appear for service in person with whatever equipment they could manage to provide. The regulations of 1529 decreed that recruits should muster as a unit in the district where they lived. If the callup affected a man in a magnate's service he was obliged to find an exempt substitute to take his place on the lord's estate when he left to join his unit. Failure to do so meant forfeiture of his holding.

A priest leasing land was subject to military service, and if he was the proprietor of a hereditary holding he must bring men with him. Positive proof of illness was required to obtain exemption. A father might send his son in his place provided he was eighteen or older, living at home, and the hetman accepted him.

THE COSSACKS

The cossacks are now mentioned with greater frequency in Muscovy and West Russia. The colonization and gradual settlement of the barren expanses of Eastern Europe and subsequently Northern Asia was one of the outstanding features of old Russian life. As is usually the case, densely settled central agricultural regions produce individuals whose character and temperament incline them to seek their fortunes in strange and unknown places. Such people prefer the new to the old and the unknown to the known; they constitute the boldest and most vigorous element in society. They play a vital role in the history of colonization because they are pioneers who open up new areas for settlement. A man who decides or feels compelled to leave his home and lose himself in the unknown quantity of the steppe needs the kind of courage that will sustain him when he undertakes a new life there. He must depend entirely upon his own resources and be constantly on guard against hostile forces. Conditions of this sort impel such people to form groups or bands, for which fighting is the main activity. Such was the nature of the cossacks, who settled on the frontier.

The immunity charters the government issued to settlers in this barren region well illustrate the origin of the cossacks. A good example is the charter (cited above) granted Naum Kobel and his associates: "Naum may receive peasants in his settlement who are not inscribed on the tax rolls, provided they are of good character, not robbers, thieves or bandits who have been expelled from towns and estates." A new settlement could always attract landless peasants not on the tax rolls, who were forced to earn their living by farming another's land, working for another, and enriching someone else by their labor. These rootless peasants became the original cossacks, but they also included many who refused to work another's land and be dependent upon someone else—men who chose to live a warlike, dangerous, independent and exciting life on the steppe frontier or beyond it. Since settlers had no right to receive them, where else might men who had fled the towns and estates hide?

Old Russia with its open borders found a frontier military population like the cossacks necessary and natural. They served on all the frontiers, but the largest number was required along the steppe frontier, which was regularly liable to savage nomad raids. Only fierce warriors constantly prepared to repulse attacks and always on guard against the enemy dared to settle there. The frontier cossacks were dependent in varying degrees on the government and showed it varying degrees of obedience, depending upon whether they lived on the frontier, where the government could keep an eye on them, or in the remote steppe far removed from the ruler's influence and scrutiny.

The chronicles have good reason to mention the Riazan cossacks first. The southeastern frontier at Riazan had suffered more severely than other areas from the attacks of the steppe nomads. During Vasily's reign Muscovy effectively employed these cossacks against the Crimeans and Turks. When the government tried to improve relations with Turkey it asked the Riazan cossacks which was the most suitable place where soldiers could meet and arrange for an exchange of envoys. The cossacks knew the steppe well and suggested a good site. A description of the embassy Morozov led to Constantinople contains the following: "Ivan Morozov is accompanied by ten groups of Riazan cossacks. He has instructions what to do with them. Four groups are to stay in Azov, four in Kaffa, and two are to go with him to Constantinople. He knows the names of the cossacks who are to stay in Azov and Kaffa and of those who are to go with him. If the Crimean khan plans to attack the Muscovite frontier, one contingent should report to the grand prince at once and the others should stay where they are gathering information. When they have done so these contingents should report to the grand prince and tell him everything they know."

Interestingly enough, the Islamic world also had its cossacks, like the Russian ones, in its own parts of the steppe. In Ivan III's reign the Tatar cossacks of Azov were described as fierce bandits. Vasily asked the sultan to forbid the Azov and Belgorod cossacks to aid Lithuania, but when Korobov, the Russian envoy, asked for guides from Azov he was told that his request could not be granted because there were no cossacks in Azov. The Tatars used the term *cossack* to designate the third and lowest order in their army, which was composed of ulans, princes and cossacks.

In Vasily's reign cossacks from Smolensk were reported operating along the Lithuanian border. King Sigismund often complained to the grand prince about the incursions they made into Lithuania.[28]

The same circumstances that brought about the emergence of cossacks in the Muscovite borderland led to their appearance in the steppelands along the Dnieper river in West Russia as well. Even in the days of the original Kievan state this area had contained numerous warlike, partially nomadic and semi-sedentary tribes who acknowledged the suzerainty of the princes. These included Torki, Berendei, Kouei and Turpei, known collectively as *Black Caps*. The chronicler states that this name is the same as *Cherkas*, the name by which Ukrainian cossacks are invariably known in Muscovite documents. These people may well have formed the nucleus of the Ukrainian cossacks, but in West Russia their numbers were augmented by many cossack bands of purely Russian origin. The geographic characteristics of the Dnieper borderlands had long favored the growth of military settlements.

This period provides interesting information about the Ukrainian cossacks. Khan Sahib-Girey complained to King Sigismund about them: "The Cherkasy and Kanev cossacks occupy positions near our settlements along the Dnieper and harass our people. I have frequently asked your majesty to restrain them but you have refused to do so. Once thirty of my men were taken ill on a campaign against the ruler of Moscow and returned home. On their way back cossacks attacked them and took their horses. Is this fair? I attack your enemy and your cossacks steal my army's horses! I hesitate to renounce my oath of fraternal friendship, but I intend to send troops to storm the fortresses of Cherkasy and Kanev. Where is our fraternal friendship? The Cherkasy and Kanev chieftains allow their cossacks to join those of the grand prince of Muscovy, your enemy and mine, and the Putivl cossacks, to occupy positions along the Dnieper near our settlements. They observe our activities and immediately report to Moscow. Your chiefs in Cherkasy supply information to the Putivl cossacks, and in this way give Moscow two weeks' advance notice of any attack we plan to undertake." The Ukrainian cossacks were under the supervision of the chief of Cherkasy and Kanev; during the period in question this office was held by Evstafy Dashkovich.

TOWNS

Vasily's reign saw no change in the function and appearance of Muscovite towns. They continued to serve as places of refuge for surrounding populations whenever an enemy attacked. The seats occupied by landowners and monasteries in the suburbs were called blockhouses. A decree issued by the grand prince to the city administrators of Tver concerned the establishment of a blockhouse on the territory controlled by the Josephan monastery in Volokolamsk. In 1508 the grand prince told Master Aleviz Friazin[29] to surround the Kremlin with a moat, reinforced with brick and stone, which would expand to form ponds at strategic points.

Here is how foreigners described Moscow in Vasily's time: "The capacious city of Moscow is built of wood. At a distance the city appears wider than it actually is because large cultivated areas surround each dwelling and magnify its extent. Works belonging to smiths and other artisans who use fire occupy outlying regions, with whole meadows and fields scattered among them. On the other side of the river Grand Prince Vasily has built a new town for his bodyguards known as *Nali*, which means *pour out* in Russian. The place is so called because only its inhabitants are freely allowed to drink mead and beer and thus have to be isolated beyond the river to prevent infecting others by their example.

"Monasteries occupy sites around the city and from a distance each one resembles an entire town. The great extent of the city makes it difficult to determine its boundaries and construct adequate fortifications. Streets in some sections are cordoned off by barriers, where guards are stationed to prevent passage after a certain time of night.

Anyone found there later receives a thrashing, has his goods seized, or is imprisoned, except for prominent and important men, whom the guards escort to their homes. Sentinels are also posted at the main gate leading into the city. The rest of Moscow is surrounded by the river of the same name, into which the river Yauza empties just below the city. The high banks of the Yauza, on which many mills are located, render the river difficult to cross. The city, which is built entirely of wood except for a few stone houses, churches and monasteries, is surrounded by these rivers. It is said to contain more than 41,500 churches, but this is hard to believe.

"This sprawling city is very dirty and its heavily populated areas are filled with bridges. One side of the brick Kremlin is protected by the river Moscow, the other, by the river Neglinnaia. At the upper end of the fortress the Neglinnaia widens to form a small lake, whose overflow fills the Kremlin moats, along which mills have been built. The Kremlin is the site of the grand prince's extensive, handsome palace, the metropolitan's residence, and the domiciles of the grand prince's brothers, his nobles, and various other persons. All of these are large wooden structures. The Kremlin also contains many churches."

Smolensk, a most important fortress at this time, was situated on the Lithuanian frontier. Smolensk and Pskov were the two strongest fortresses Muscovy possessed. In 1517, 280 feet of the city wall of Smolensk collapsed. Master Ivan Friazin [Gian-Battista della Volpe] restored it, but, even though priests carried stone and the people of Pskov brought sand and dug a barrier, the reconstruction cost the grand prince 700 rubles. Great efforts went into protecting the towns on the southeastern borderlands from the Crimeans and threats from Kazan.

A wooden fortress was built in Tula in 1509 and replaced by a stone one in 1520. A stone fortress was erected in Kolomna in 1525; wooden ones appeared in Chernigov and Kashira as did a stone fort on the Osetr river in 1531. To the east Master Peter Friazin put up a stone fortress in Nizhny Novgorod in 1508; the new wooden city of Vasilsursk has been mentioned previously. In 1508 the grand prince sent a boyar to Novgorod with instructions to survey the market squares and mercantile sections and measure the streets in the Muscovite manner. In 1531 he sent officials to measure the streets on the Sophia side. They measured the main street from the Vladimir gate to its terminus and all other streets from outside the city to the river bank. Identifying locations where danger of fire was great the officials erected barriers all over the city and posted watchmen, who took up their stations on October 1 and produced good results. Formerly the city had been the haunt of numerous criminals, who plundered, stole and murdered, but now the entire city was peaceful. As a result of these new measures many criminals departed, while others reformed and became honest workmen.

During Vasily's reign serious fires were rare in Moscow. In 1508 the artisan district and the clothing merchants' quarters burned down. In 1531 a gunpowder factory belonging to a foreigner, Master Aleviz, caught fire and in an hour more than 200 workmen perished in the blaze. A great fire broke out in Novgorod in 1508, killing more than 5,000 people. Another one occurred in Nizhny Novgorod in 1531. Fires are mentioned twice in Pskov, and Izborsk burned to the ground.

In West Russia some towns obtained new charters under Magdeburg law[30] and such existing charters were renewed. Inhabitants of towns along the Dnieper river complained to King Sigismund that they were badly treated by the officials he sent to collect outstanding taxes. They were forced to maintain the officials' deputies for years on end at their own expense while the latter extorted huge sums of tax money from the districts. The officials also imposed unconscionable exactions. Their behavior caused many to flee, and those who were left could not fulfill even half of their demands. They asked the king to resume the practice of the time of Vitovt and of the earlier time of Sigismund, whereby the inhabitants themselves collected the taxes in coin, beaver and marten skins, and forwarded them to the treasury, supplying the king's local representative with nothing save freshly brewed mead. The king granted their petition.

THE RURAL POPULATION

When the authorities wished to colonize areas in West Russia they exempted settlers from taxes for several years. King Sigismund instructed Radziwill, governor of Vilna, to settle the territory around Kleshcheliazy, in the Belsk district. Quite a few people were already there, but as soon as the governor decided to place them under the jurisdiction of the royal demesne at Kleshcheliazy, many of them departed. Observing their behavior Gastold, the new governor, seeking to carry out the king's instructions, granted the settlers rights which transferred the authority of the royal estate at Kleshcheliazy to collect imposts from them to the district chief, magistrates, and the local council. The district chief supervised two magistrates. One was attached to the royal estate, the inhabitants of which chose him from among the burghers of Kleshcheliazy and made him responsible for collecting estate revenues. The other performed local functions, and both of these officials were elected annually.

The inhabitants paid 25 kopecks and a barrel of oats per each tract of forty acres. Brewers paid a like amount. Four kopecks from court fines were earmarked for the king's estate and two kopecks went to the district chief. Merchants paid an annual tax of nine kopecks. Butchers had to supply the king's estate with a shoulder of mutton. Taverns were a royal monopoly; wine merchants paid 83 kopecks. Unindentured peasants willing to settle the virgin lands around Kleshcheliazy received a ten-year exemption from the acreage tax of 25 kopecks and a barrel of oats, but a settler on cultivated lands was exempted from these imposts for no more than two years.

Life in towns under Magdeburg law was far from tranquil. Citizens complained of the governors, princes, magnates and boyars. In 1527 King Sigismund was obliged to tell Peter Kiszka, governor of Polotsk, to cease violating the Magdeburg statutes. His edict declared that the mayor, his magistrates, the councillors, and the entire citizen body had frequently complained to him that Kiszka's officials and attendants murdered, robbed and stole from them. Repeatedly Sigismund had ordered the governor to desist from such practices, but instead he had redoubled his harassment. The populace also complained of the Polotsk princes, magnates, and boyars, as well as of the abbot and brothers of the Benedictine monastery. Townsmen who sought to purchase land from boyars and officials were ordered to appear and state their case before the governor. He seized many craftsmen and forced them to work for him. Kiszka also took into custody individuals who had deliberately renounced Magdeburg law to avoid paying the military assessments, Horde Pence and other town imposts. A further device was to make various people indenture themselves to the bishop, princes and boyars, who were delighted with the arrangement. New toll bridges were established on the rivers. Many of the governor's boyars and attendants married townspeople and thereby acquired homes and lands in the town, but they refused to pay town taxes or accept Magdeburg law. The governor applied local statutes to persons living in villages or inside the fortress.

The inhabitants of Vilna openly clashed with their rulers, including the mayor and his magistrates, and the council. The people, dissatisfied with the existing statute, demanded that it be revised. The king refused and ordered the original statute to remain in force, but he agreed that the people of Vilna might continue to pay military assessments and Horde Pence at existing rates and did not raise them. During Alexander's reign a certain Hoppen had obtained the right to administer Belsk on hereditary tenure. Hoppen sold the privilege to a local individual, who in turn sold it to Nicholas Radziwill, governor of Vilna. Radziwill's son and heir, Jan, sold a lifetime interest in the right to Ivan Segenevich, a resident of Belsk, for 150 rubles. In 1526 the mayor and his deputies, the councillors and the people of Belsk asked King Sigismund to allow the city to levy a general assessment on the inhabitants in order to buy the patent of authority from Radziwill, and to permit the citizens thenceforth to choose their own district chief. The king assented to their proposal.

The entire district of Kiev sent an interesting communication to King Sigismund which shows that all the districts along the Dnieper usually took part in repairing the city fortress. When Khan Mengli-Girey destroyed Kiev in King Casimir's time these districts, and even those beyond the Dvina and around Toropets, sent men to help rebuild the city. More than 20,000 workmen were engaged in the task and a special nobleman assigned to supervise the construction was given the title of town chief.

The Jews were once expelled from Lithuania, but they soon returned and were granted the right to reclaim their homes and lands, which had been occupied by Christians during their exile. Originally the Jews were supposed to furnish 1,000 warhorses, but later they were excused from all military service and finally, in 1533, all their former rights were restored.

A charter to the peasants of Artemovo in the Pereiaslavl district has survived. It provides information about the peasant population of Muscovy in Vasily's time. The charter specified the supplies the peasants must furnish their district chief, his bailiff, and his juridical officers three times a year, at Christmas, Easter, and St. Peter's Day. When a proprietor first took up residence on his estate he accepted only voluntary contributions from the peasants. New settlers, who were registered but had not yet occupied their lands, or who arrived after enrollment had begun, paid no taxes to the proprietor, his bailiff or his juridical officers for a specified interval, but on its expiration they were obliged to pay the same taxes as other, established villagers. The proprietor kept the same bailiff and juridical officers for a year. Neither he nor his bailiff heard cases unless a village elder and his chief men were present.

When a murder occurred and the murderer was not detected, the peasants on the estate had to pay the owner a fine of four rubles. When a murderer was apprehended and surrendered to the proper authorities, no fine was assessed. Peasants similarly paid no fine in cases of drowning and the like, where no one was at fault. Unless invited, no one, not even the proprietor's assistants, stewards and boyars, might attend peasant celebrations and family affairs. A man who came without an invitation was merely asked to leave, but if the unwelcome guest refused, forced himself on the company, and created a disturbance he was fined double on the spot and the grand prince required him to make good any damage he had caused. Beggars were not allowed on estates. On his daughter's marriage a peasant had to present two kopecks to his proprietor, and if a daughter married someone from another estate her father had to give his proprietor six kopecks. Strolling players were not allowed to perform on estates. The proprietor took a kopeck from both buyer and seller in transactions involving horses.

Princes, boyars, commanders and soldiers were forbidden to behave violently on an estate. They were not to force peasants to supply them with food, guides or fodder, and had to pay for what they needed at regular prices wherever they stopped. Such was the content of a charter issued by Yury, the appanage prince of Dmitrov, to beaver hunters in the village of Kamenny, whose superior was a hunting master. The latter's privileges compared with those enjoyed by proprietors as described above, but this charter specified how the hunters were to meet their obligations. The group determined the amount of coin and produce necessary to support the hunting master, land officials and bailiffs, and to make contributions to the estate. The larger the area sown or planted, the greater the amount of supplies it must furnish. The elder and his assistants collected the assessment and conveyed it to Dmitrov on a holiday, where they handed it over to the hunting master or his steward and bailiff, who never went in person to the villages to collect it.

Were a land official or bailiff invited to attend a peasant celebration or family gathering he might have some refreshment at the house but was not to take a measure of beer or other spirits with him when he left to spend the night in another village, as he was required to do. Quarrels and fights breaking out at such gatherings were to be settled in accordance with the Dvina charter once proclaimed by Grand Prince Vasily Dmitrievich:[31] "When a quarrel or a fight occurs at a celebration and the hostile parties resolve their differences on the spot, a hunting master or bailiff is not to interfere. If the contending parties later come to terms through an intermediary officials may only impose a small fine."

Neither charter quoted above alluded to the judicial function possessed by peasant corporations to which the Pskov Law Charter refers: "A corporation has the power to render judgments." A circuit judge visited villages twice a year, at Christmas and on St. Peter's Day. He travelled in a sled, accompanied by an attendant, and was not supposed to spend the night in a house where he dined, and vice versa. An interesting agreement made by a certain Vlas Friazinov when mortgaging his estate sheds some light on the status of the dependent population. The people on his estate are listed by name, and "all of us promise to repay this loan and all of us accept responsibility for it."[32]

The king's charters show that the rural population in West Russia was divided into free, tax-paying subjects and slaves. One charter says: "If a peasant refuses to obey the orders of his master or his designate and misses a day's work he must forfeit a ram. If he is intransigent he may be punished with a whip or a switch."

Crop failures struck three times during Vasily's reign—in 1512, 1515, and 1525. A violent storm causing rivers to overflow and sundering communications occurred in 1518, as did severe droughts in the years 1525 and 1533. Plague broke out several times in Novgorod and Pskov, in 1507-1509, 1521, and 1532. The inhabitants of the central part of the country escaped this misfortune and gradually forgot the terrible epidemics of the fourteenth and fifteenth centuries. Foreign accounts of Muscovy in Vasily's time state: "The climate of Moscow is so salubrious that no one can remember an outbreak of plague. There are occasional incidents of an illness resembling cholera, which they call the *Flame*. It strikes a man internally and affects his head. After a few days of sickness the patient dies."

FOREIGN ACCOUNTS OF MUSCOVY

Foreigners described Muscovy as a broad plain covered with forests and intersected by large rivers, full of fish, running in every direction. In spring, swollen with melting ice and snow the rivers turned fields into swamps and covered roads with dirty water that remained until the next winter, when the savage frost formed bridges of ice in the swamps and rendered the roads passable. The chief products of the country were grain, timber, honey, wax and furs. Pine trees grew to an unbelievable size. Oaks and maples were of finer quality than those found in Western Europe. Bees collected honey and deposited it in trees everywhere. A story tells that a peasant, investigating a hole in a huge tree, fell in and was buried up to his neck in a cache of honey. For two days he waited vainly for help with nothing but honey to eat and was finally extricated from his desperate situation by a bear, which thrust its hind legs into the hole. The peasant flailed at the bear with his fists and yelled so loudly that the terrified creature jumped out of the hole, pulling the man with him.

Masses of furbearing animals lived in Muscovy's forests. The value of sable fur was determined by the darkness of its texture and its length and thickness. The time when the animal was caught might increase the value. Sables were comparatively rare around Uglich and in the Dvina region, but large numbers of high quality skins were obtained in the Pechora district. Sableskins sold for one or two rubles apiece in Moscow. Fox fur, particularly black fox, was costly; ten furs might occasionally fetch fifteen gold pieces. Beaver fur was also very expensive. Squirrelskins were common, particularly in Siberia. The best ones came from around Kazan, but others came from Perm, Viatka, Ustiug, and Vologda. They were usually bundled together in batches of ten, in which two skins were excellent, three were good, four were average, and one was of markedly inferior quality. There was some traffic in lynx, wolf and white fox fur. The forests also contained moose, bear, and big black wolves. Wild oxen lived in the west. The high mountain country inhabited by the Yugrians and Voguls was the home of splendid falcons and hawks.

The fields abundantly produced wheat, corn and other cereals, as well as a wide variety of vegetables. The sandy soil around Moscow was not fertile, and the slightest imbalance of drought or moisture could kill the crops. The cold sometimes killed the crops after planting. Stumps of huge trees, still visible everywhere at that time, proved that the whole country had been covered with forests until comparatively recently. The land around Vladimir and Nizhegorod was very fertile; an acre would occasionally produce twenty or even thirty bushels of grain. Riazan was considered the most fertile area in Muscovy. Horses could not force their way through its thick cornfields and it produced much finer fruit than Moscow. There was an abundance of honey, fish, fowl, and game. Besides agriculture, hunting, fishing and beekeeping, foreign writers mention iron-smelting at Serpukhov and salt-panning at Staraia Rus, at Solovki near Pereiaslavl-Zalessky, and adjacent to Nizhny Novgorod. They state that a lake not far from Beloozero contained sulfur, which was removed by a river that rose in the lake, but the natives were unable to take advantage of this gift from nature. Among secondary industries foreigners mention the manufacture of fretted wooden cups and other utensils, which were sold in Moscow, Lithuania and nearby countries.

Russian sources tell of whole fishing villages located in places suitable for that pursuit, such as the shores of Lakes Galitsky and Pereiaslavl. The Pereiaslavl fishermen were under a rural district chief of court rank, whose rights were specified by a charter, like the one given to the district chief of the village of Artemovo cited earlier. Another of Grand Prince Vasily's charters has survived. It was issued to falconers, under the falconry office, who lived in their own quarter in Pereiaslavl. They were exempt from control by vicegerents and land officials, and held no responsibility for building roads or maintaining any except the main highway. Their sole contact with the people of Pereiaslavl involved such affairs as the construction of fortifications and rendering military service. Either the grand prince or the master of falconry judged their cases. The twenty falconers paid an annual quitrent of fifty kopecks each, and their number included four widows, two journeyman shoemakers, a saddler, and a woman baker.

A letter from appanage Prince Semen to the Trinity monastery refers to the grand prince's hunting. Monasterial peasants living in Bezhetsky Verkh had to provide five men whenever Vasily hunted bear, moose or elk. This assignment was considered a privilege.

Foreign accounts state that Muscovy carried on an extensive trade in raw materials, shipping large amounts of pitch, wax and valuable furs to Europe via Livonia, where these commodities were in demand. Muscovy was not alone in this enterprise, for West Russia under Lithuanian control exported a great deal of pitch and wax. Muscovy also supplied the west with timber, excellent flax, hemp, and hides. Lithuania and Turkey imported hides, furs, and walrus tusks. The Tatars imported saddles, bridles, cloth, hides, linen, knives, axes, arrows, mirrors and bags. Muscovy's imports consisted largely of silver ingots, cloth, raw and processed silk, precious stones, jewels, decorative gold objects, pepper, saffron, and wine. Oriental traders supplied the silk. Tatar merchants furnished horses and bolts of good-quality woollen yardage used to make attractive ponchos that kept out the rain.

A famous fair was held at Kholopgorod on the Mologa river. The popular Makarevsky fair started during Vasily's reign. Seeking to embarrass Kazan, which was hostile to him at the time, the grand prince in 1524 forbade Russian merchants to attend the fair held near Kazan on what was known as Merchant's Island, and arranged to hold a fair near Nizhny Novgorod. Muscovy initially suffered from this action. A major shortage developed in goods brought through the Caspian Sea and up the Volga from Persia and Armenia. The absence of salt fish from the lower Volga area proved especially unpopular.

Foreign writers were interested in trade routes. They mention traffic on the Moscow river, which was winding and difficult to navigate, particularly the section between Moscow and Kolomna. Donkov, situated on the Don river 120 miles from Riazan, was the place where merchants loaded their boats to go to Azov, Kaffa and Constantinople. They usually set out in the rainy fall season because the rest of the year the Don was too shallow to float their craft. The Viazma river, passing below the town of the same name to empty into the Dnieper, was the starting point for freight boats ascending and descending the Dnieper to and from Viazma. Dmitrov was situated on the Yakhroma river, a tributary of the Sestra, which in turn flows into the Dubna, a tributary of the Volga. This waterway system facilitated extensive commercial development. Foreigners give interesting accounts of trade that had been quietly going on prior to the sixteenth century with the Lapps on the far northern borders of European Russia, and in the Ob district beyond the Ural mountains.

An agreement made in 1514 with the seventy Hansa towns allowed their merchants to trade in Novgorod in all commodities, including salt, silver, tin, copper, lead and sulfur, while Novgorod merchants obtained equal rights to trade in Germany in all goods, including wax. If a German bought wax which proved to be impure from a trader in Novgorod the latter had to exchange it. If a Novgorod merchant bought or sold at short weight in Germany and later bought or sold at full weight, he had to make up the difference. A German merchant selling salt, herring or honey in Novgorod at short weight would similarly be obliged to make up the difference. If a German paid for merchandise with adulterated silver he would have to exchange it.

Herberstein speaks of interest charges which ran as high as ten and twenty percent. The speed at which freight moved in those days cannot be ascertained, but Herberstein has provided information about passenger service: "When I was proceeding from Novgorod to Moscow the station master had thirty, forty or fifty horses ready for me. I needed no more than twelve, and so each of us was able to choose the horse he wanted. Everyone was free to use post horses. If a horse became exhausted or fell on the way we could requisition another at the first house we found or from the first passer-by we encountered, unless he was one of the grand prince's couriers." It was the station master's responsibility to rescue an abandoned horse and to locate the owner of a commandeered horse in order to compensate him; the owner usually received fifty kopecks for each six to twelve miles. Herberstein's attendant covered the 360 miles between Novgorod and Moscow in 72 hours. Such speed, concludes the author, was all the more remarkable because the horses were rather small and by no means as well cared for as horses in his own country.

An order from the grand prince to repair the Ergolsk station also contains information on the internal transport system: "Station masters have been saying that the buildings, living quarters, sheds and station at Ergolsk are in utter disrepair and fences have fallen down. As many peasants as are necessary, two from each taxpaying plot in the Belozersk district, are to rebuild all of them without exception. They are also to repair the roads and the bridges over the rivers, swamps and mudholes between Ergolsk and Naporozhsk. They are to replace bridges in danger of collapse with new structures. Bridges over rivers must have supports to prevent the current from sweeping them away. The station master and his men are to assign portions of the land belonging to the station for farming, haymaking, and pasturing post-horses. They are to separate the sections by digging pits which will be covered by latticeworks." The word *yam (pit)* is not derived from these boundary pits, which were very common, but either from the Russian verb *emliu (I take)* or, more probably, from the Tatar word *yam*, meaning *road.*

In West Russia in 1511 King Sigismund granted the people of Vilna exclusive trading privileges. Merchants coming to the city could trade with no one save its inhabitants, except on fair days, when visiting merchants might also trade with foreigners.

CULTURE

There is some interesting information concerning the arts during Vasily's reign. The chronicles mention restoring ancient icons bearing Greek inscriptions. The icon of the Savior and the Virgin was brought from Vladimir to Moscow for this purpose and triumphantly welcomed by Metropolitan Varlaam and the whole people in 1518. The work of restoration was carried out in the metropolitan's residence, and, so the story goes, the metropolitan often participated personally in the work. After the icon was restored and refurbished it was solemnly returned to Vladimir. Two icons were sent to Moscow for restoration from Rzhev in 1531. One portrayed Parasceve as a saint, the other, as a martyr.[33] The Russian master Fedor Edikeev was outstanding for church wall paintings; Alexis the Younger of Pskov was known as an icon painter. The New Virgin monastery, commissioned in honor of the capture of Smolensk, is the most remarkable structure in Moscow that has survived from Vasily's time. Vasily continued to invite foreign artists and physicians. In 1534 Nicholas the German was asked to cast a bell weighing 3600 pounds. During Vasily's reign Master Aleviz Friazin built eleven stone churches in Moscow and Bon Friazin put up the Ivanov belltower. Two doctors, the Germans Nicholas Bülow and Theophilus, attended Vasily during his final illness. A third doctor was a Greek named Mark.

All during this time, while Muscovy was endeavoring slowly and hesitatingly to appropriate the fruits of European civility, the Russian people maintained their thrust to the northeast and continued to propagate Christianity, the essential element of civilization, among the savage tribes inhabiting the forest regions. Herberstein, who frequently dilated upon the dark side of Muscovy, could not refrain from observing that during his visit Russian monks set out for a variety of northeastern destinations, overcoming formidable obstacles on their way, enduring hunger, and risking their lives, solely in order to disseminate the Christian faith. In his description of Perm, Herberstein observed that St. Stefan's mission[34] had failed to convert all the inhabitants of the region, but the monks who subsequently came there succeeded in disabusing the rest of the pagans lurking in the forests of their errors. Feodorit the Anchorite converted the Lapps of the Kola peninsula, while Trifon spread the Gospel among those dwelling on the Pechenga river.

CHURCH AFFAIRS

Two remarkable individuals, Joseph of Volokolamsk and Maxim the Greek, played leading roles in the Russian church during Vasily's reign. Vasily's accession guaranteed Joseph's triumph over the heretics [the Judaizers][35] and assured him the constant protection of the throne. Far more a man of deeds than words, Joseph was a worthy successor to the illustrious ascetics whose personal example had advanced the cause of Christianity in Muscovy. Whenever a peasant needed seed or had lost his draught animals or his equipment, he went to Joseph, who provided him with everything he required. When a famine assailed Volokolamsk the people sought refuge with Joseph. He fed some 700 of them, as well as their children, and established a camp containing a church and a hospital near his monastery to receive strangers, tend the sick, and feed the poor.

When Joseph had exhausted the monastery's resources he borrowed money to feed the poor and constantly appealed to Yury, prince of Dmitrov, to help the starving people: "My lord, in the name of God and the Virgin Mary, protect the Orthodox Christian inhabitants of your ancestral realm, as did the Orthodox tsars and princes of old, who succored their subjects in times of famine. Any of those rulers who had ample stocks of grain available distributed them among the needy or ordered them sold cheaply at a price he and his boyars considered proper, and he strongly condemned those who refused to obey, as your brother, Grand Prince Vasily of all Russia, has just done. If you act thus in your realm you will be an inspiration to its poor. Many are presently starving; only you have the power to alleviate their suffering. Others are powerless to act unless you manifest concern and use your princely power to set prices."

Joseph had to fight other campaigns as well. He was obliged to wage bitter struggles with his opponents. During the struggle with the heresy of the Judaizers in Ivan III's time Joseph called for stern measures against its proponents. His attitude aroused many powerful people against him. The dispute over the policies he advocated carried over into Vasily's reign. Joseph's opponents, including the monk, Vassian Kosoy, who had been Prince Vasily Patrikeev in secular life, once more insisted that repentant heretics should be pardoned but Joseph uncompromisingly maintained his position. Citing examples of stern punishment meted out to the guilty from the Old and New Testaments, he wrote the grand prince: "Our sovereign, we pray that you will employ your royal power utterly to extirpate the wicked tare of heresy." Elders in the Kirillov monastery and the monasteries of Vologda prepared a caustic refutation of Joseph's views. Historians of the church believe the tract was composed by Vassian. The grand prince supported Joseph, but his enemies were not entirely vanquished. Vassian moved to Moscow, effected a second rapprochement with the court, and enjoyed some temporary success in his campaign against Joseph.[36]

A contemporary account asserts that Vassian's hostility, fueled by the long-standing animosities resulting from their dissimilar views, was so intense that he tried to destroy the monastery over which Joseph presided. Fedor Borisovich, the appanage prince of Volokolamsk, had his own reasons for attacking the monastery.[37] Here is Joseph's own description of the ways in which the prince harassed the monastery: "Prince Fedor Borisovich will stop at nothing. He will not let us keep what God has given us. He declares that some of the goods he seizes are gifts to him, and he pays only half their value for others. If we fail to obey him he threatens to beat our monks with a knout and assails me. We have fear of him. We have surrendered to him all the gifts pious people have bestowed upon the monastery, such as horses, armor and clothing, but this is not enough. He wants and demands money. We sent him sixty rubles, but he asked for more. Then we sent him forty rubles, which he held for ten years. We decided we wanted this money back, but he refused and threatened to knout our emissary, the monk Gerasim Cherny. He tries to appropriate all the money we receive to distribute as alms or to say masses for the dead. No sooner had Prince Semen Belsky sent us 75 rubles to honor the memory of his parents than Prince Fedor was there demanding the money. No sooner had we spent 150 rubles on the purchase of precious stones to adorn our robes than the prince was there to demand them. He told our monks: 'I guarantee to maintain any of you who want to get away from Joseph and settle on my lands, but I shall take action against all who refuse my offer and remain with Joseph. I shall shatter Pavel's head with my knout or I am not the son of Prince Boris Vasilievich.'

"Fedor's threats made several monks leave the monastery. I realized that Prince Fedor was determined to destroy the monastery, and I decided to escape. I told the brothers of my intention, but they said to me: 'God will punish you if you forsake the church and the monastery of the Virgin Mary, because it was the Virgin who built the monastery, not Prince Fedor. We have bestowed all our earthly goods upon the Virgin and yourself and hope you will take care of us before we die and remember us when we are dead. We have devoted all our energies to the monastery, and now, when we are penniless and feeble, you intend to desert us. You know we cannot reach agreement with Prince Fedor. Even your presence here fails to deter him from beating and robbing us. You are well aware that Prince Fedor stole all the money belonging to the monasteries in Vozmishche, Selizharov and Levkiev. He will fleece us just as thoroughly. When the monks in those monasteries took their vows they retained their estates, where they now can seek refuge, but when we took our vows we surrendered all our possessions to you and the Virgin Mary.' I feared the judgment of God and dared not abandon the monastery to robbers. I myself begged the prince's men to ask their suzerain to spare us and leave us alone, but they answered: 'Our lord is free to do whatever he wants with his monasteries. He can spare them or plunder them.'

"After that I petitioned our sovereign, the Orthodox autocrat and grand prince of all Russia, to show his mercy to the Virgin's monastery and deliver it from Prince Fedor's attacks. If he was unwilling to do so the monks would flee and the monastery would be abandoned. The sovereign grand prince acted immediately. He took counsel with all his princes and boyars and conferred with most holy Metropolitan Simon and his whole sacred council. Following their advice and with their blessing he placed the monastery, myself, sinner that I am, and all our brothers under his mighty protection and refused to allow Prince Fedor to attack us further. For two years we lived quietly and peacefully."

Two years later further trouble arose. Prince Fedor refused to give up his plan to control Joseph's monastery. He and three close associates decided that their only hope of success lay in securing the cooperation of the archbishop of Novgorod, to whose diocese an ancient political division had assigned the Volokolamsk area. Prince Fedor prevailed upon Archbishop Serapion of Novgorod to send Joseph a notice of excommunication during Easter week.[38] This move produced a violent reaction. Prince Fedor's supporters rejoiced, saying: "We have won Joseph's monastery. Our bishop has thwarted Joseph, and Moscow as well." Moscow lost no time demonstrating that the matter was not so simple. Serapion was summoned to the capital, deprived of his office, and banished to the Trinity monastery upon conviction on a charge of excommunicating Joseph without prior consultation with the grand prince and the metropolitan, who had approved Joseph's transfer of allegiance.

The affair caused considerable stir and was variously interpreted. Joseph had many enemies, who let him know that a substantial body of opinion in Moscow believed he would have been better advised to leave the monastery and the area rather than to have petitioned the grand prince. Their strictures aroused Joseph to compose a lengthy treatise justifying his behavior, which contained a detailed exposition of the entire incident. His pupil, Nil Polev, also wrote in defense of his patron.[39]

MAXIM THE GREEK

Joseph died in 1515. Vassian Kosoy survived him and continued the struggle against Joseph's views. This old contest had begun under Ivan III, but the intrusion of the distinguished figure of Maxim the Greek further complicated the affair during Vasily's reign. The year Joseph died Grand Prince Vasily sent Vasily Kopyl to Mt. Athos with a letter addressed to the superior, and to all the abbots and monks of the eighteen monasteries on the holy mountain, in which he asked them to send the elder Savva, a translator, from the Vatoped monastery to Moscow for a time. The abbot of the Vatoped monastery replied that age and infirmity made it impossible for Savva to go, but he would send another monk in his place. The choice fell on Maxim, who was skillful and capable of interpreting and translating all kinds of church books, including Greek.

Before entering the Vatoped monastery Maxim, a Greek from the Albanian town of Arta, had travelled in Europe and studied in Paris, Florence and Venice. These were the hands that took control of the splendid collection of Greek manuscripts preserved in the grand prince's library in Moscow, which had not been used due to the lack of persons able to take advantage of them. Maxim knew the essential languages of Latin and Greek. Unfortunately, at this stage he had not yet learned Church Slavonic or the Russian vernacular, although he had begun studying them before he left for Moscow. This deficiency did not prevent Maxim from rendering signal service to the cause of Russian enlightenment in the sixteenth century.

The first thing Maxim did was to render the commentary on the Psalmbook. He translated it from Greek to Latin and two Russian interpreters then proceeded to translate it from Latin to Russian. After completing this assignment Maxim was entrusted with the task of correcting the liturgical books, which transcribers had filled with clumsy errors. Then he translated Chrysostom's commentary on Matthew and John, and the commentary on the Acts of the Apostles. By now he was able to translate the Psalmbook directly from Greek to Russian. Maxim's activities ranged far beyond these assignments. In olden days the number of apocryphal compilations had multiplied, for such works were in intense demand by those who desired to acquire the most precise information possible on matters of religion. People were fascinated by these books, but they lacked the capacity to distinguish the true from the false and believed anything they found in a book.

It was inevitable that such an undertaking would compel Maxim to criticize apocryphal writings and the superstitious practices countenanced in books and disseminated by ignorant people. These considerations led Maxim to refute Papias' tale about Judas Iscariot,[40] the fable about those who proclaimed that the sun stood still and never set during the first Easter week,[41] and Aphroditian's story of the birth of Christ.[42] To support his analysis Maxim established three rules to determine a work's veracity: 1) was it written by a pious and well-known churchman, 2) did it agree with Scripture, and 3) was it internally consistent? Maxim wrote a treatise, "Against the insane God-hated conceit of philosophers who claim that burying drowned and murdered men shames and destroys the earth's vegetation." Maxim strongly opposed the belief in astrology, fate, and the wheel of fortune common in his day. He asserted that the guiding force in the world was God's providence, not stars or a wheel of fortune making the stars move. Maxim's interpretation of the Greek inscriptions regularly found on icons of the Virgin Mary constitutes his best commentary on the learning possessed by his contemporaries. He declared the words meant *Mother of God,* not *Marfa* or *Mirfa,* "as some people have vainly asserted."

VASSIAN KOSOY

The learned Greek monk inevitably came in contact with Vassian Kosoy (Prince Patrikeev), the eminent Russian monk distinguished for his relatively high degree of enlightenment. Ivan III had accused Vassian of arrogance. In reality he had the habit of expressing himself bluntly on matters of which he disapproved. He censured contemporary society for its ignorance and boldly reserved the right to criticize the moral qualities of prominent individuals. He refused to consider a man truly moral or religious if he thought him uncultivated and base born. Maxim had found a dangerous ally.

Both men agreed on the central issue dividing the Russian clergy: whether it was proper for monasteries to own landed estates. A pupil of Nil of Sorsk, Vassian opposed the practice. A pamphlet almost certainly attributable to Vassian has survived, in which he says: "When did the Gospels or the traditions of the apostles and the fathers ordain that monks should acquire populous villages, enslave peasants, and unjustly appropriate their gold and silver? As soon as we become monks we do everything we can to acquire villages and estates which do not belong to us. We importune noblemen with shameless flattery and buy their estates. Instead of maintaining a vow of silence and supporting ourselves by our own labors we travel constantly around the towns. We cozen wealthy men, flatter them, and slavishly seek to win their favor in order to obtain some paltry settlement or a handful of coins. The Lord enjoins us to give alms to the poor; instead we harass poor people living in our villages in every way we can—unless they pay. We steal their cows and horses. We debase them and their wives and children, and drive them from their homes. Whenever we hand a man over to the secular authorities we sign his death warrant. We insult, rob and sell our Christian brothers and beat them savagely, like wild beasts. Self-proclaimed miracle-workers order us to show no mercy to peasants who fail to fulfill their obligations to the monasteries—as long as we torture them outside, away from the monastery. They deem it no sin to execute a peasant off the monastery premises! . . .

"I do not corrupt Christ-loving princes with God's word; it is those who follow the ways of the world and pagan customs that dazzle and confuse pious people. You say it is I alone who wrongfully intercede on behalf of heretics. Had you reasonable intelligence or honest judgment you would realize that I am not defending wicked heretics but fighting for salvation and righteous teaching when I declare that we must punish heretics but not put them to death. Tell us which heretics of old were beheaded, immolated or drowned? Did not the holy councils of the fathers simply invoke anathema upon them and pious rulers merely imprison them?" Maxim joined the chorus of protest against monasterial landholding in such writings as *A Strange and Remarkable*

ASCENSION CATHEDRAL

Kolomenskoe near Moscow (1532)

Tale, which offered the poverty of the Cartesian monks as an example, and the *Dialogue Between a Possessor and a Non-possessor.*

Vassian and Maxim were unable to make their views prevail. Their opposition to his divorce cost them the favor of the grand prince. Both were subsequently charged with crimes of an ecclesiastical nature. Errors were detected in the translations Maxim had made and a court convicted him. At first he was immured in Joseph's monastery, where he was subject to serious indignities, and later in the Otroch monastery at Tver, where he was allowed to read and write. Among the charges made against him were his criticism of monasterial landholding and the lack of respect he showed the metropolitans when he censured them for assuming office without the blessing of the patriarch of Constantinople. The first of these two counts was the sole charge made against Vassian at his trial. Maxim appeared three times before the council deciding his case. He invoked God's mercy and human frailty when beseeching forgiveness, and tearfully begged the judges to pardon the errors which had been found in his books.[43] Vassian behaved differently and refused to admit his views were mistaken. He too was confined in Joseph's monastery.

The ideas of Joseph of Volokolamsk had triumphed. Monasteries continued to own land, which they leased out on lifetime tenure or for which they received quitrent. A charter issued by Grand Prince Vasily to the nunnery of the Dormition monastery in Vladimir contains some interesting information on monasterial landowning. The abbot, elders, five priests and two deacons of the place informed the grand prince that the estate and village they controlled did not provide sufficient income to support the nunnery. They asked him to purchase the estate and village from them and set the money out at interest. The grand prince paid 2142 rubles for the estate and village and instructed his state secretaries to let the money out at a rate of ten kopecks to the ruble. The revenue derived therefrom was to be returned to the nunnery in the following manner: the abbot received ten rubles, 50 quarters of rye, 50 quarters of oats, and 360 pounds of salt. Each elder received one ruble 50 kopecks, twelve quarters of rye, twelve quarters of oats, and some 100 pounds of salt. Priests got ten rubles, thirty quarters of rye, thirty quarters of oats, and 360 pounds of salt. Deacons received six rubles, twenty quarters of rye, 20 quarters of oats, and some 200 pounds of salt.

MONASTERY LIFE

Archbishop Makary of Novgorod issued an interesting charter to the Dukhovsky monastery, which tells something of monastery life in Vasily's time. He set the monastery's complement at a priest and a deacon from the black clergy and ten brothers. In addition to reciting the regular offices, the monks were to pray on Sundays, Mondays, Wednesdays, Fridays and holidays for the health and safety of the grand prince and princess, imploring the Lord God to grant them children, for good order in the world, and for all Orthodox Christians, and all the monks were to recite the prayers. After vespers on Mondays, Wednesdays and Fridays they were to sing a requiem mass for the dead. The abbot should not dine in his cell, with or without guests, or entertain them there. The place for him to dine or entertain was the refectory or the pantry.

The abbot was responsible for providing the monks with clothing, shoes, and all the equipment they needed in their cells to meet the requirements of communal life. He was required to have a secretary, a treasurer, and three or four lay brothers to fill administrative positions, and he was supposed to take the best possible care of the rest of the brothers. He was in charge of all income and expenditure and he disciplined anyone who disturbed church order or harmed the monastery. No brother might leave the monastery without the abbot's blessing. Laymen were not allowed to visit elders in their cells. The abbot might have one or two novices in his quarters, but no laymen. Young men were not permitted to reside with the abbot and elders, nor were their servants to live in the monastery.

It was the bishop's duty to keep the metropolitan and grand prince informed about monastery affairs. One detailed report, composed by the archbishop of Novgorod, has survived. It begins with a striking invocation to the grand prince: "To the noble, Christ-loving, omnipotent tsar, lord, grand prince, and autocrat of all Russia. Sire, the right hand of almighty God made you autocrat and sovereign of all Russia. You it was, sire, whom God chose to be His vicegerent on earth and sit upon His throne. When He elevated and set you upon His throne He empowered you to uphold and champion the mighty realm of Orthodoxy. It behooves us to acknowledge you as our sovereign and autocratic tsar in all your intelligence and God-given wisdom."

Archbishop Makary was responsible for introducing coenobitic life into most of the monasteries in Novgorod. The chronicle asserts that before his time monks had lived a communal life only in large monasteries; elsewhere each monk sat alone in his cell "overwhelmed by the sorrows of life." Major monasteries formerly housed six or seven monks; the others but two or three. When Makary ordained the communal form of life the number of monks increased; where once there had been two or three, now there were twelve or fifteen, and where formerly there had been six or seven, now there were twenty, thirty or forty. Only two prominent Novgorod monasteries refused to introduce the coenobitic life. The archbishop said to their abbots: "God will requite your action." Makary issued an important regulation pertaining to nunneries. He substituted abbesses for abbots in the interest of decorum. During Vasily's reign a census was held of the clergy to assist in determining the metropolitan's revenues. Metropolitan Daniel persuaded the grand prince to send lay brothers to visit all dioceses and survey all the parishes. They were charged to find out how many military servitors, peasants and land belonged to each church; which churches enjoyed but little revenue and needed their taxes reduced, and which churches disposed of ample revenue and should have their taxes increased.

Vasily's reign saw closer relations with the eastern churches than had been the case in his father's time. In 1515 the grand prince granted the eighteen monasteries on Mt. Athos permission to send monks to Muscovy to ask for alms. In 1518 Patriarch Theoleptos of Constantinople sent representatives to Moscow in quest of alms. The document he sent with them called the grand prince "the most exalted and meekest tsar and great king of the whole Orthodox land of mighty Russia." Patriarch Joachim of Alexandria sent emissaries for the same purpose, and his letter notes that eastern monks and nuns regularly came to Muscovy to seek alms. The friars of Mt. Sinai came as well. A letter from Archbishop Nil of Tver to Vasily Andreevich Korobov when the latter was setting out for Constantinople contains interesting information about the kind of assistance the Russian clergy rendered their impoverished eastern brethren.

The letter enumerates articles which Nil sent to the Byzantine Patriarch Pachomius. It affords insight into the artistic taste of the time and shows the resources at the disposal of the Russian clergy: "Nil, archbishop of Tver, to his son, Lord Vasily Andreevich. I wish you to take the following objects to my lord and brother Pachomius: three icons.[44] The first is large and quite thick. It contains incised representations of the prophets with sixteen holy days etched below them in the Sinope manner [Soloviev is uncertain of the meaning of this phrase]. The second is only half as thick and it also contains representations of holy days. The third, smaller and thinner, contains similar representations. A gold icon divided into four panels, inscribed with minuscules. A book telling of the creation of the world. A gold icon. A carved ivory icon inlet with twelve holy days. Two baptismal robes. A string of beads chased with holy scenes in silver and gold: on the front, Sophia in all her wisdom; on the back, the Transfiguration of our Savior; on the right, the Entrance into Jerusalem and the Birth of Christ, and on the left, the Resurrection of Christ and Epiphany. A piece of lacework a foot wide inlaid with gold and tiny jewels. A blue silk cloth with representations, woven in gold and silver, of Christ above and the Virgin Mary and St. John the Baptist below; beneath them the Archangels Michael and Gabriel, the twelve Apostles, and the saints, all embossed in three places on both sides. Further: a bale of forty sableskins; five single sableskins; 740 squirrelskins; fifteen large tusks; 25 medium and small tusks; a silver cup weighing seven pounds; a heavy plain silver goblet, shaped like three apples, with a cover; a silver cup gold-plated on the inside, with an incised image of an ox's head; five woven tablecloths; six Novgorod tablecloths including their makers' names; a 24-hour German clock with a bell and weights; a sable coat with a black velvet collar; nine white, eight red and two black squirrelskin coats; a piece of black and a piece of red satin; Russian towels and washcloths; 120 combs; 2,000 pumice stones; 440 *khamiaki*;[45] 43 bone knives; five ivory combs chased in gold with representations of animals; 94 straight knives; ten short leather coats; ten fox-fur hats; three plates from Kaluga; three plates from Tver, and 200 silver buttons."

In West Russia King Sigismund responded in 1511 to a request from Metropolitan Joseph[46] and Prince Konstantin Ostrozhsky to confirm the charters by which his predecessors Vitovt, Casimir and Alexander had permitted the Orthodox clergy to maintain their own ecclesiastical courts and freely to dispose of church revenues. The king appointed bishops and approved their transfer to different dioceses. For example, Pafnuty, bishop of Vladimir [in Volynia], asked the king to make him bishop of Lutsk. The king willingly granted his request because Prince Ostrozhsky and Lord Yury Radziwill had asked for Pafnuty. Again in 1511 the king settled a quarrel between the bishops of Polotsk as to which one of them held higher rank.

In 1522 the king received a petition from the abbot, clergy, attendants and monks of the Kiev monastery of the Caves urging him to help them repair their establishment, which had been ruined by Tatar raids, and the king agreed. They also complained that whenever an abbot died the governors of Kiev administered the monastery and took advantage of the opportunity to appropriate the deceased's effects, including books and other church equipment, until the king designated a new abbot. The king decreed that henceforward the elders might claim the abbot's possessions for the monastery upon his death, and join the princes, magnates and leading citizens of Kiev in electing a new abbot, whom they would ask the king to confirm. The elders would remain in charge of the monastery until the confirmation was received. They were to pay the king fifty gold pieces in recompense for his services every time an abbot was elected.

The monks also complained that whenever the governors of Kiev made one of their frequent visits to the monastery the abbot and elders were obliged to entertain them and make them gifts, a practice which strained their resources. The king decreed that a governor might visit the monastery no more than once or twice a year and then only when the monks invited him. They should entertain him, but were under no compulsion to present gifts to him.

The king exempted monasteries from the obligation of providing food and shelter for Tatar envoys and couriers. They were required to furnish ten armed mounted men whenever a war broke out. Royal charters have survived which dealt with repairing the Mezhigorsk and Zlatoverkh Mikhailovo monasteries and ordered them to establish the communal mode of monastic life. Taking these monasteries under his protection, the king allowed them to choose their abbots. Monasteries continued to own land and peasants.

In 1509 Metropolitan Joseph convoked a council of bishops, abbots and archpriests in Vilna. It condemned in the strongest terms those who, while an incumbent was still alive, offered bribes and intrigued at court to obtain an episcopal see without the advice and consent of the Orthodox metropolitan, bishops, princes and magnates. The only persons deserving of the office would be consecrated priests; the council would refuse to approve unworthy men even if the king demanded it. Should this happen the metropolitan and the bishops would visit the king and disclose to him the unworthiness of the man he had chosen. No priest might move to another diocese unless he had obtained a release from his bishop. Unmarried priests could not say mass; they would have to become monks in order to officiate. If they refused to take this step they were declared laymen. In this instance West Russia imitated the example of Muscovy.

Princes and magnates enjoyed no right to bar a priest from his church on their estates unless they had communicated his guilt to the bishop and a church court had sifted the charges against him. Were a prince or boyar to undertake such action against an innocent priest without ecclesiastical sanction, a bishop was not to appoint a successor until the innocent man had been granted compensation. In the event a prince or boyar left a church on his estate without a priest for three months the bishop would appoint one. A prince or boyar who stole from a church and defied the metropolitan's court would be excommunicated. A priest who was persuaded by a prince or boyar to perform actions without the bishop's blessing would be deprived of his office. Should the king or any member of the nobility demand that the metropolitan or the archbishop quash any statute approved by the council, the entire group should make common cause, join the metropolitan in an appeal to the king, and fearlessly support the decisions the council had taken. The Orthodox clergy participating in the council of Vilna were clearly seeking to formulate regulations designed to resist the insidious inroads made by a secular authority of a different [Catholic] faith.

LEGISLATION

Ivan III's Law Code had stipulated that local governors and district chiefs could not hold court unless a representative of the grand prince, an elder, and leading citizens were present. Vasily also embodied this regulation in his charters. Here is a chronicle entry for 1508: "The grand prince has decreed: 'I have heard that decisions made by my governors and tax collectors in Novgorod have been influenced by bribes. I have instructed my representative and the court secretaries to swear in 46 prominent citizens from the quarter. We have ordained that henceforward the mercantile administrator will sit with the governors, and four members drawn from this special panel, rotating each month, will sit with the tax collectors.' "

The remote Lapps complained that representatives of the Novgorod governors served notice upon them to appear at trial. Then groups of thirty or more men without official status charged them ten rubles or more for bail, and their trials were scheduled during their busiest season. This complaint led the grand prince to order his officials in Novgorod to protect the Lapps from the governors and to cancel the governors' and tax collectors' authority to cite the Lapps before a court. The prince's officials were to assume the task of supervising them and hearing their cases. Their assistants, who visited the Lapps to collect taxes, were told to consider the Lapps' interests when selecting trial dates. As a result March 25 was designated for that purpose. The assistants were forbidden to supply the Lapps with alcoholic beverages, to force them to attend assemblies, issue them bail bonds, or collect more than the stipulated amount of taxes.

An interesting correspondence developed between the elder Job, chief lay brother of the Solotchinsk monastery in the Riazan district, and Fedor Zamiatnin, who had sued the monastery over timber rights. It sheds light on the activities of the arbitration court in this period. In an affidavit Job and Zamiatnin stated: "We have both agreed to station two referees, the junior boyars Kondyrev and Kashkaldev, in the wood to adjudicate our dispute over timber cutting, and we shall abide by their decision. We shall take up positions in the disputed area together with those of our men who live there, and the referees will question them under oath. The inhabitants will show the referees the boundary line, and the latter will tell them to cast lots. If their lot comes up the monastery people will move forward in procession and designate a boundary line where Zamiatnin and his men will dig holes and set markers. The line they draw will be the boundary. If the lot of Zamiatnin and his people comes up they will proceed to designate the boundary. Both plaintiffs will accept the findings, even if only one referee appears."

An instructive act of the period refers to the institution known as the judicial duel. In a dispute over land Ivan Mashkov hailed the elder Pavel, chief lay brother of the Pechersky monastery, before an officer of the grand prince who was conducting a cadastral survey in the Nizhegorod area. As custom required, both sides produced witnesses, who were longtime inhabitants of the area. Mashkov brought three military servitors and three peasants from one of the grand prince's estates, while Elder Pavel brought six of the monastery's peasants. The latter demanded a duel with Mashkov's witnesses, but the three military servitors replied: "We will not fight a duel with the likes of them. Bring us men who are our equals and we will show you what we can do." The peasants on their side agreed to the contest. The judge ruled in the monastery's favor on the grounds that half of Mashkov's witnesses had declined to fight a duel. His decision was clearly in error. The military servitors had merely refused to fight peasants. They were quite ready to fight men of a standing equal to their own.

Two interesting wills of Vasily's time have survived. In one, made by Ivan Alferiev, the testator divided his estate equally between his son and grandson on condition that neither dispose of his share, sell, exchange, dower, alienate, lease, or hire it out without the other's concurrence. The other will belonged to Peter Molechkin. A childless man, he bequeathed his estate to monasteries and relatives. His testament contained this clause: "If my wife bears a son after my death I devise all my property to said son, provided he distributes the sum of fifty rubles among the churches to say masses for my soul. If a daughter is born my estate is to pay her the sum of eighty rubles to provide her dowry. I bless my wife with my lands (which are enumerated), which she may exchange, sell or alienate, but she may not remarry and must continue to dwell in the village of Molechkin until her death, at which time the village will pass to the Trinity and Joseph of Volokolamsk monasteries." When the testator died the grand prince took charge of the estate and ordered the treasury to pay its debts. Later he returned it to the widow, requiring her to pay the debts and granting her the right to sell or alienate it.

Grand Prince Vasily made some observations on the theory of inheritance to Herberstein. When Vasily insisted that King Sigismund hand over towns which had belonged to Grand Princess Elena, Herberstein objected that the Muscovite sovereign had no right to them. Vasily told him: "We believe that our brother Maximilian and other rulers are aware that rulers great and small in many states, the common people, and the holy fathers in their canons have established the principle that the law of succession means that a man's progeny inherits his wealth and lands. If a man has no issue his next-of-kin inherits." This fully accords with the principle enunciated in Ivan III's Law Code: "All the property of a man dying intestate who has no son passes to his daughter. If no daughter survives the next-of-kin inherits."

Molechkin's will reflected the force of ancient tradition, according to which a daughter could not inherit and was entitled to no more than a dowry enabling her to marry. Molechkin gave his only daughter a paltry eighty rubles. This provides an excellent commentary on the section in the Russian Law[47] which asserts that a daughter's right of inheritance is inferior to that of a bondman.

King Sigismund told the diet meeting in Vilna in 1522 that Lithuania possessed no written statutes, and as a result custom and judicial arbitrariness influenced the outcome of cases, a state of affairs which had led to frequent complaints. The king promulgated a universal general statute designed to end such abuses. The statute, written in Russian, was approved in 1529 and became effective January 1, 1530. It consisted of thirteen articles. The first article dealt with state crimes. It reaffirmed an old law which provided that no guilty verdict might be returned unless the accuser was present and that those who brought false charges would incur the very penalty they had sought to mete out to the accused.

In 1509, after conferring with the council of magnates, the king had decreed that his treasury might seize the property of a defector and that he was free to decide whether to restore the defector's estate to his children. Where brothers lived on an estate in joint tenure and one defected, his portion was confiscated and the king decided whether the rest of the brothers might retain the balance. If their tenure was personal the defector lost his portion but the others kept theirs. The statute declared that a defector's property, whether inherited or acquired through service or by purchase, escheated to the crown. Neither his children nor relatives might inherit it. When a father fled to the enemy abandoning minor children, he forfeited his estate, but his children or brothers might keep their portions, provided they could prove that they had not participated in his treachery.

Those forging royal decrees or making facsimiles of the king's seal were to be burned at the stake. Those assaulting the king's officers in the performance of their duties were to be put to death, although it was reiterated that criminals' relatives and servants were not subject to punishment. Distinctions of rank and wealth among the king's subjects were not to influence the court. While present in Poland the king was prohibited from assigning estates or confirming previous distributions in Lithuania. He could do so only in conjunction with the council of magnates meeting in a general diet on Lithuanian soil. Litigation involving property was subject to a ten-year statute of limitations.

The second article contained decrees having to do with national defense; the third defined gentry rights, and the fourth dealt with family relationships. Ancient customs affecting the property rights and status of widows remained influential in both parts of Russia but were undergoing modification as a result of the increasing demands of the state. A husband desiring to settle a sum on his wife needed to estimate the value of his estate and assign to her an amount equal to one third of its total value in compensation for the dowry she had brought him.

A good example of the practice is found in Molechkin's will, in which he assigned his wife lands equal in value to her dowry. When a husband died after making such a disposition and his wife remarried, the surviving children of the original marriage might redeem the portion which their father had assigned to their mother by paying her an equivalent sum. Children who decided not to redeem the portion must wait for their mother's demise in order to inherit. When that occurred they had to pay the equivalent of her dowry to the person she designated in her will as the one to receive it, and her will must specifically mention the portion. When there were no children this obligation devolved on the husband's relatives. A husband need not bequeath his moveable property, including gold, silver, and the like—all except his arms—to his wife, but he was obliged to leave her two thirds of his flocks, slaves and cattle, which were considered part of the estate, not moveable property.

A man contemplating a marriage for his daughter and considering her dowry was well advised to find out whether one third of his future son-in-law's estate was equivalent to the amount he proposed to settle on his daughter. If it was not the father had to supplement his daughter's dowry in order to make up the difference. When a wife who had received a portion from her husband did not remarry after his death and had adult sons, she had to subsist on her portion. Her sons entered into full possession of their father's estate, which was the basis for calculating the amount of service they owed. A wife who had received no portion was entitled to share equally in an estate with her sons. If she remarried she had to surrender her share to her sons without compensation.

Childless widows who controlled their late husbands' estates caused the government concern. An estate managed by a woman who wasted its substance to the detriment of the male legatees was a poor source of service. To correct this condition the king decreed that a childless widow could receive no more than her portion. If she had no portion she might enjoy a third of the estate during her lifetime or until she remarried, when it must pass to her first husband's relatives.

At his death a husband might entrust his children and his estate to a friend, who might not be a relative. He served as guardian of the children and the estate, and the deceased's wife had only her portion. Were a man to die without entrusting his children to a guardian, his wife took care of them and managed the estate until they attained their majority. When they became adults the estate was apportioned equally among them and their mother. A mother with one son had to give her son two thirds of the estate and retain one third. When a widow with minor children remarried, responsibility for their care was transferred to the relatives of her deceased husband. If it were proved in court that the widow had administered her children's estate improperly, she lost her right to remain their guardian. In the absence of relatives the king or the magnates designated an honorable third party to serve as the children's guardian. When parents died after their first daughter had married, leaving other minor daughters, the latter were to be given the same dowry their sister had received. A will in which parents had specified the amount of their daughters' dowries was valid, but if the parents died intestate their estate was appraised and the daughters received one quarter of its value. A sister, no matter how many brothers she had, received one quarter of an estate. When a brother had numerous sisters, each female received a quarter share, and they divided these equally among themselves.

A Lithuanian woman who married in Poland or Mazovia could not inherit an estate in Lithuania. A girl who married without her parents' consent was deprived of her inheritance even though she was an only child, and her estate passed to relatives. When a minor orphan married without the consent of her uncles and brothers she was deprived of the family estate. If she was of age and her uncles or brothers arbitrarily refused her permission to marry, she could complain to other relatives or to the authorities. If both approved she might marry without losing her share of her estate, but if she married with the approval of neither she forfeited her share even though she was of age. When a father controlled an estate his sons inherited in direct line exclusively, but when a mother controlled, a sister was entitled to an equal share.

Parents enjoyed the right to deprive children of their inheritance, but only on condition that they informed the authorities and stated valid reasons for their action. A father who deprived his son of his inheritance and had no other children had to leave two thirds of his estate to relatives but was free to dispose of the remaining third as he wished. A widow possessing a portion from her first husband who remarried could not claim another portion from her second husband, but she was entitled to share with his children at his death. If no children issued from the marriage she held the right to lifetime use of a third of the estate. The king pledged that he would not force widows and young girls to marry against their will.

The fifth article in the statute defined guardianship. A guardian's responsibility followed the ancient provisions encountered in the Russian Law. The same article also provided that anyone was free to make a will disposing of goods he had purchased or acquired. The only persons debarred from making wills were minors, monks, children residing with their parents, individuals under foreign jurisdiction, criminals, and the insane. This formed a major legal difference between East and West Russia. In the former, beginning with Oleg's treaty with the Greeks, the law never undertook to interfere with the right of inheritance. The state intervened only when a deceased person left no will or a testator disposed of his inherited and acquired property arbitrarily. Lithuanian jurisprudence restricted the right of testament to acquired or moveable property. It has been thought that the Lithuanians had followed the example of all Slavs in rejecting the influence of Roman or Canon law on their own law of succession, but there is reason to believe that testaments going as far back as Oleg's treaty with the Greeks display traces of the influence of Roman law, because, as is well known, Russians had lived in the Byzantine empire and served the emperor. A question arises as to why the eastern Slavs easily admitted the influence of Canon law while the western Slavs stoutly resisted it. A possible explanation is that corporate and government interests early achieved predominance over the personal predilections of testators and served to limit individual testamentary rights among the western Slavs and in Lithuania. This was not the case in Muscovite Russia.

The sixth article discussed the administration of justice. A governor, administrator or royal prefect would select two prominent, honorable and trustworthy men in his district and have them swear an oath. When the officials themselves were unable to hold court these sworn deputies, assisted by a court officer, could substitute for them, provided they observed the general law of the land. Everyone participating in a trial was required to make full disclosure and at that stage a case could not be transferred to the king or the diet. After a decision had been rendered, either party, if it felt aggrieved, possessed the right to appeal the case to the royal court or, in the event the king was unavailable, to the diet court. The council of lords was obliged to meet twice a year in Vilna to discharge this responsibility.

The seventh article prescribed penalties for attacks on members of the gentry. A man who forcibly entered a house to commit murder was put to death and his estate had to compensate the slain man's relatives and pay a fine to the treasury. Even if the master of the house managed to escape and survived, the perpetrator had to pay the same penalty and his estate had to make reparations for his crime. Where the master resisted and slew the attacker and anyone in his company he was not charged and received a reward, taken from the estate of the dead assailant. Sixteenth-century jursiprudence thus can be seen firmly upholding the dispositions found in the Russian Law. Anyone who raped a woman or girl was put to death, although the victim could save the rapist if she declared she was willing to marry him. Death was the penalty for parricide, matricide, or murdering a brother or sister, and highwaymen were also to be executed. The estate of a man who murdered a member of the gentry must pay the slain man's relatives fifty rubles, while another fifty rubles went to the royal treasury. Anyone who harbored or furnished assistance to lawbreakers was liable to the same penalty that was meted out to them.

The eighth and ninth articles codified procedures to resolve disputes over land. Among other items it provided that only Catholic or Orthodox

Christians who went to confession, received communion each year and possessed a good reputation might be witnesses, not Jews or Tatars. The tenth article dealt with estates encumbered with debts or indentures. The eleventh established penalties for wounding or killing common people. No Jews or Tatars might have Christian slaves, but Tatars were allowed to keep slaves whom the king's predecessors had assigned them as a part of their estates. A free man could not be enslaved, no matter what crime he had committed. If a master refused to maintain his slaves and drove them away at a time of famine, but they managed to survive through their own efforts, they became free men. Slave status derived from four sources: 1) those who had been slaves from time immemorial, and their offspring; 2) prisoners of war; 3) persons sentenced to death who chose servitude instead, and 4) individuals of both sexes who married slaves.

The twelfth and thirteenth articles treated the crime of theft. The first time a member of the gentry was charged with theft and there were no witnesses to his action, he swore an oath that he was not guilty. Were he charged a second time, even though there were no witnesses, his unaided oath no longer sufficed; two other members of the gentry, men with good reputations, must support his oath of innocence. If he was charged a third time he needed the support of six members of the gentry, and if a fourth charge was brought the accused was hanged. A thief caught in the act was beaten three times in one day. If he maintained his innocence after enduring such punishment his accuser had to pay him ten kopecks for each beating. Should he die from the beating without admitting guilt his accuser had to make recompense for him depending upon his rank. If the accused cast spells to obviate the pain of the punishment his accuser swore an oath to that effect and recovered his losses from the accused. Long before the promulgation of the statute King Sigismund and the council of lords had drawn up regulations governing retrials. When a man filed suit but failed to establish his case the plaintiff was not liable for costs; but if a man filed suit and established and won his case, he was liable for the costs of a retrial at a rate of ten kopecks to one ruble, one ruble to ten rubles, and ten rubles to 100 rubles.

INTERNATIONAL LAW

A noteworthy treaty made by the governors of Novgorod and Pskov with the Germans of Livonia in 1509 contains information on international law. As the treaty notes, the previous practice had been for an envoy from Novgorod visiting the Livonian master to give his guide a ruble in Narva, and likewise the master's envoy had to give his Novgorod guide a ruble in Ivangorod. Now neither side was to expect payment and both were to provide guides free of charge. A comparable practice had been for both sides to charge for maintaining each other's envoys in their towns. In future both sides were to maintain envoys free of charge.

A treaty of 1521 provided that if a man from Novgorod sued a German in Livonia the case should be settled locally if the sum involved was ten rubles or less. If the sum exceeded that amount the suit could not be filed in Livonia. The defendant, if from Novgorod, put up bail or was held under guard until the governor of Novgorod was informed. The governor appointed a time for both litigants to meet on an island of the Narova river under the joint jurisdiction of both countries, where both governments were to send judges to hear the case. This procedure was also to be followed in criminal cases. A German in Novgorod or a man from Novgorod in Germany was not to be punished unilaterally. The litigants were to appear before a tribunal composed of judges from both countries. If this court required oaths the defendant was sworn.

A treaty made with the seventy Hansa towns in 1514 provided that if a Novgorod merchant was a victim of piracy on the high seas and the pirates came from the Hansa towns the corporation would track down, arrest and execute the pirates, and restore his goods to the Novgorod merchant. If the pirates were not from the Hansa towns the government of Novgorod assumed responsibility for the investigation. If a German merchant suffered loss in the land or on the waters under Novgorod's control, the governor had to discover, apprehend and execute the perpetrators and restore their goods to the merchants. When informed of acts of piracy the Hansa towns were not to imprison merchants from Novgorod, and German merchants were not to be imprisoned in towns under Novgorod's control. If merchants from Novgorod and Germany had cargoes on a ship and their merchandise was damaged on the high seas the merchants were to divide the remainder fairly under oath. When a vessel from Novgorod ran aground in Germany or a German vessel ran aground at Novgorod during a storm the ship was inspected and returned to its owner upon payment of a transfer fee of one ruble per ten rubles of value.

In his discussions with Herberstein, the Imperial envoy, the grand prince enunciated this principle concerning the safety of envoys: "According to custom envoys of major rulers transact their masters' business under a mutual agreement that their persons are inviolate. During the reigns of our ancestors, our father and ourselves, Polish kings have sent envoys to seek resolution of important problems. Those whose efforts met with success departed freely, and those who failed to obtain the results they desired were also free to leave." Such regulations obviously did not apply to Tatars.

MORALS AND CUSTOMS

Certain events occurring in Vasily's reign afford some insight into the morals and customs of the period. The chronicles describe church festivals in detail. The grand prince personally took a very active part in them. Describing the day when the holy icons were returned to Vladimir after they had been restored, the chronicles report that the grand prince joined the senior clergy, princes and boyars in a gay and joyful celebration, provided an elaborate entertainment, and distributed alms to the city priests and poor. In fulfillment of a vow, in 1531 the grand prince built a church in honor of St. John the Baptist in the Old Vagankov section. He laid the first stone himself; workmen set to immediately, and the church was built and consecrated in a single day. The grand prince attended the ceremony with his family, the boyars, and a large number of the people. He was most probably fulfilling a vow he had made when his son Ivan was born.

The grand prince consecrated a church in the village of Kolomenskoe with a three-day celebration, making gifts to his brothers and the metropolitan. Sources for the period often mention family or communal celebrations on holidays. They were of the opinion that the origin of such practices must be sought in pre-Christian times. In special circumstances, which will be discussed later, brotherhood groups in southwestern Russia advanced this concept in a significant way.

Grand Prince Vasily presided at a court session held in 1525. Peasants from the village of Yurev, which recently had come under the control of the metropolitan, led by Klimko Nasonov and his associates had sued Kozel, Sukhoy, Khromy and other peasants belonging to Akinf Chudinov. Klimko complained: "Kozel and his friends stole four of our cows and twenty sheep and took them to their village. When my comrades and I asked Kozel to return our animals he and his friends beat us and set dogs on us. I escaped with two comrades, but Kozel and his men beat our third comrade, Dobrynka Andreev, to death. We do not know where they have hidden his body, but the cattle Dobrynka and we lost are worth four rubles fifty kopecks." The defendants and their master, Akinf Chudinov, denied the charges and tried to indict their accusers.

They failed to substantiate the charges they made. The grand prince convicted them, fined Kozel and his associates four rubles fifty kopecks, made them pay four rubles for killing Dobryna and settle Dobryna's outstanding debts, and awarded court costs to Klimko and his associates.

In 1513 the grand prince told the district chiefs, their deputies and the peasants of the Belozersk districts: "The elders of Nil's hermitage have asked me to protect them from thieves and robbers. It is your duty diligently to guard them against wicked thieves and robbers and see that no one harms them. A monk who causes scandal in their community by refusing to obey their rules must be immediately dismissed. If he will not listen and refuses to leave at once, as I have commanded, and the elders tell you to remove him, you must expel this person and see that he never returns." The *Life of St. Daniel of Pereiaslavl* mentions several cases of aggrieved assault occurring on the road from Moscow to Pereiaslavl. The chief miscreant was a certain Simon Voronov.

When Misiur Munekhin, the well-known state secretary in Pskov, died, his effects yielded a notebook in which payments to specific boyars, secretaries and military servitors in Moscow were listed. The grand prince took charge of these records and summoned Misiur's relatives to Moscow. Artiush, a native of Pskov who had been Misiur's principal undersecretary, was tortured.

Foreign visitors, mainly envoys, began a series of elaborate descriptions of Muscovy during Vasily's reign. The first was Herberstein's famous *Commentary.* According to them parents arranged marriages and young people of the upper classes rarely saw their betrothed until the actual marriage ceremony because it was thought proper for girls to lead sequestered lives. They seldom went to church and even less frequently appeared in mixed company. They might occasionally be seen in the presence of older men, whose motives could not be suspect. On great holidays girls and women were allowed to assemble in the fields, where they would sit on swings and sing while they clapped their hands. The statement that noblewomen rarely went to church is explained by the fact that almost all wealthy men maintained chapels in their homes; thus, members of their families had little need to attend service in the cathedrals, monasteries, and other institutions frequented by the public.

Herberstein is responsible for the tale that Russian women accused their husbands of coldness if they failed to beat them. He said the same thing about servants; that they thought their masters were angry with them when they did not get a thrashing. He complained that men of the highest rank were arrogant and indolent and incapable of behaving in a manner consonant with their positions on important occasions.

Although moderate at table, they drank to excess. Rich men led a sedentary life; it was considered a disgrace to go about on foot.

Noblemen possessed numerous retainers, both freemen and slaves. A free retainer usually spent his entire life in the service of a single master because no one would receive him if he left his master's employment against the latter's wishes. A master who treated a devoted retainer poorly acquired a bad reputation and free men would not enter his service. At their death masters often manumitted their slaves, but the slaves would immediately sell themselves to other masters. A father might sell his son into slavery. If the son gained his freedom his father could sell him into slavery again to a maximum of four times. The grand prince reserved the exclusive right to inflict capital punishment on anyone, whether slave or freeman. In general the death penalty was seldom invoked. A death sentence for robbery was unusual, and this was even true of murder, unless it was committed in the course of a robbery. Torture was common. People were beaten about the heels, doused with cold water and had wooden slivers driven beneath their nails. Bribery was rampant. Herberstein complained of the Muscovites' commercial cunning, excessive fondness for sharp practice, and their habit of procrastination. He was especially critical of the people of Moscow in this regard and praised the people of Pskov because they eschewed such practices.

Herberstein has left a description of one of the mock battles which young people enjoyed when he was in Moscow. Assembling on a broad square they started punching each other, trying to hit their opponents in painful places, often so hard that men were killed in these encounters. After mass on holidays the common people resumed their regular work because they were forbidden to drink mead and beer except on such high holidays as Easter, Christmas, Holy Trinity Day, and a few other occasions.

In Herberstein's description of Russian dress in the sixteenth century it is easy to recognize the caftan, fastened below the stomach with a sash, and short red sandals reaching to the knee. A Russian source, the testament of appanage prince Dmitry Ivanovich, enumerates in some detail the articles of clothing and adornment worn by women and men. Here is a list: women's outer garments inset with jewels; long dresses of soft material with precious stones attached to the lower end of the petticoat and purple silk borders; an elegant woman's overcoat with little pearls attached to the flounces; a gold necklace; pendants set with rubies and other precious stones; tall headdresses with the same kind of adornments; long silver and gold pendants; a necklace of gold pendants;

woman's earrings and rings set with pearls and precious stones; neck-laces shaped like crosses, icons and beads; aprons sewn with pendants, and gold ornamental knobs. Among men's garments were smooth over-coats decked with lace patterns inset with pearls; smocks of rich fabric; pointed hats, and buskins adorned with pearls and other precious stones.

The will also mentions utensils with gilded rims. Their covers had representations of various objects, such as a fortress or a bird, incised upon them. There were plain or gilded pitchers decorated with geometric designs; utensils shaped like an ox, a boat, a cockrel, or a horn; cups; ladles with etched animal shapes or patterns; tureens; dishes shaped like swans or geese; bowls; mustard pots; forks; spoons; platters; salt shakers; pepper mills; cruets, and gold frying pans. The wills speak only of clothing and table utensils; the description of Vasily's death refers to chairs next to his bed on which the grand prince sat during his final illness.

These were the objects detailed in a prince's will. It will also prove of interest to see the objects enumerated in the testament of a wealthy merchant; "I bless my daughter Uliana with a gold icon of the Annunci-ation and another with the twelve Stations of the Cross etched on it in silver. I also give Uliana a marten coat, a light silk dress, a green-colored coat, a necklace sewn with beaver fur, a new light purple dress made from Asian silk, another of the same covered with decorations, and a white dress with a ruffle. I bless my second daughter Anna with three gold icons, and I give her a little bronze jug, a washstand, three kitchen boilers, and a wine-making apparatus with pipe attached. I bless my youngest daughter, Praskovia, with five gold icons. To my three daugh-ters jointly I give eight pewter tankards, receptacles, a bronze pitcher, pewter table settings, and four white copper frying pans. I have given my mother-in-law an old marten coat, and I have given my daughters a marten coat, a squirrelskin coat, a blue garment fashioned like a pair of trousers, a long-sleeved purple robe, two chests, a box from Novgorod, nine pewter plates, four iron candlesticks to hang on the wall, and two copper candlesticks to stand on the table. I have given Praskovia a copper tub to brew beer, and Anna a silver cup valued at two rubles."

Herberstein has provided a brief description of the houses. According to him they had broad high entryways but the doors were so low that one had to stoop in order to pass through them. Every section of the forecourt contained pictures or statues of saints.

In West Russia the government restricted the ecclesiastical courts and diverted criminals from their jurisdiction. This policy was deleteri-ous to general morality. When he was named metropolitan Joseph complained to the king that many Russians led immoral lives, contracted illegal marriages, refused to have their children baptized, and never came to confession. When he sent men to arrest them local officials such as district administrators, their associates, and councillors, as well as ordinary citizens, refused to hand them over for trial in church court. The king dispatched a circular letter ordering such practices to cease immediately. In charters issued to the prefects and tax collectors in Samogitia the king admitted that his subjects in those regions had been woefully misused and cruelly burdened by the officials; as a result many had fled, leaving their lands vacant.

A letter composed by the distinguished hetman of Lithuania, Prince Konstantin Ostrozhsky, is revealing of the customs followed in West Russia. He wrote it before he was married a second time to Princess Alexandra of Slutsk. Obliged to postpone the wedding because he had to campaign around Minsk, Prince Konstantin promised to appear for the ceremony as soon as he returned unless he became ill or the king gave him a new assignment. The bride's parents had to settle 1,000 Hungarian gold pieces on her personally and provide her with a dowry of no less than 1500 rubles, which was proper for someone of her high rank. For his part Prince Konstantin agreed that when he received the money he would assign his wife her portion of his lands. In the interim he could not assign, sell or give them away. Her portion was to be a third of all the lands the prince owned. Konstantin pledged to maintain any children from his second marriage as he maintained his son, Ilia, by his first wife. On his death they were to inherit equally with their elder brother. In the event these obligations were not fulfilled the side that failed to perform its part of the bargain had to forfeit 4,000 rubles— 2,000 to the other party and 2,000 to the king.

LITERATURE

Literature remained almost exclusively the preoccupation of the church. There has been some discussion of the issues agitating the Russian church during Vasily's reign, the leading figures involved, and their works. The controversial anchorite, Nil of Sorsk, who had raised the question of monastery landowning during Ivan III's reign, died in 1508. A monk of the Kirillo-Belozersk monastery, Nil spent some years in the monasteries of Mt. Athos and in Constantinople, where he became familiar with the writings of the desert fathers, writings which extolled the contemplative life. On his return home he tried to introduce this practice among Russian monks. Nil's injunction to his followers has

survived. Several quotations from it reveal the attitude of its framer:
"Here is the awesome tradition the holy fathers have handed down to
us. We must earn our daily bread and supply all our needs by our own
righteous toil. We must work with the sweat of our brow. When we
cannot obtain what we need from our own toil we may seek alms from
the pious, but we must ask only for what we need, not luxuries. Goods
amassed from the repression of others who toil can never benefit us.
How can we keep God's commandments if we possess such things? If a
man goes to court to take your clothes, give him the shirt off your back
and anything else he wants if he is humble and in need.

"Like lethal poison we must resist and avoid [the desire for earthly
goods]. When we buy what we need or sell the fruits of our labor we
must not cheat our brothers. Even worse is to covet the things of this
world. We have no need of luxury. Do not turn away in loathing from
beggars and debtors, says the great Basil,[48] they are sent to test the
greedy. A man who has no more than he needs is not required to give
gifts. If he declares 'I have it not,' he has told no lie, says the great
Barsanuphius.[49] A monk is still a monk even though he is unable to
give alms. He can say in all honesty: 'Lo, we have forsaken everything
to follow in Thy footsteps.' St. Isaac[50] has written that 'it is greater to
have nothing than to give alms.' We have no need of even the most
hallowed gold and silver vessels or other unnecessary trappings. We need
only to render the church its due.

"Above all, at time of prayer, as Nilus of Sinai[51] has said, it is essential for us to make our minds deaf and dumb and empty our hearts of
all thoughts, even pious ones, as Hesychius of Jerusalem[52] says. Believing that we must think pious thoughts has permitted contrivance to
enter into us; wherefore we must not allow our minds to think even
righteous thoughts. Concentrating silently on our inner hearts we cry:
'Lord Jesus Christ, Son of God, have mercy upon me.' We may pro-
nounce this standing up, seated, or lying down. We should merge our
minds with our hearts, hold our breath as long as we can, and breath
infrequently, as Symeon the New Theologian[53] tells us. Since saints
such as these have told us to hold our breath, breathe infrequently, and
acquire these skills quickly such practices must obviously be highly
beneficial to our mental condition. St. Gregory of Sinai[54] has said of
skills that have helped or will help a man in his search for truth, 'he
need not recite psalms; he must be silent, pray constantly, and behold
visions.' When writing of these mighty mysteries St. Isaac tells us:
'Whenever a man experiences ineffable joy prayer dies on his lips. Shut
are his lips and tongue and heart, the abode of thought, and his mind,

the nurturer of emotion. Intelligence is a pure fleet bird, but neither it nor movement nor self-control have any place in prayer. Prayer comes from a different force. It may not appear or it may be captured for no more then a fleeting hour. It is found in incomprehensible things and knows not where it is.' "

Occasional reference has been made to Misiur Munekhin, the grand prince's official long in charge of Pskov. Like other able intellects of his time Munekhin was strongly attracted to the monastic life. He discovered the Pechersky monastery, a poor and unknown institution situated on the German border some 25 miles from Pskov. Growing interested in it he used to visit it on holidays with a large entourage, and helped the brothers. He enhanced the monastery's reputation and added buildings to it. After that, says the chronicler, the monastery grew famous both in Russia and "among the Latins," by which he meant Germany as far as the Baltic Sea.

Misiur was the recipient of interesting communications from Filofey, a monk in the Elizarov monastery. In one of them Filofey dealt with questions that greatly exercised learned men of the time. Maxim the Greek had condemned astrology, and Filofey adopted a similar position. He declared that stars could not determine the fate of the world and its inhabitants. If God had created evil days and evil hours wicked people should not be punished, because if they had been born on an evil day they could not incur guilt. Men must place their hopes in God, Who bestowed everything. Stars could not help at all; they neither added nor subtracted a jot to or from the total.

Filofey was of the opinion that it made no difference whether one calculated time from the creation of the world or the birth of Christ. He opposed the Catholics and eventually delivered an observation on the role of Muscovy: two Romes have fallen; Moscow is the third, and a fourth never shall be.[55] Another of Filofey's epistles to Misiur mentioned the methods the capable official had employed to prevent the spread of plague—barricading roads, quarantining houses, and ordering the dead buried at a distance from town.

As previously had been the case, the clergy remained the sole source of instruction. Describing Archbishop Makary's arrival in Novgorod the chronicler says: "Endowed with strength from God he conversed with the people, telling them many stories. All were amazed at the scriptural learning God had given him, and everyone understood his words." In a letter to a bishop Metropolitan Daniel defined the nature of pastoral instruction: "You are not to talk about yourself. Your instruction must be based on holy writ, not what you think yourself."

According to the testimony of foreign writers the clergy preached no sermons. Fear that a preacher might utter heretical opinions was the reason. Metropolitan Daniel's regulations (quoted above) are proof of this. In his own writings Daniel scrupulously adhered to the rule he had promulgated and his sermons were usually filled with citations from the holy fathers. Daniel was a follower of Joseph, and in view of his attitude to Vassian Kosoy it is not surprising to find the metropolitan urging the government in one of his precepts to persecute heretics: "God's servants must be vigilant in upholding God's laws, preserving mankind from soul-destroying magicians, and refusing to grant men licence to do wrong. Thieves, robbers and other malefactors are condemned. People who have altered or spat upon a representation of the earthly tsar are executed. We should much more relentlessly pursue those who insult God, His Son, and the Virgin Mary. Protect us from charlatans; protect us from dogs; protect us from swine; protect us from evildoers; do not let them plunder and devour Christ's flock. You will have to render awesome account at Christ's Last Judgment. Take care you do not destroy yourself and others by seeking to please."

Daniel's precepts contain allusions to some curious practices of the time. Here is an example: "When you entertain immoral people you will produce a remarkable impression if you change your clothes. You should put on bright red narrow slippers that squeeze your feet, and wear bright-colored clothing. You should prance about and neigh like a horse. You should shave your head and body with a razor and even pluck out hairs with a pair of tweezers. To attract women you should make your appearance more feminine by washing, and applying rouge and perfume the way they do . . . [then you say] why do you put on silk slippers and wear rings on your fingers? Why do you waste time with birds? Why do you keep many dogs? Do you expect praise for frequenting low haunts? We also have silk slippers, and under our shirt, where no one can see, we have gold and silver girdles."

IV

THE REGENCY OF GRAND PRINCESS ELENA

ELENA'S RIGHT TO RULE

The Russian Law had provided that when a father died leaving minor children a mother became their guardian and had the right to dispose of their property. Like Olga in olden times[1] the grand princes' mothers continued to play important roles and influence their sons both when they were minors and even when they became adults. Such precedents established Grand Princess Elena, Vasily's widow, as guardian of her minor son, Ivan, and entitled her to administer the grand duchy as a matter of course. Since this custom was universally acknowledged and understood, the detailed description of Vasily's death, which quotes his last words and outlines his final dispositions with such care, made no direct allusion to the fact that the grand prince had designated his wife to be the interim successor, and merely noted that Vasily had instructed three intimates, Mikhail Yurevich, Prince Mikhail Glinsky and Shigona, how Elena was to act after his death and how the boyars should treat and report to her. This observation should be considered a direct reference to Elena's new status in the government. It required the boyars to appear before her in order to make reports.[2]

A chronicler describes young Ivan's elevation: Metropolitan Daniel, all the clergy, princes, boyars and city people installed him as grand prince in the cathedral of the Assumption. Blessing him with a cross the metropolitan cried: "God blesses you, sovereign, Grand Prince Ivan Vasilievich of Vladimir, Moscow, Novgorod, Pskov, Tver, Yugorsk, Perm, Bulgaria, Smolensk and many other lands, tsar and lord of all Russia. May you flourish as grand prince on your father's throne." The princes and boyars invoked long life for the new ruler and approached him laden with gifts. Afterwards they dispatched junior boyars to every city and town to administer an oath of allegiance to the entire population.

As he lay on his deathbed Vasily had good reason to fear for his young son's future. The child had two surviving uncles. They had renounced their claim to the succession, but if they had an opportunity they might well forswear an oath they had been obliged to take against their will and reassert their original claims, which were rendered all the more formidable by the fact that other noble descendants of princely families grumbled about their old rights and were discontented with the new order which Vasily and his father had established. The dying man said to his brothers: "Prince Yury and Prince Andrei, my brothers, you must remain true to your vow, to which we swore a solemn oath." Vasily also considered it necessary to remind the boyars that he descended from Vladimir of Kiev and right of birth entitled him and his son to rule. Vasily was well aware that should disturbances break out and his brothers prevail the disorders associated with the reign of his grandfather, Vasily the Dark, would be repeated, and his minor children could expect no mercy from the victor. In hope of preventing this, Vasily appealed to the man whose kinship and capacities obliged and enabled him to protect the royal family: "Prince Mikhail Glinsky, you must stand ready to shed your blood and have your body cut to pieces in defense of my son, Grand Prince Ivan, Grand Princess Elena, and my son Georgy."

DISTURBANCES AND THE FALL OF PRINCE YURY

The dangers Vasily apprehended in his last moments came to pass. The grand prince's obsequies were scarcely completed when Elena was informed that a conspiracy had formed. The chronicles are not in agreement. One states that the two Shuisky princes, Ivan Mikhailovich and Andrei Mikhailovich, had sought refuge with Prince Yury during Vasily's lifetime, but when the grand prince ordered his brother to surrender them Yury hastened to comply. Vasily sent them under house arrest to different towns, but when Elena came to power the metropolitan and boyars intervened on their behalf, and she released them. On his return to Moscow Andrei Shuisky lost no time concerting another intrigue and urged Prince Boris Gorbaty to defect. He claimed Prince Yury had asked him (Andrei) to come over to him and that he was anxious to do so. "Let us both go," he said to Gorbaty. "You have no future serving here. The grand prince is a stripling and people are already talking about Prince Yury. If we are the first to go over to him and he becomes ruler we shall be duly rewarded." Gorbaty refused to defect and advised Shuisky not to do so. Shuisky realized he had failed and was afraid that he had spoken too openly to Gorbaty. He decided to forestall him. Securing an audience with the grand princess he declared that although Prince Yury had suggested he come over to him, it was Prince Gorbaty who had urged him to take such action. When the truth was discovered

Prince Shuisky was again arrested. This time the boyars told Elena she should apprehend Prince Yury as well, and she said: "Do what you think is best." The boyars were convinced this was a splendid opportunity to settle accounts with Yury once and for all. They arrested him and his boyars, and confined Yury in the same house where his nephew, Ivan III's unlucky grandson Dmitry, had been incarcerated.

A second version states that Yury sent Tretiak Tishkov, one of his secretaries, to ask Prince Andrei Shuisky to enter his service. Shuisky told Tishkov: "Your prince has just sworn solemn fealty to the grand prince, but now he is asking the grand prince's men to leave him." Tretiak replied: "The boyars forced Prince Yury to swear that oath but did not administer it to him personally in the name of the grand prince. One can only regard such an oath as involuntary." Andrei Shuisky related this conversation to Prince Gorbaty, who told the boyars, and they in turn informed the grand princess. Elena replied: "You have just sworn a solemn oath unconditionally to serve and support my son. You must honor your pledge. Whenever one detects the presence of evil one must take steps to eradicate it." She issued orders to arrest Yury.

Which account is more credible? In an effort to justify Prince Yury the first places the entire blame on the boyars and Prince Andrei. As its author puts it: "The devil made men think wicked thoughts—'The realm can never be stable as long as Prince Yury is free. The ruler is a child; Yury, a man of mature years, has the qualities of a leader. People will flock to him and he will try to undermine the grand prince.' This is what the devil wanted people to think because he knew that were Prince Yury left at liberty the program of robbery, bribery and murder he (the devil) craved would never be carried out."

The last words indicate that this narrative was composed after the acts of robbery, bribery and murder which the boyars committed had provoked outbursts of universal indignation. The same source goes on to say that before the boyars decided to tell the grand princess to arrest Yury the devil, realizing that his plan might fail, entered wicked Prince Shuisky and made him plot to defect. Such an idea had never entered Prince Yury's head, because he had sworn fealty to the grand prince and would never betray him. Prince Andrei was solely responsible. *Many* were supposed to have said that junior boyars and even some boyars had advised Prince Yury to proceed to Dmitrov as quickly as possible: "Go to Dmitrov, where no one will dare lay a hand upon you. Do not stay here, for there is a lot of talk that you will soon be arrested." Yury's answer was: "When I came to my sovereign, Grand Prince Vasily, he, for his sins, was ill. I swore an oath to him and his son, Grand Prince

Ivan, which I cannot transgress. May I die if I am not telling the truth." The author of this account was undoubtedly convinced of Prince Yury's innocence, but unfortunately he has provided no satisfactory proof. Yury's oath is no proof, for Andrei Shuisky had sworn an oath as well. Little credence can be given to the reports of the *many* who reported the answer Yury was supposed to have given the senior and junior boyars.

The second account carries greater conviction because of its detail. Its author knew precisely whom Yury sent to Andrei Shuisky, the secretary Tretiak Tishkov, and he knew the arguments Tishkov used to justify his master's violation of his oath. The fact that Andrei Shuisky was convicted and remained in prison until Elena's death is sometimes used as an argument to disprove this version, but the account contains no information exonerating Shuisky. Shuisky may have criticized Yury for having so recently sworn an oath of fealty but this does not necessarily mean that he subsequently refused to accept the arguments advanced by Tishkov, remained insensible to the advantages that might accrue to him by going over to Prince Yury, and did not invite Gorbaty to join him. The version of these particulars given in the second account in no way contradicts the first, but the former sought only to explain why Prince Yury was arrested and thus had no reason to provide detail about Shuisky.

Both accounts further refer the arrest of Prince Yury to December 11. The second has Andrei Shuisky upbraid Tishkov with the words "*yesterday* your prince swore an oath," and has Elena say to the boyars "*yesterday* you swore fealty to my son." The oath-taking ceremony occurred as soon as Vasily died, or, in other words, it took place on the morning of the fourth, because Vasily had died the preceding midnight. This could only mean that Yury had been in touch with Shuisky, or that Shuisky had opened negotiations with Gorbaty, and Elena had learned of their activity as early as the fifth. This was simply not enough time for Elena to release the Shuisky princes and for them to return to Moscow, where "after a little while" (as the first account says) Andrei started planning a second defection.

The date of the fifth in the second account is in error and the first chronicler's assertion that Andrei Shuisky was not released from prison until after Vasily's death is similarly suspect. In the brief interval between the fourth and the eleventh Elena is supposed to have pardoned the Shuisky princes, sent a courier with her authorization to the town where Prince Andrei was a prisoner (and there is no reason to assume he was confined near Moscow), and Andrei to have made the necessary

arrangements to return to Moscow, where "after a little while" he formed a conspiracy.

The short interval between Vasily's death and Yury's arrest also rules
out any question that Yaganov's report (cited earlier) could refer to
plots hatched by Prince Yury prior to his arrest. It is far more probable
that Yaganov was speaking of junior boyars of Dmitrov in Prince Yury's
service when he declared that people were complaining about their
prince and inveighing against the government in Moscow. Here is what
Yaganov says in his petition: "My lord, the junior boyar Yakov Mesh-
cherinov in Prince Yury's service, who had previously rendered certain
services to your father, told me to meet him in a certain village to discuss a matter of state. I informed Ivan Yurevich Shigona, who told me
to meet with Yakov: 'If he has something important to say, both of you
are to come to Moscow at once, and I shall tell the sovereign what he is
doing.' I met Yakov, immediately wrote a letter about what he told me,
and had my man take it to Prince Mikhail Glinsky and Shigona. I stayed
with Yakov to learn all I could from him. Shigona sent my man back
with instructions for us to proceed to Moscow and you, my lord, also
dispatched men of your own with orders to bring us to Moscow. There
in the presence of your boyars Yakov denied the statements he made to
me about what he had heard from the junior boyars in Prince Yury's
service. I supplied your boyars with an outline of the conversations I
held with Yakov about affairs in Dmitrov, but he denied that any such
discussions had taken place. We related to your boyars the substance of
hostile remarks Yakov and I had heard the junior boyars utter at a
carouse. I do not know whether they were drunk or crazy when they
made them, for in those days whatever I heard stuck to my ears like
pitch." His report was thought to be false, and Yaganov was arrested.
Such a punishment for filing a false report shows that the government
was not inclined to pay attention to all it heard about appanage princes.
The authorities must have had good reason for arresting Prince Yury.

OBOLENSKY'S RISE AND GLINSKY'S FALL

Yaganov's petition indicates the identities of the most trusted and influential persons at court immediately after Vasily's death. They were
Prince Mikhail Glinsky and Shigona Podzhogin, the men with whom
Yaganov filed his reports on state affairs. Glinsky had managed to
achieve approximately the same position in Moscow that he had enjoyed
in Lithuania during Alexander's reign, but soon a formidable rival appeared in the person of Prince Ivan Ovchina-Telepnev-Obolensky. The

grand princess displayed exceptional favor towards him and formed a
close alliance with him. This was doubtless due to the influence exercised
by the grand prince's nurse, Agrafena Cheliadnina, who was Obolensky's
sister.

Obolensky and Glinsky had been close associates. Elena was forced
to choose between them, and she chose Obolensky. Glinsky and his
supporter, Mikhail Semenovich Vorontsov, were charged with coveting
supreme power. This accusation is comprehensible, because Glinsky's
prior behavior had shown him to be a man incapable of restraining his
ambition or of selecting suitable means in order to achieve his goals. It
was ambition, not moral conviction, that led Glinsky into a contest with
Obolensky, but the charge had to be framed differently to suit contemporaries. Glinsky was accused of poisoning Grand Prince Vasily in
Moscow, just as he had earlier been charged with poisoning Grand Prince
Alexander in Lithuania. Both accusations were groundless, but Glinsky
could scarcely complain. The man who had murdered Lord Zaberezski
was in no position to defend himself. Glinsky's coadjutor, Vorontsov,
was the nobleman Grand Prince Vasily had forgiven before he died.
Glinsky was arrested in August, 1534 and confined to the house where
Vasily had previously consigned him, where he soon died.

FLIGHT OF NOBLES TO LITHUANIA

A little earlier that month Prince Semen Belsky and Ivan Liatsky (who
belonged to the Koshkin family), two men of the highest rank, fled to
Lithuania. On suspicion of sympathizing with the defectors Elena ordered the arrest of Prince Ivan Fedorovich Belsky, Semen's brother, and
Prince Ivan Mikhailovich Vorotynsky and his children. No action was
taken against Prince Dmitry Belsky, and this circumstance indicates that
there was good reason for arresting Ivan Belsky and Vorotynsky. The
flight of Semen Belsky and Liatsky and the arrest of Ivan Belsky,
Vorotynsky, Glinsky, and Vorontsov occurred within less than a month.
This is conducive to the view that all these events were manifestations
of a sense of outrage which the nobility felt against Elena and her
favorite, Obolensky, an attitude which was to have substantial repercus-
sions.

When Vasily died and his vigorous rule was succeeded by the regency
of a feeble woman everyone who witnessed the transfer, sensing that
now there was opportunity to realize personal ambitions, gave wholehearted and unanimous approval to the swift moves that effectively
thwarted Prince Yury. Later, when the situation began to clarify, this

euphoria evaporated and the interested participants realized with growing disappointment that they could never achieve their goals. Telepnev-
Obolensky had acquired Elena's full confidence and occupied the chief
administrative position.

PRINCE ANDREI'S FLIGHT AND ARREST

The sources insist that the boyars were primarily responsible for the
fall of Prince Yury and that Elena acted on their advice. The fall of
Ivan's other uncle, Prince Andrei Ivanovich, is attributed to Prince
Telepnev-Obolensky and the grand princess personally. Prince Andrei
was never suspected of concerting with his brother Yury. He lived
tranquilly in Moscow until Vasily died, at which time he decided to
return to his appanage. He asked Elena to add some towns to his holding. She refused, but in accordance with custom gave him various coats
and cups, and some race horses and trotting horses equipped with
saddles, in memory of the deceased.

Andrei was unhappy when he reached Staritsa. Some people communicated his feelings to Moscow, while others told him that the authorities there were planning to arrest him. Elena sent Prince Ivan
Vasilievich Shuisky and an official, Menshoy Putiatin, to Staritsa in
order to convince Andrei that the rumors were without foundation. Not
satisfied with their assurances Andrei insisted that Elena give him a
written guarantee. After receiving it he went to Moscow for a personal
meeting with the grand princess, which Metropolitan Daniel arranged.

Andrei declared he had heard rumors that Elena and the grand prince
intended to place him under official displeasure. Elena replied: "We
too have heard a rumor that you are angry with us. You must stand firm
and refuse to listen to gossipmongers. Let us know who they are, to
prevent future misunderstandings between us."

Prince Andrei was unwilling to provide names but added that he
shared Elena's opinion. She reiterated that she harbored no hostility
towards him. Andrei apparently signed a document in which he swore to
fulfill the terms of the understanding he had reached with his nephew
and agreed to divulge anything his brother, the princes, boyars, royal
officials or his own attendants said to him about the grand princess and
her son, and to avoid troublemakers, but to report to the grand princess
and her son what such people said. One feature of this document is
remarkable. For the first time it limited, or rather nullified, the right
appanage princes had always enjoyed to accept other princes, boyars
and free serving men into their entourages. The right had been infringed

during the reigns of Ivan's father and grandfather, but it was invariably stipulated in treaties between the grand princes and the appanage princes. Andrei pledged not to receive princes, senior or junior boyars, other officials, or anyone whose departure harmed the grand prince. Yet a man's desire to depart was, in virtually every instance, a signal that he was dissatisfied, since conditions of service with an appanage prince were invariably inferior to those enjoyed by those in the grand prince's service. The grand prince had no way of knowing, when a boyar left to serve his uncle, whether it was to his detriment or not; thus, every time one did so he was bound to suspect the worst and insist the defector be returned.

After he returned to Staritsa Andrei's suspicion and apprehension did not abate and he continued to be annoyed with Elena because she refused to assign further towns to his appanage. More reports reached Moscow that Prince Andrei was planning to defect. The chronicle asserts that Elena refused to credit them and summoned Andrei to attend a council planning a campaign against Kazan. Andrei replied that he was unable to come because he was ill, and asked for a physician. Elena sent him Theophilus, who has figured in this narrative. On his return Theophilus reported that Andrei's illness was not serious. He had a growth on his thigh and had taken to bed. His report made Elena suspicious and wonder why Andrei had refused to take part in a council debating so vital an issue as Kazan. She sent others to check on Andrei's health, secretly charging them to ascertain the latest rumors about him and discover the reason for his refusal to come to Moscow. Those she sent reported that the prince of Staritsa was surrounded by a great many people who were not normally present at his court. They were afraid to talk, but there were others who believed that Andrei was feigning illness in order to avoid going to Moscow.

Elena again summoned him to Moscow and he pleaded the same excuse. The third request was a peremptory order to come at once regardless of his condition. Andrei had Prince Fedor Pronsky convey his reply to Moscow. It has survived. Although the man who was the ruler's uncle and an appanage prince humbly referred to himself as the grand prince's slave, Andrei could not refrain from reminding his nephew of the old customs. He told him: "Sovereign, you have strictly enjoined me to appear before you at once regardless of circumstances. My lord, we are filled with sorrow and sadness because you refuse to believe we are genuinely ill and bid us appear before you forthwith. Ere this, sire, no ruler ever had us carried before him on a litter. My illness, my misfortune and my unhappiness have upset me dreadfully.

My lord, you should show me favor and mercy; warm your slave's heart and body with your favor, and let your slave feel assured that in future your generosity will free him from misery and sorrow, as God so moves you."

Before Pronsky arrived in Moscow Prince Goluboy-Rostovsky, one of Prince Andrei's junior boyars, secretly informed Prince Telepnev-Obolensky at night that Prince Andrei was certain to quit his appanage the following day. Elena immediately dispatched three members of the clergy, the bishop of Krutitsa, the abbot of the Semenov monastery, and the archpriest of the Savior convent, to say to Andrei in the metropolitan's name: "We have heard a rumor that you intend to abandon your patrimony, your ancestors' graves, your sacred realm, and the generous protection of your sovereigns, Grand Prince Vasily and his son. I bless you, and I pray that you will remain with your sovereign and unconditionally observe the oath you swore. You need not hesitate to appear before your sovereign and his mother. We offer you our blessing and will escort you there." The envoys were told to lay a curse upon Andrei if he refused to heed the metropolitan's adjuration.

In case the churchmen's threats and admonitions proved inadequate the Muscovite government moved strong forces to Volok under the command of two Obolensky princes, Nikita Khromoy and Ivan Ovchina-Telepnev. Prince Pronsky, Andrei's representative, was intercepted en route, but when he was captured a member of his retinue, the junior boyar Satin, managed to escape. Hastening back to Staritsa he informed Prince Andrei that Pronsky had been arrested and the grand prince's forces were on their way to apprehend him as well. Word came from Volok that government forces were in the area.

Without further hesitation Andrei left Staritsa on May 2, 1537, although it is uncertain that he had decided to go to Novgorod to stir up a revolution there. To judge from the pattern of Andrei's behavior it is logical to assume that he never intended to wage open civil war against his nephew. Flight to Lithuania appeared the most promising solution to his difficulties, but when he learned that the Muscovite units in Volok intended to interdict his escape route southwest to the Lithuanian frontier he had no choice but to flee due north into Novgorod territory.

He sent letters of exhortation to landholders, junior boyars and villagers: "The grand prince is a boy. The boyars are in charge. Whom can you serve? I shall be glad to show my favor to you." Many rural landholders came over to him, but this gain was more than offset by treachery in the ranks of Andrei's personal retainers. Some junior officers fled from one of Andrei's camps, located on the Desna river. One of them was captured and brought before the prince, who assigned a courtier, Kasha, to guard him. Kasha bound the fugitive hand and foot and immersed him, clad only in a shirt, in a lake, leaving just his head above water to prevent him from drowning. Using such means he tried to discover how many others had planned to flee with him. The man named so many fellow-conspirators that Prince Andrei ordered an end to the investigation, because (as the chronicler puts it) it was impossible to hang all of them.

Judged by the standards of the time, Andrei's commander, Prince Yury Obolensky, displayed rare devotion. When Elena first came to suspect that Andrei harbored hostile intentions, in an attempt to divert his forces she ordered him to send Prince Yury with a large detachment to Kolomna. In the chronicle account, when Obolensky learned that Andrei had fled, he prayed to God, eluded the grand prince's officers, and quitted Kolomna. After crossing the Volga below Degulin he sank his boats to deny them to his pursuers, and linked up with Andrei at a point on the Berezna river just short of the Edrov station.

While his partner, Prince Nikita, had gone to strengthen Novgorod's defenses, another Obolensky prince, Ivan Ovchina-Telepnev, overtook Andrei at Tukhol, some two and a half miles from the Zaiach station. Now accounts diverge, for some chroniclers supported the Muscovite government while others favored the appanage prince. Muscovite versions state that when both armies were ready for battle Prince Andrei, hoping to avoid the encounter, opened negotiations with Prince Obolensky and promised to lay down his arms if the latter swore that Elena and the grand prince would not arrest or disgrace him. Acting on his own authority Obolensky gave the desired assurance and both men set out for Moscow. Elena severely criticized Obolensky for reaching an understanding with Prince Andrei without her permission. She had Andrei arrested and imprisoned in a move to eliminate further outbreaks of civil disturbance, which were affecting the loyalty of many in her realm. Other versions declare that Elena had given the Obolensky princes a prior authorization to invite Prince Andrei to Moscow, promising that the grand prince would show him favor and augment his holdings. When the armies met, Prince Andrei was eager to fight; it was Obolensky who sent the offer to avoid hostilities and promised that Andrei could return in safety to his appanage.

Andrei entered Moscow on a Thursday and was arrested the following Saturday. This means that Obolensky did reach an understanding with Andrei, with or without the regent's approval, and the decision to break it was not taken immediately. Andrei's wife and his son, Vladimir, experienced the same fate. His boyars, including Prince Pronsky, the two Obolensky princes, Ivan Andreevich and Yury Andreevich, members of the Peninsky family, Prince Paletsky, and other princes and junior boyars on Andrei's estates who were privy to his plans were tortured, beaten about the ankles, and put in prison. Thirty Novgorod landholders who had gone over to Andrei were knouted in Moscow and hanged at fixed intervals along the highway all the way to Novgorod. Andrei died in prison six months later.

WAR WITH LITHUANIA

Lithuania might have been expected to take advantage of the tension and disturbances in Moscow during the grand prince's minority, but the Lithuanians had miscalculated the likelihood of factional strife when Vasily came to the throne and had been forced to concede to his son all the territory Ivan III had taken from them and even to give up Smolensk. When the truce was on the point of expiring the aged Sigismund had no desire to go to war with Vasily. As custom required, his council sent an envoy, Klinowski, to the Muscovite boyars Prince Dmitry Fedorovich Blesky and Mikhail Yurevich Zakharin, urging them to persuade the grand prince to send ambassadors to the king before the truce expired, to conclude a permanent peace or arrange a new truce. In the event the grand prince proved unwilling to send envoys to the king he should dispatch a courier to Lithuania bearing a safe-conduct for the king's envoys, as the custom had been in the past.

Vasily died before Klinowski arrived. The new administration decided that the boyars should send an envoy to the magnates with a safe-conduct. The new grand prince simultaneously dispatched the junior boyar Zabolotsky to inform Sigismund of his father's death and his own accession. Zabolotsky's charge contained these instructions: "If you are asked where the grand prince's brothers, Prince Yury Ivanovich and Prince Andrei Ivanovich, presently are, you are to answer: 'Prince Andrei Ivanovich is at the court in Moscow. Immediately after our father's death Prince Yury Ivanovich grossly transgressed the oath he had sworn to his sovereign. Our sovereign has placed him under official displeasure and confined him.' " Zabolotsky was to ascertain whether the king planned to stay long in Vilna and whether he intended to dispatch envoys to the grand prince.

Moscow had good reason for apprehension on the latter score. Reports of Vasily's death and his minor son's accession, which implied a weak government and presaged domestic disturbance, had aroused the hopes of the king and his council. Instead of sending ambassadors under the terms of the safe-conduct, Sigismund issued a safe-conduct of his own for Muscovite envoys and told Zabolotsky: "I desire to enjoy exactly the same fraternal friendship with the grand prince that our father, King Casimir, enjoyed with his grandfather, Grand Prince Ivan Vasilievich. If he desires fraternal friendship with us on these terms he must send ambassadors to us with all dispatch." The council gave the Muscovite boyars a similar answer.

The grand prince was annoyed when he received this safe-conduct from the king, because he had not asked the king to issue it and had no wish to send envoys to him. The truce expired and relations were broken off. In summer, 1534 Hetman Yury Radziwill and the Tatars devastated regions around Chernigov, Novgorod Seversk, Radogoshch, Starodub and Briansk. The king received the following intelligence: Moscow was rent by serious strife among the boyars, who were often at each other's throats. Pskov had no forces except its ordinary citizens and some merchants transferred from Moscow. Its people frequently met in assembly, a practice the governors and their staffs had forbidden, for they did not know what the people discussed when they met.

The king was greatly encouraged by the arrival of distinguished defectors such as Prince Semen Belsky and Ivan Liatsky. They wrote that were he to make them properly welcome many Muscovite princes and noblemen among the junior boyars would imitate their example. Sigismund understood and rewarded Belsky and Liatsky lavishly.

That autumn Hetman Radziwill sent Andrei Nemirovich, the commander at Kiev, and Vasily Chizha, court master of horse, to the Seversk region. They burned Radogoshch, but sustained losses and had to withdraw from Starodub and Chernigov. Prince Alexander Vishnevetsky experienced similar misfortune near Smolensk. Meeting with resistance when attacking towns, Lithuanian commanders avoided pitched battles with Muscovite armies.

More fearful of the Crimean khan than of Lithuania, Moscow held forces on the alert in Serpukhov, but found it difficult to raise and move armies while coping with domestic discord and events such as the defection of Semen Belsky and Liatsky, and the disgrace of Ivan Belsky, Vorotynsky and Glinsky. Not until September were administrative lines finally determined and not until late October was a Muscovite army in a position to invade Lithuania. The main detachment was commanded by Princes Mikhail Gorbaty-Suzdalsky and Nikita Obolensky, and the vanguard by Boyar Prince Ivan Ovchina-Telepnev-Obolensky, master of horse. Prince Boris Gorbaty brought units from Novgorod to link up with Prince Mikhail. The Muscovite armies met with no resistance from the king's forces and freely ravaged Lithuania up to 25 or 35 miles from Vilna. Moving in another direction, Prince Fedor Ovchina-Telepnev-Obolensky advanced from Starodub as far as Novgorod Litovsky.

The following year, when Moscow learned that the king had made substantial preparations for a campaign, an army set out with the main detachment under Prince Vasily Vasilievich Shuisky and the vanguard again commanded by Prince Ivan Telepnev-Obolensky. Its target was Mstislavl. The Novgorod courtier Buturlin and soldiers from Pskov were ordered to erect a fortress on Lake Sebezh, in Lithuania proper. The Lithuanian army, under the command of Hetman Yury Radziwill, Andrei Nemirovich, the Polish Hetman Tarnowski, and Semen Belsky, the fugitive from Moscow, again attacked the Seversk region, took Gomel without resistance, and besieged Starodub. The commandant, Prince Fedor Telepnev-Obolensky, resisted stoutly, but the Lithuanians secretly mined the town and blew it up. The commandant and many of his soldiers were captured and 13,000 inhabitants perished. The Russians voluntarily abandoned and destroyed Pochap. Delighted with the capture of Gomel and Starodub, the Lithuanian commanders halted. Their armies contained numerous foreign mercenaries, bombardiers, musketeers, and sappers. The Muscovites had no such experts. This is why they were unable, after destroying most of Mstislavl, to take the fortress and had to be satisfied with laying waste adjacent areas. Buturlin managed to build a strong new fortress, which was called Sebezh.

Early in 1536 the Lithuanian commander, Andrei Nemirovich, appeared before Sebezh, but his artillery performed poorly. It inflicted no damage on the fortress and injured his own men. The besieged made a sortie and handily defeated the Lithuanians when the ice on the lake gave way beneath them. Encouraged by this success the Muscovite commanders attacked the Liubech district of Lithuania. They razed the town of Vitebsk, seized many estates and villages, took many prisoners, confiscated much wealth, and returned home in good order with few casualties. In addition to Sebezh, the Muscovites constructed the fortresses of Zavoloche in the Rzhev district and Velizh in the Toropets area along the Lithuanian frontier, and restored Starodub and Pochap, which the Lithuanians had abandoned.

Having assumed the accession of Vasily's infant son would cause domestic chaos and drastically weaken the government's effectiveness, Lithuania was unprepared for warfare on so large a scale. Sigismund made the same error in his calculations that his brother Alexander had made when Ivan III died, and he was anxious to terminate this futile war. As early as September, 1535 Andrei Gorbaty, representing his brother, Prince Fedor, a prisoner in Lithuania, came to Moscow to see Prince Ivan Telepnev-Obolensky. Gorbaty stated that Hetman Yury Radziwill had told him the king wished to reach fraternal peace with the grand prince and had asked him to communicate the king's desire to the boyars and officials in Moscow. Other magnates had expressed similar sentiments.

The boyars resolved that Gorbaty should convey to Prince Fedor a letter which Prince Ivan composed. Obolensky wrote to Fedor: "As you know very well, Moscow did not begin the war. The grand prince sent Timofey Zabolotsky on a mission of peace and fraternity. The king gave him an unfriendly answer to bring back to our sovereign and, instead of sending an envoy, ordered his forces to invade our sovereign's land. As befits a true Christian prince, our sovereign has not wanted and does not want to shed Christian blood and strengthen the forces of Mohammed. Our sovereign wishes Christians to dwell together in peace and tranquility. If the king entertains similar sentiments and sends an envoy as a token of his sincerity, such an exchange will produce beneficial results."

Four months went by. Early in February of 1536 Smolensk reported that Gajka, a representative of Hetman Radziwill, was on his way to Moscow to see Prince Obolensky. The envoy displayed a safe-conduct which the king had issued, authorizing Muscovite envoys to proceed to Lithuania. Radziwill in a note to Obolensky stated that the prisoner, Prince Fedor Ovchina-Obolensky, had begged the magnates to encourage the king to seek peace and he had issued the safe-conduct as a result of their intervention. The grand prince's council rejected the document and gave its reasons: "By alleging that he sent them a petition the Lithuanian authorities are trying to incriminate Prince Fedor. He is in their power and they can say anything they like about him." The council advised Obolensky to authorize a representative to accompany Radziwill's man with a letter stating that Prince Fedor was not entitled to submit petitions. The boyars also decided, in accordance with traditional custom, to transmit a safe-conduct that envoys from the king might use. Their action impelled Obolensky to dispatch a representative to keep negotiating channels open.

It was February 27, the day Obolensky dismissed Gajka to return home from Moscow, that the Lithuanian army suffered its defeat at Sebezh. The Lithuanian authorities realized this meant that Moscow was certain to refuse to entertain the king's proposal to send envoys to

Lithuania, and it led them to adopt a new strategy in order to satisfy the demands both sides had put forward. In May Radziwill sent a further communication to Obolensky in which he said: "You write that our ruler must send envoys to your sovereign. Consider who has the stronger obligation to take the first step—our ruler, who is far advanced in years, or your sovereign, who is still very young. Like a son showing respect to a father, your sovereign should take the initiative, but if your sovereign sends envoys to our ruler with a set of non-negotiable demands the result might easily be that our ruler would reject them and your envoys would return empty-handed. The same situation might also occur if our ruler sent envoys to you in Moscow. To deliver us from the impasse you should consult with your fellow princes and boyars and your sovereign, and persuade him to send envoys with a grant of full authority to the frontier. The king will respond by sending envoys with plenipotentiary authority, instructed to negotiate until peace or a truce is achieved."

The victory at Sebezh doomed this compromise also. The grand prince, Elena, and the boyars agreed there was no need to dispatch envoys either to the king or to a designated meeting place, for his father had never done so. The pope and the emperor frequently had recommended the latter course, but his father, Grand Prince Vasily, had steadfastly refused to adopt it. Once the decision was taken Obolensky again sent a representative to Radziwill bearing a letter in which he observed that in a ruler's relations with other sovereigns his principal duty was to maintain the dignity of his position without regard for questions of age: "As you are fully aware, our sovereigns exercise their authority in direct succession from their predecessors in accordance with God's will. The mighty sovereign Vasily, our ruler's father, inherited his domain from his father and ruled it in his own right. Now his son reigns where his father and grandfather reigned. Our sovereign is young at present, but merciful God will grant him long years of rule as an adult. You suggest that envoys meet on the frontier. Only a person who does not wish our rulers to arrive at accord would offer such an unprecedented proposal. The rulers of our ancestral realm ordained that the kings' envoys must always come here to negotiate."

The king did not allow matters to rest there. In July he sent Nikodim Tekhanovsky, governor of Krevo, as his personal representative to Ivan to reiterate his proposal for the grand prince to send envoys to Lithuania, and included a safe-conduct. The council refused to deal with Nikodim, but in a move to prevent the negotiations from breaking down sent a high-ranking junior boyar to the king, for to ignore his overtures would preclude further opportunities to achieve peace. The junior boyar, Khludenev, took safe-conducts valid for the king's envoys with him, and returned by November to report that a major Lithuanian delegation headed by Jan Jurewicz Glebowicz, governor of Polotsk, would arrive in Moscow at Christmas time. Khludenev also mentioned that he had been made most welcome on his journey, had received ample maintenance, and accorded tokens of esteem.

NEGOTIATIONS AND TRUCE

Jan Glebowicz arrived at the appointed time to open negotiations. A dispute immediately arose over whether it was the Russians or the Lithuanians who had begun the war. The boyars frequently returned to and debated this issue at length, claiming the king was responsible, while the envoys maintained the opposite, asserting that when the king sent his hetman to take the towns in the Seversk area he was simply recovering his property. King Casimir had assigned the towns to Shemiakin and Mozhaisky, but they had betrayed him by handing them over to Moscow. The boyars countered this argument by stating that the Seversk towns had belonged to Kiev, which was part of the grand prince's patrimony. This issue caused intense strife, but the arguments led nowhere. The envoys declared they had not come to debate history but to find a satisfactory way to arrange peace between the rulers.

When the boyars agreed to take up immediate issues a quarrel at once arose over who should be first to present his demands. The boyars insisted the envoys speak first, and they obliged by demanding Novgorod and Pskov. The boyars replied: "We have heard this demand before. It was idle then and it is idle now. Stop talking foolish nonsense. You know where these cities are. Such talk is a waste of time." After much more inflammatory rhetoric the envoys said: "There has been a lot of talk, but now it is time to get down to business." They called for a peace treaty embodying the terms of the agreement which had been made by Casimir and Vasily the Dark.[3] The boyars refused to entertain the proposal. The envoys next mentioned the treaties between Ivan III and Alexander, and Vasily and Sigismund. The boyars grew angry and walked out. The grand prince told the envoys to retire to their residence.

The envoys came to the second session and sat quiet for a long time. Annoyed at their silence the boyar, Mikhail Yurevich, said: "My lords, even if there were twenty-four hours in the day you would accomplish nothing by sitting silent, but as it is the days are short and you should speak. There is not much time left." The envoys replied: "We have already been speaking for two days; we have defined our position in

accordance with our sovereign's instructions, but you have utterly failed
to respond. Tell us how your sovereign proposes to achieve permanent
peace with our sovereign." The boyars answered that permanent peace
could be concluded only on the basis of the terms which had formed
part of the truce made between Sigismund and the late Grand Prince
Vasily; namely, that Moscow receive Smolensk in perpetuity and issues
which had arisen since Ivan had ascended the throne form part of subsequent negotiations. To this the envoys said: "Consider what you have
said. Why should our sovereign cede his patrimony and sign a treaty to
that effect?" The boyars again berated the envoys, and the latter retired
to their residence.

The third session opened with the same inflammatory rhetoric with
which the second had closed. Finally one of the envoys said: "There is a
lot of talk but not much action. Let us seek a compromise; our ruler
will never accept any unequivocal formula acknowledging the loss of
Smolensk." The boyars inquired what an "unequivocal formula" meant.
The envoys explained: "If your sovereign intends to keep Smolensk he
should hand over a town as large and rich as Smolensk to our ruler."
The boyars conveyed this proposal to the grand prince, and returning
formally stated in Ivan's name: "God granted our father that portion
of his patrimony and our father bequeathed it to us. We are determined
to keep Smolensk and will not cede it to the king under any circumstances. We are under no obligation to give him another town in its
place. Smolensk has always formed part of our patrimony, which we
inherited from our predecessors. Our predecessors lost it temporarily,
but God has restored it to us. We shall not give it up."

Realizing that permanent peace could not be achieved, the envoys
proposed a truce. The grand prince conferred with his boyars and
wondered whether it was sound policy to make a temporary truce with
the king. He favored the move: "We have other enemies. It is true that
Khan Sahib-Girey has not regained his strength, Islam-Girey is a weak
and unstable man and thus the Crimea remains an unknown quantity,
but the people of Kazan have deceived us and we have been in no position to punish them. The need to deal with our problems in these areas
makes it advantageous to come to terms with the king."

The truce negotiations bogged down when the boyars demanded the
retrocession of Gomel and an exchange of prisoners. Since they were
determined that the war had to show a few gains for their side the
envoys absolutely refused to consider these proposals. When the prisoner
issue arose they reminded the boyars, as their predecessors had done
in Vasily's time, that the king still held some Muscovite noblemen and

could discern no advantage in exchanging them for Lithuanian soldiers. The boyars asked what benefit could possibly accrue from refusing to exchange prisoners: "Surely these men are human, and, being so, are mortal. They are alive now, but they will die some day; thus, there is no advantage in holding them. Gomel forms part of our sovereign's patrimony, and the king has no business to keep what does not belong to him. Your ruler holds a few brave men captive, but the men our sovereign holds are both numerous and young. It is foolish to refuse to exchange a handful of noblemen for a large number of soldiers. Both the mighty and the humble alike are mortal and all of them will die. Neither side will profit from such a policy." The envoys were adamant in their refusal and additionally demanded that the grand prince dismantle the fortresses in Muscovy and Lithuania that he had built during the war.

Finally it was agreed that there would be no prisoner exchange, Gomel would remain under the king's control, and the new fortresses of Zavoloche and Sebezh were to belong to the grand prince, but then a bitter quarrel broke out over where the frontier line should be drawn. No solution could be found and the talks were broken off. The envoys took leave of the grand prince, but as they were departing they said to their escort: "Surely the boyars wish to negotiate with us further, as we do with them. Your sovereign's generosity has provided us with comfortable accommodations and abundant supplies. Perhaps we might spend a little more time exploring the issues. May God grant a successful outcome." The escort told the boyars what the envoys had said; they were invited to a further session, and both sides managed to hammer out a truce to take effect on the day of the Annunciation [March 25] of the year 1537, for a period of five years.

CRIMEAN AFFAIRS

The council was strongly of the opinion that the truce with the king constituted an essential prerequisite for dealing with the problems of Kazan and the Crimea. As soon as Vasily died the authorities dispatched the junior boyar Chelishchev to inform the Crimean khan that Ivan had ascended the throne. Chelishchev was instructed to ask Sahib-Girey for his indulgence towards the new grand prince and to consider the latter his friend and brother, as Grand Prince Vasily had regarded Mengli-Girey, and to say: "If you offer a solemn covenant to this effect our ambassador, Prince Strigin-Obolensky, is waiting in Putivl with handsome presents. He will come to you soon." Like his predecessors

Chelishchev was authorized to promise splendid gifts in order to secure a covenant, but he was forbidden to pay tribute or guarantee that the grand prince would make regular presents. The envoy set out for the Crimea in January. In May the Tatars attacked Russian settlements on the river Prona but were driven off.

The Crimea soon became a scene of rivalry between Khan Sahib-Girey and Islam, his potential successor, with elements in the Horde supporting both contenders. This development was highly advantageous to Moscow. Both leaders were inveterate bandits and neither one could be counted a trustworthy ally, but now their strength was fragmented. Islam promised to support Sigismund "against all his enemies," which specifically meant the prince of Muscovy, but he simultaneously conveyed an offer of alliance to Moscow, which, of course, was designed to elicit maximum financial support: "You must send me as much money as you have given Sahib-Girey. The Turkish sultan has recognized me as khan and you ought to send him some fine gifts too."

Moscow considered it sound policy to furnish pecuniary support to Islam, for Sahib's hostility had become painfully obvious. He stole effects from Chelishchev and all the members of his party. In retaliation Prince Strigin-Obolensky was instructed to proceed from Putivl to the Crimea, where he was to hand over his gifts to Islam. The prince knew what invariably awaited Muscovite envoys there and apparently tried to avoid going to the Crimea. He thought of all sorts of excuses, and the one he finally chose seems strange. He wrote to the grand prince: "Sire, Islam has sent his envoy, Temesh, to you. Temesh is unknown in the Crimea. No one has ever heard of him. You and God dispose of everything; you may have me disgraced or executed, but I shall not budge as long as Temesh serves as Islam's envoy." The grand prince placed Strigin under his displeasure and told Prince Mezetsky to go to the Crimea.

The exchanges which followed assumed their regular form. The Muscovite authorities insisted that Islam conclude a binding alliance directed against Lithuania, while Islam kept demanding money and protested that the grand prince had failed to fulfill the terms of his father's will, in which Vasily, to prove his friendship, had supposedly earmarked half of his revenues for Islam. While Muscovite units were marching to protect the Seversk region from Lithuania the Crimeans attacked the Oka defense line. They were repulsed, but they succeeded in diverting Muscovite forces from Seversk and facilitated the king's capture of Gomel and Starodub. Moscow retaliated by arresting Islam's representatives. The khan claimed it was Sahib, not he, who had invaded Muscovy. The envoys were released.

Muscovites serving in the Crimea continued to suffer the same indignities their predecessors had endured. Ambassador Naumov informed the grand prince: "When your cossacks appeared before Islam, his princes and nobles began tearing their clothes off and demanding sableskins. I told Islam what his men were doing. The princes and nobles complained because Islam refused to give them a free hand and had not ordered the grand prince to send presents to them. Islam's reply to me was: 'No brotherly feelings exist between us. Your grand prince has deliberately chosen not to send us gifts because he does not care to enjoy fraternal friendship with me.' He has told his princes to do as they please. Every one of them has tried to sell your cossacks into slavery."

Moscow did all in its power to avoid offending the khan. When the khan's envoy was impaled on a horn during a quarrel in Novgorod Seversk, all the ringleaders were sent to the Crimea. Whenever an envoy from the Crimea presented his credentials he received two sets of clothing and the grand prince served mead to him and his retinue with his own hands, although he insisted that the envoy fall on his knees and remove his cap, actions the khan had forbidden him to perform.

BELSKY'S INTRIGUES IN CONSTANTINOPLE

Moscow's relations with the Crimea soon assumed a new dimension. Prince Semen Belsky, the defector, saw that Moscow was decisively winning the war with Sigismund, a situation he had promised the Lithuanians to prevent. Alleging a need to fulfill a vow, he obtained the king's permission to journey to Jerusalem. He went instead to Constantinople, where he tried to concert an alliance among Lithuania, the sultan, and the Crimea against Moscow. With help from Turkey and Lithuania Belsky planned to restore the independent duchies of Belsk and Riazan. His mother had been a princess of Riazan and a niece of Ivan III. Since the male line of Riazan princes had become extinct Belsky considered himself the sole heir to the principality.

After the truce with Moscow Sigismund received a letter in which Belsky stated that the sultan had agreed to aid him. He claimed the sultan had ordered Sahib-Girey and the pashas[4] of Silistria and Kaffa to accompany Belsky on the campaign, and the pashas probably had more than 40,000 men under arms, not to mention Sahib-Girey's forces and the Belgorod cossacks. Sigismund was to order his chief hetmen and all his forces to invade Muscovy. Belsky asked the king to issue him a safeconduct granting him free access to and return from Lithuania to attend to his affairs and allowing men on his Lithuanian estates to visit him in Perekop.

The king found Belsky's communication altogether untimely because the war with Moscow had just ended. He replied: "You asked our permission to go to Jerusalem in order to fulfill a vow. You said nothing about a visit to the sultan of Turkey. We shall take appropriate action when you come in person to show us the sultan's letter. You ask us to furnish you a safe-conduct to enter Lithuania. You are in our service and your estate lies in our realm. You have no need of such a document. Our princes and magnates come to us freely. We have ordered your retainers to report to you at once."

Islam-Girey took the opportunity of informing Moscow about Belsky's manoeuvres to demonstrate that he was well-disposed to the grand prince. Apparently Sahib-Girey had told the sultan that he (Islam) was dead. This report led the sultan to approve Belsky's campaign, for which the latter had recruited 100,000 troops. When Belsky reached Belgorod he learned that Islam was not dead and informed the sultan, who said: "Since Islam is alive our project will fail." Belsky sent a man to Islam with a request to grant him passage and be his friend, but Islam refused. "You must realize," he wrote the grand prince, "that the Ottomans are crafty. The sultan has undertaken this project without the slightest regard for Prince Belsky's interests. He does not care whether Belsky acquires a principality or not. His sole concern is to stir up trouble, from which he may derive advantage. The sultan harasses us constantly. He covets territory. It makes no difference to him who provides it. He may be the basest of slaves—as long as he can make good his undertaking."

The Muscovite authorities rewarded Islam for his friendly action and asked him to arrest or murder Belsky, but they essayed another method to divert Belsky from his dangerous course. One of Belsky's men had told Naumov, the Muscovite envoy in the Crimea, that his master wished to return to Moscow were the grand princess to forgive him and grant him a safe-conduct. Acting on this information the government sent Belsky a document which contained this statement: "We desire to show our favor to you and we lay aside our wrath. We intend to forget the crime you committed while young, and we shall show our great favor to you more abundantly than we have in the past. You know that in times gone by certain of our retainers forsook us in order to enter the service of our enemies. When they came back to us their action did not cost them their patrimonies. Our ancestors pardoned them and restored their rank and estates. You need not fear to come to us now."

For some reason Belsky chose not to come. The Muscovite government continued to negotiate concerning him with Islam, and also with

Sahib, to whom it sent occasional missions. Sahib regularly sent envoys to Moscow in an attempt to supply his wants: "You must send us clothing; three sable coats, three foxfur coats, three falcons, and falconeers. We are quite ready to be your brother. Send us five black foxes and five black walrus tusks." Sahib's son wrote: "You must provide whatever we ask. This will keep my father on good terms with you."

Sahib's courier was given this answer in the grand prince's name: "When our brother sends us a man of rank as envoy we shall designate an ambassador of our own to accompany him and keep our brother informed of developments in our realm. You, Sahib's representative, have called Belsky our friend. Is your master so poorly informed that he told you to refer to Belsky as our friend? Belsky is not our friend; he is our slave. If our brother wishes to prove he is our friend, he will hand Belsky over to us or kill him on the spot. This is the best token of friendship he can provide us." The courier replied: "The Turkish sultan sent a letter to our khan with Belsky. Belsky is raising an army to attack the Muscovite borderlands, but he calls himself your sovereign's friend and brother. People who used to know him in Moscow, where he was the grand prince's slave, abuse and spit on him, but young men, ignorant of the past, flock to him, anxious to join his expedition. You know the Horde; it is full of all kinds of people. One says one thing; another says another. Our khan says what he has to say, but he knows perfectly well that Belsky is a slave."

The departure of Sahib's courier coincided with that of Islam's representatives. The latter had observed to the boyars: "Certain boyars advocate that the grand prince should become Sahib's friend and brother and abandon Islam. We are aware that if the grand prince comes to terms with Sahib it will bode ill for our ruler Islam, but the grand prince will derive no benefit from such an action. He should pay no attention to anything Sahib's men have to say." They were told that the grand prince had no intention of forsaking Islam; the boyars knew nothing about such a plan and did not care to hear about it. Moscow had no wish to abandon Islam, for his promise to surrender Belsky rendered him too valuable. He failed to make good his pledge. Then one of the Nogay princes, a friend of Sahib, suddenly attacked and killed Islam and seized Belsky, whom Sahib ransomed on the sultan's orders.

Now the undisputed ruler of the Crimea, Sahib informed the grand prince: "We shall be pleased and stay friends with you if you send me what you have traditionally sent us, but if we receive no gifts this winter and you delay and procrastinate until spring, we shall put our trust in God and come in person to get them. You will have no reason to be angry if we do so. Do not wait for us to send you an envoy or use that as an excuse for tardiness. If you delay you will have good cause to fear us. We are no longer the ragged mob of Tatars we were in the past. Besides my own artillery I shall bring 100,000 cavalry, which the Felicitous Khan (the Turkish sultan) has placed at my disposal. Do not imagine that you have merely the feeble forces of Mohammed-Girey to contend with; I am far stronger than he was. Kazan belongs to me and Khan Safa-Girey is my brother. This means you may no longer attack Kazan, for if you do I shall descend on Moscow."

CRIMEA AND KAZAN

Now that Sahib was sole ruler, the Crimea resumed its interference in Kazan affairs. To detach Kazan from Moscow and unite all the Tatar hordes, or at least to bring them under a single ruling dynasty, had always been the ambition of the house of Girey, which embodied this policy and sought every opportunity to accomplish it. During Grand Prince Vasily's later years Kazan had been a docile satellite of Moscow under Khan Enaley. He transferred his friendship to Vasily's successor and remained the loyal ally of Moscow he had been previously, but the parade of rulers and the divergent influences emanating from Moscow and the Crimea had rendered the people of Kazan adept at taking sides and choosing opportunities to defeat their opponents. The party favoring the Crimea saw the major war with Lithuania as a splendid chance to get rid of Moscow's supporters; accordingly, a conspiracy was formed in the fall of 1535, led by Mohammed-Amin's sister and Prince Bulat. Enaley was assassinated and Safa-Girey was proclaimed khan.

One faction had triumphed, but the other was not vanquished. The Tatars of Gorodets, known as the Volga cossacks, came to Moscow and stated that some sixty princes, nobles and cossacks had come to their fort from Kazan, told them Enaley had been assassinated, and added: "The princes, nobles and others involved in the conspiracy number some 500 individuals. We remember the favor Grand Princes Vasily and Ivan have shown us and the oath we swore, and we wish to serve our sovereign grand prince. As a sign of his favor the sovereign should pardon Khan Shig-Aley and allow him to come to Moscow. When Shig-Aley arrives in Moscow we shall join our sympathizers and drive the Crimean khan out of Kazan." After receiving this information Elena and the boyars decided to release Shig-Aley, and in December he was brought from Beloozero to appear before the grand prince. The khan fell on his knees and proclaimed: "When I was a boy your father, Grand Prince Vasily, showed his favor to me. He was like a father and made me ruler of Kazan. Then, for my sins, the princes and people of Kazan fell out, and I went back to your father in Moscow. Your father was generous and assigned me towns. Sinner that I am, I was guilty of manifesting to my sovereign a proud and fickle mind. God exposed me and your father punished me for my transgressions, humbling me with his official displeasure. Sire, remember your father's favor to me and be merciful to me." The grand prince bade the khan rise, invited him to approach his person to offer a greeting, and told him to sit on a bench to his right. He then gave him a coat and dismissed him to his residence.

Shig-Aley asked for an audience with the grand princess as well. Elena consulted the boyars as to the propriety of his request. The boyars decided that she might receive the khan, for the grand prince was young and she was in full charge of the administration. Elena received Shig-Aley on January 9, 1536. Two boyars, Princes Vasily Vasilievich Shuisky and Ivan Fedorovich Telepnev-Obolensky, and two state secretaries met him at his sleigh, and the grand prince himself, attended by his boyars, met him at the chamber entrance. Elena was accompanied by her ladies-in-waiting and boyars were seated on each side of her, the regular custom at the reception of envoys. When Shig-Aley entered he bowed his head to the ground and said: "Mistress, Grand Princess Elena, my sovereign, Prince Vasily Ivanovich, took me into his service as a young man. He was generous to me, he nurtured me like a puppy, and conferred his mighty favor upon me. He was like a father to me and made me ruler of Kazan. For my sins the people of Kazan expelled me and I returned to my sovereign. My sovereign was generous to me and assigned me towns in his realm. I betrayed him, and I stand convicted of my actions in my sovereigns' sight. My lords, you have shown your favor to me, your slave; you have forgiven my fault; you have spared me, your slave, and have allowed me to behold your regal eyes. I, your slave, have sworn an oath; by its terms I shall support you to my dying day and be ready to die to keep your royal favor. I stand prepared to die, as my brother died,[5] to atone for my guilt." Elena gave him this reply: "Khan Shig-Aley, Grand Prince Vasily Ivanovich laid his displeasure upon you, but my son and I have been generous to you, have shown you our mercy, and have permitted you to behold our eyes. Forget the past; if you behave in future in the manner you have promised, we shall continue to manifest our mighty regard and concern for you."

The khan bowed his head to the ground in honor of the grand prince and princess, received additional gifts, and was escorted to his residence. His wife Fatima also asked permission to behold the sovereigns' eyes and

Elena received her. Boyars' wives greeted Fatima at her sleigh and on the staircase; the grand princess met her at the chamber entrance, greeted her, and conducted her to the reception room, where the grand prince soon joined them. When he entered Shig-Aley's wife arose and stepped away from her place. Young Ivan said to her in greeting, "*Tabug salam*," and took his seat near his mother to the right of the visitor. Boyars were stationed on both sides of him and their wives stood near the grand princess. Later that day Fatima dined with the grand princess, and Ivan and his boyars joined them in his mother's chambers. After the meal Elena presented the khan's wife with a cup and other gifts.

While Moscow was entertaining and making gifts to Shig-Aley in an attempt to encourage the anti-Crimean party in Kazan, war broke out with Safa-Girey. The Muscovite commanders failed to mount a vigorous offensive; the Tatars destroyed villages near Nizhny Novgorod, but were beaten back from Balakhna and their attacks on other points were unsuccessful. Next they invaded the Kostroma region. The man responsible for its defense, Prince Zasekin, attacked the Tatars with inadequate forces, and was defeated and killed; only the approach of substantial fresh units compelled the Tatars to withdraw. The danger of this situation was the principal circumstance that constrained Moscow quickly to conclude the truce with Lithuania. Once the western frontier was secure the government early in 1537 transferred its military forces east to Vladimir and Meshchera. Safa-Girey appeared off Murom and burned the environs, but he could not take the fortress and withdrew when he learned detachments were on their way from Vladimir and Meshchera.

Such was the situation when Sahib-Girey consolidated his position, which posed a further obstacle to a successful Muscovite attack on Kazan. His threats had made an impression. Moscow told his envoy that his master's demands would be met in spite of the offensive remarks the khan had made in his letter, and if Safa-Girey initiated peace negotiations with the sovereign the latter was prepared to make a suitable response. Sahib-Girey reiterated: "You must send us a prominent man, such as Prince Vasily Shuisky or Ovchina, as ambassador, together with a substantial sum of money. You must reach an agreement with Kazan and stop extracting revenue from it. If you dispatch forces to attack Kazan and send no envoy to us I shall be your enemy." The council gave its opinion: "If we ignore the khan and attack Kazan he will invade our borderlands, and the Crimea and Kazan will damage the cause of Christianity on two fronts at once." Therefore it urged: "Do not attack. Have one of Sahib-Girey's men go from here to Kazan with a junior boyar to take a note to Safa-Girey."

The grand prince replied to Sahib: "My brother, your representations have led me to restrain my army and send a man to Safa-Girey. If he wishes peace, let him send us responsible men. We desire to treat him in the same way as our father and grandfather treated previous rulers of Kazan. You tell us Kazan belongs to you. You should examine your old chronicles. A realm belongs to him who takes it. You never forget how certain khans lost their dominion in the Horde, went to Kazan, and wrongfully appropriated it through war, but you refuse to remember that God's favor enabled my grandfather to take Kazan and expel its ruler. Our brother, you should remember your own history and not forget ours."

PEACE WITH SWEDEN AND RELATIONS WITH OTHER COUNTRIES

Elena's administration was preoccupied with Lithuania and the Tatars, but a peace treaty was concluded with Sweden in 1537. Gustavus Vasa[6] agreed not to come to the aid of Lithuania or the Livonian Order in the event either went to war with Moscow. Both sides affirmed the principle of free trade and pledged to return deserters. Existing agreements with Livonia were maintained in force. The extent of Moscow's relations with the Empire is unknown. As far as Poland was concerned, Moscow sought by an exchange of envoys to remain on good terms with Peter Stepanovich, the hospodar of Moldavia, who was an enemy of Sigismund. The sultan of Turkey continued his previous habit of sending Greeks to Moscow to purchase goods.

FORTRESS CONSTRUCTION

Domestically the government's first priority was the construction of towns and fortresses; the danger of attack from three quarters rendered this action imperative. Construction of new fortresses along the frontier and inside Lithuania, and the reconstruction of older ones damaged during the war, have been mentioned above. A fortress was built in Perm in 1535, on the site where the old one had burned down, and a wooden fortress was put up at a place called Murunza on the Moksha river in Meshchera because, as the chronicler reported, there was no other nearby. In 1536 the districts of Korega, Likurgi, Zalese and Borok Zhelezny in the Kostroma area petitioned the grand prince and his mother for the sovereign to show them his favor by having a town built: the districts were populous but located far from any towns. Buigorod was founded in response to this petition. An earthen fortress was erected at Balakhna on the Solia river, because adjacent settlements were numerous and contained a substantial population. A fortress was built on the river Prona, and the new town of Ustiug was constructed entirely of wood. Yaroslavl burned to the ground, but in the very same month orders went out to erect a new town on the old site. A great conflagration damaged the city wall of Vladimir, but it was soon restored. Similar action was taken in Tver when several major fires occurred there. New fortifications were built in Novgorod and Vologda. In Moscow, Grand Prince Vasily decided to enclose an area with a stone wall, which received the name of *Kitay* or *Middle* Town. The builder was Peter Friazin the Younger, who started work on the wall on May 16, 1535. The policy of increasing the population by attracting immigrants from foreign lands remained in force. In 1535 three hundred families came from Lithuania at the invitation of the sovereign.

MEASURES TO IMPROVE THE COINAGE

In the last years of Vasily's reign a serious problem arose involving clipped and counterfeit coins.[7] A *grivenka* was supposed to equal 250 Novgorod *dengi*, or, in the Muscovite system, two rubles, six *grivni*, but debasement had reached such proportions that a *denga* was now worth no more than half its original value and 500 or more debased *dengi* were needed to make a *grivenka*. As a result shouting, arguing and cursing had now become a feature of every business transaction. Shortly before Grand Prince Vasily died numerous persons from Moscow, Smolensk, Kostroma, Vologda, Yaroslavl and other towns were executed in the capital for adulterating coins; lead was poured into their mouths and their hands were cut off. In March of 1535 Elena forbade the circulation of clipped or counterfeit coins, changed their composition, and had them reminted at a rate of one *grivenka* per three rubles, or 300 Novgorod *dengi*. The value of the *grivna* was increased. These measures were taken, as the chronicler reports, because if left unchecked the debasement of the coinage would have caused people to suffer serious losses. In Grand Prince Vasily's reign coins had born a representation of the grand prince on horseback holding a sword; now he was represented holding a spear (*kope*), and henceforward the coins were known as kopecks (*kopeiki*).

JUNIOR BOYARS IN COUNCIL

Aside from decrees like these, noted in the chronicles, other trends first discernible during Elena's regency merit attention. As an example, the view persists that prior to the reign of Ivan IV no one but boyars and lords-in-waiting could sit in the council and that it was Ivan's struggle with the nobility that opened the council to a third group composed of men of lesser rank, the so-called service gentry of the council. The description of the reception the regency accorded the Lithuanian envoy Tekhanovsky contains the observation: "The grand prince sat in a timbered room surrounded by his boyars, lords-in-waiting, major-domos, *junior boyars who live in the council*, and merchants of the first guild who do not live in the council." If the term *council* denotes the grand prince's advisory body and the word *live* possesses its normal meaning of *existing*, or *being present*, it becomes clear that junior boyars were admitted to the council even before Ivan IV began to rule independently. It is also entirely possible that Elena's administration was not the first to admit them.

A description of negotiations with Polish envoys demonstrates that lords-in-waiting were primarily court officials, like court boyars, who closely supervised court functions and ceremonies: "The grand prince told the escort, Fedor Nevezhin, to tell the envoys on behalf of the lords-in-waiting to come to the court." Junior boyars assigned to escort the envoy Tekhanovsky met him when he arrived in Moscow and said: "The grand sovereign's lords-in-waiting have designated us to accompany you and show you to your residence." After the envoy was installed in his residence he was provided with supplies from the *storehouse*, which here meant the grand prince's palace. The clerks in charge of the storehouse made a list of the supplies he was furnished.

THE ONEGA CHARTER

In 1536 a charter comparable to those granted by Ivan III to Belozersk and by Grand Prince Vasily to the peasants of Artemovo was issued to the elders and people of the Onega district. The Belozersk charter had stated: "The governor and his deputies are forbidden to collect taxes in the villages; they must obtain them from the town officials." The Onega charter declared: "They are forbidden to circulate among the villages in order to collect taxes; they must obtain the taxes from the village elders. The elders will collect taxes and maintenance for the governor and his officials from outlying villages and remit it to the governor and his officials at the district seat." Both the Belozersk and Onega charters affirmed: "If anyone in the district or the district seat is mistreated by the governor, his officials, members of his party, or their visitors, they are entitled to designate a time when both parties must appear before the grand prince." This clause is absent from the Artemovo charter.

Both the Belozersk and Onega charters prescribed: "The circuit judge must tour his district alone and on foot." The Belozersk charter stated: "No one on the governor's staff may attend parties or celebrations without an invitation." The Onega charter declared: "Among the various officials belonging to the governor only the circuit judge may attend a party or celebration uninvited." The people of the Onega district were permitted to deny the people of Belozersk and Vologda access to the sea to pan salt. The latter had been poaching on the former's preserves, but now they had to come to Kargopol in order to obtain salt from the Onega inhabitants.

THE CHARTER TO THE BEAVER TRAPPERS OF VLADIMIR

A charter was issued to the beaver trappers of Vladimir in 1537. It was much the same as the one promulgated by Yury, appanage prince of Dmitrov, cited above, but a few differences are discernible. Yury's charter permitted the circuit judge to tour the villages twice a year accompanied by two attendants and three horses; Ivan's charter stipulated that the judge must tour the villages alone, with one horse and no attendants. The charter to the Vladimir beaver trappers further stated: "These trappers must understand the terms of their service to the grand prince. They may trap beavers in the Kliazma river from its tributary, the Orzhavka, as far as the Sudogda river. They may trap all along the Sudogda and the Kolaksha rivers. They must bring the pelts of any beavers they catch to my treasury. If they catch no beavers they must pay an annual quitrent of one third of a ruble. No one may levy a toll on the traps they set, and no one may levy a toll on or confiscate necessary supplies from the two or three of their number who bring pelts or quitrent to Moscow."

OBOLENSKY AND THE DEATH OF ELENA

These charters were issued in Grand Prince Ivan's name. The description of the negotiations conducted with the Polish envoys states that the grand prince conferred with his boyars and made decisions, but these remarks are purely formal. Behind them lie indications that Grand Princess Elena was in full charge of the government. Her chief coadjutor is known. Endeavoring to begin peace negotiations, Hetman Radziwill of Lithuania dispatched representatives to Boyar Prince Ovchina-Telepnev-Obolensky, master of horse. A courier from Kazan who wished to escort a Tatar home similarly asked the master of horse to bring the matter to the attention of the grand prince and his mother. Obolensky had no serious rivals or enemies left after Glinsky, Belsky and Vorotynsky were disgraced, but those who believed they had a stronger claim to the position of first place which Obolensky occupied were bound to resent his preeminence. No change could be anticipated as long as Elena was alive, but she died on April 3, 1538. Herberstein was sure she was poisoned.

V

THE BOYAR REGIME

BOYAR RIVALRIES–SHUISKY AND BELSKY

The primacy of Obolensky was bitterly resented. The other boyars believed they were entitled to the position of first place into which chance had thrust Obolensky. Prince Vasily Vasilievich Shuisky had been first among the boyars during the last years of Vasily's and the beginning of his son's reign. It will be remembered that Shuisky's bold move had saved Smolensk for Moscow after the battle of Orsha. Acting vigorously he had hanged the Smolensk nobles who supported the king in full view of the Lithuanian army. This deed affords insight into the man; he might be expected to make similar moves in order to fulfill his own ambitions. A week after Elena's death Prince Vasily, his brother Ivan, and others combined to arrest Boyar Prince Ovchina-Telepnev-Obolensky, the master of horse, and his sister Agrafena, the grand prince's nurse. Obolensky starved to death in close confinement, and his sister was shorn and exiled to Kargopol. Princes Ivan Belsky and Andrei Shuisky, imprisoned during Elena's regency, were freed.

Belsky's release brought an end to Shuisky's ascendancy. Like the Patrikeev family, the Belsky family was descended from Gedimin. Its members took equal pride in their origin and were determined to achieve first place. Prince Fedor Belsky's marriage to a princess of Riazan who was a blood niece of Ivan III facilitated these pretensions. Prince Fedor's eldest son Dmitry, although he held a prominent position, took no part in the frequent intrigues, but this was not true of his brothers, Ivan and Semen. Ivan had taken part in Vasily's campaigns against Kazan. Semen's restless nature is revealed by his actions after Vasily's death. He dreamed of reconstituting the duchies of Belsk and Riazan and launched intrigues in Lithuania, Constantinople and the Crimea in an attempt to restore these patrimonies. His brother's flight had led to Prince Ivan's disgrace. There must have been ample provocation, for Prince Dmitry was not involved. Once free, Belsky had no intention of standing idle while Shuisky held power. He was determined to win power himself.

The chief task facing Shuisky, the leading boyar, and his rival Belsky was to strengthen their respective factions and promote their supporters, particularly their relatives. This inevitably caused the first clash between them. The chronicler reports that hostilities began when Princes Vasily and Ivan Shuisky expressed anger because Prince Ivan Fedorovich Belsky and Mikhail Vasilievich Tuchkov advised the grand prince to bestow the rank of boyar on Prince Yury Mikhailovich Golitsyn of the Patrikeev house and the rank of lord-in-waiting on Ivan Ivanovich Khabarov. The Shuisky princes opposed this plan. The move showed how anxious their opponents were to promote their relatives, and it proved a fertile source of friction. Intent on private concerns, no one gave a thought to matters of state or the condition of the country.

Belsky numbered Metropolitan Daniel and Fedor Mishurin, a state secretary, among his supporters, but the Shuisky faction prevailed. Belsky was returned to prison and his followers were banished to different villages. His prominent supporters were usually imprisoned or exiled, but a cruel fate overtook Mishurin. This official had been one of Grand Prince Vasily's closest confidants. The fact that the chronicler names him with Metropolitan Daniel, Belsky and Tuchkov among those who incurred the wrath of the Shuisky faction further attests to his ability and great influence. Without authorization from the grand prince the Shuisky faction ordered princes, junior boyars and courtiers in their service to seize Mishurin at his residence, flay him, and expose his naked corpse on a block near the prisons, where it was beheaded.

STRIVING FOR POWER

Vasily Shuisky soon died. His brother Ivan followed in his footsteps and continued his program. The only enemy with whom Vasily had failed to deal was Metropolitan Daniel. In February of 1539 Ivan expelled him and appointed Ioasaf Skryptsyn, abbot of the Holy Trinity-St. Sergius monastery, to take his place. Ioasaf did not remain a Shuisky partisan for long. In July, 1540 he obtained the grand prince's authorization to release Belsky, whose appearance at court caused consternation among Shuisky and his supporters. Prince Ivan was furious. He ceased visiting the sovereign or conferring with the boyars. Belsky and Metropolitan Ioasaf assumed control of the administration.

The chronicles assert that the metropolitan and boyars were the ones who freed Evfrosinia and Vladimir, wife and son of Prince Andrei of Staritsa. At first they were allowed to reside only at Prince Andrei's residence in Moscow, but on Christmas Day, December 25, 1541, they were permitted to have an audience with the grand prince at the palace. His father's appanage was restored to Vladimir, who was also assigned boyars and junior boyars of his own, but those who had served his father were not transferred to him. At the same time that Prince Vladimir Andreevich and his mother were freed, better treatment was accorded another appanage prince, Dmitry, son of Andrei Vasilievich of Uglich, a nephew of Ivan III who had been held in close confinement some fifty years,[1] but although his fetters were removed the unfortunate man was not released from prison. The fact that Vladimir Andreevich had numerous supporters explains the unequal treatment; no one was interested in Dmitry's fate any longer.

The chronicles recount that a second piece of good fortune for Prince Vladimir came about through the intervention of Metropolitan Ioasaf and the boyars, where the latter term means Prince Belsky and his friends. While Belsky and the metropolitan were demonstrating their influence by restoring the disgraced prince to his appanage, a serious conspiracy formed against them. According to the chronicle their close association with the grand prince had alienated the rest of the boyars from Belsky and the metropolitan. The disaffected included Princes Mikhail and Ivan Kubensky, Prince Dmitry Paletsky, the treasurer, Ivan Tretiakov, many lesser princes, courtiers and junior boyars, and the whole city of Novgorod. Members of this group either favored Shuisky and wanted him to return to power, or else planned to invoke the name of this influential boyar to cloak their own activity. They entered into negotiations with Shuisky while he was in Vladimir in charge of the defense of the eastern region against Kazan. The name of Shuisky undoubtedly explains why the people of Novgorod participated wholeheartedly in the conspiracy; one member of the family had been the last governor of independent Novgorod. Later examples will further illustrate Novgorod's unceasing attachment to this family.

The conspirators told Ivan Shuisky and his confederates to come from Vladimir to Moscow on January 3, 1542. Shuisky made many of his junior boyars swear to support him and without informing the grand prince entered Moscow with his men the night of January 2. His son, Prince Peter, and Ivan Bolshoy Sheremetev with a band of 300 men had preceded him. Belsky was apprehended that night at his residence. Next morning he was exiled to Beloozero, but even so far away he was considered dangerous as long as he remained alive. In May three Shuisky partisans travelled to Beloozero and slew Belsky in prison. Two of his principal coadjutors were banished—Prince Peter Shcheniatev to Yaroslavl, and Ivan Khabarov to Tver. Shcheniatev was seized in the grand prince's own room and dragged out through the back door. Metropolitan Ioasaf was awakened by stones the conspirators threw into his cell. He ran through the palace, a shouting pack of conspirators at his heels, and burst into the grand prince's bedroom, waking him at six in the morning. The terrified grand prince could not protect him in the palace. Ioasaf fled to the local sanctuary of the Trinity-St. Sergius monastery, hotly pursued by junior boyars and men from Novgorod. They reviled him, and the men from Novgorod, not satisfied with curses, might have killed the metropolitan if Abbot Alexis, invoking the name of St. Sergius, and Boyar Prince Dmitry Paletsky had not restrained them. Ioasaf was eventually apprehended and exiled to the Kirillo-Belozersk monastery. Makary, archbishop of Novgorod, became metropolitan in his place. The people of Novgorod had participated enthusiastically in the overthrow of Belsky and Ioasaf, and Makary enjoyed previous ties with Shuisky.

Ivan Shuisky did not live long after the *coup,* and power passed to three of his relatives, Princes Ivan Mikhailovich and Andrei Mikhailovich Shuisky, and Prince Fedor Ivanovich Skopin-Shuisky. The leader was Prince Andrei, whose relationship with appanage Prince Yury has been discussed. After Belsky's fall and death the Shuisky faction had no more rivals with a base of power of their own to face, but now difficulties arose in another quarter. The grand prince was maturing and might promote men who, although no threat themselves, might become dangerous were the grand prince to place trust in them, now that he was no longer a child. Next the Shuisky faction learned that Ivan had in fact bestowed his favor on Fedor Semenovich Vorontsov, brother of the Mikhail Semenovich who has figured in this narrative. On September 9, 1543 the three leaders of the Shuisky family and their confederates, Prince Shkurliatev, the Pronsky and Kubensky princes, Paletsky, and Alexis Basmanov, burst into the palace dining room where the grand prince and the metropolitan were in conference, seized Vorontsov, scratched his face, tore his clothes, and tried to kill him. Ivan asked the metropolitan and the Morozov boyars to dissuade them from killing Vorontsov. They refrained, but they led him from the room, a sorry figure, later beat and punched him, and locked him up. The ruler again asked the metropolitan and the boyars to request the Shuisky princes to send Vorontsov and his son to serve in Kolomna if they were not allowed to remain in Moscow. The princes felt it was too dangerous to have Vorontsov and his son so near and exiled them to Kostroma. The chronicler adds: "While the metropolitan was on his way to the Shuisky princes Foma Golovin trod on his cloak and tore it."

THE YOUNG IVAN

Ivan, now thirteen years old, was endowed with splendid talents. His susceptible, highly impressionable and passionate temperament was most probably innate, but without question his upbringing and the experiences he endured enormously intensified his sensitive and irritable temper, if not actually creating it. Generally a gifted boy left to his own devices in a difficult and painful situation develops rapidly, if not prematurely. After his mother died Ivan was surrounded by persons who, determined to advance their own interests, manipulated him in order to achieve their individual goals. Constantly thrown among men pursuing their own ends Ivan withdrew into an inner world, where an intense personal development took place.

Had his father lived Ivan would have taken no part in affairs for some time. In a tranquil environment and under careful supervision his character would have developed and matured in a normal way, but at the age of three Ivan became grand prince. He could not actually rule, but the necessary formalities he had to observe, such as receiving ambassadors, were constant reminders of his position. He was obliged to become deeply involved in affairs of state and serve as the focus of vital issues, although he was no more than a passive spectator mutely following protocol. He witnessed the struggle of factions. Intimates to whom he was strongly attached were snatched away and his pleas were scorned as confidants were brutally and unceremoniously led off to prison. He would subsequently learn they had been put to death.

He formed a clear conception of the high dignity of his office when he observed the men who ignored him as they harassed and tormented his intimates in his presence yet behaved like lackeys at receptions for ambassadors and on other ceremonial occasions. Seeing them bow before him and invoke his name in everything they did, he grasped the nature and extent of his power. Furthermore, he was constantly surrounded by people whose lust for gain and hatred of the faction in ascendancy made them charge their rivals with violating the law and showing disrespect for the ruler. The boy realized that those around him were enemies, bent on filching his power, with whom he was incapable of struggling overtly. Ivan could strike back at them only in his thoughts and imagination. This is the most serious, dangerous and deadly kind of struggle a man can wage, to say nothing of a child. The boy was ceaselessly preoccupied with this contest, the question of his power, and his enemies' usurpations. He pondered means to enforce his rights, expose the lawlessness of his foes, and condemn them.

Young Ivan's inquisitive mind required nurture. He read voraciously and omnivorously. Studying Scripture, Roman history, church history, and the writings of the Fathers he sought support for his position in everything he read. He tried to discover means to prevail in the struggle which absorbed all his energies. He ransacked Scripture and other sources for precedents to assert his authority over the lawless minions who had stolen his power. His precocity provides a key to understanding Ivan's later actions, such as assuming the title *tsar*, or desiring to rule in Moscow as David and Solomon had ruled in Jerusalem, or as Augustus, Constantine and Theodosius had ruled in Rome. Ivan IV was the first tsar not simply because he was first to adopt the title, but because he was first to comprehend fully the authority such a title conferred. It might be said that whereas his father and grandfather had been content to take practical steps to increase their power, Ivan was the first to devise a theory justifying such action.

Ivan's mind was obsessed with discovering ways to recover the authority rightfully his, which others had impudently trampled upon, in order to render his position invulnerable, but his emotions were swayed by other powerful forces. He was surrounded by men in pursuit of their own goals, who ignored and insulted him, attacked their rivals mercilessly, and behaved violently in his presence. As a result Ivan grew accustomed to disregarding others, formed a low opinion of the human condition, and set little value on a man's life. As Ivan grew up no attempt was made to develop his good qualities or repress his evil tendencies; he was left free to indulge his emotions and lusts. He was praised for doing things that merited censure.

In advancing their own interests the boyars harmed the young prince and assaulted the tenderest and most sensitive parts of his nature. They defamed and calumniated the memory of his parents and destroyed those close to him. Ivan was exposed to double insult; he was a ruler whose authority was flouted and he was a man whose pleas were ignored. The combination of indulgence, flattery and scorn stimulated two tendencies which became characteristic of Ivan: scorn for slavish flatterers and hatred for his enemies, the refractory nobles usurping his authority, or anyone who demeaned his person.

Here are memories of his childhood which Ivan mentioned in his reply to Kurbsky:[2] "Our mother Elena died and we and our brother Georgy were orphans. Our subjects behaved as they wished and our country had no sovereign. They showed no concern for us, their rulers. They strove for wealth and renown and quarrelled with one another. What evil they wrought! How many boyars and commanders who had loyally served our father they slew! They appropriated and occupied homes, villages and estates that had belonged to our ancestors. They transferred my mother's personal holdings to the treasury, savagely kicking her possessions with their feet and stabbing them with sharp implements. They apportioned the remainder among themselves. Your grandfather, Mikhail Tuchkov, did things like that!" After describing what the Shuisky princes did to Secretary Mishurin, Prince Ivan Belsky, and two metropolitans, Ivan continued: "They treated us and our brother Georgy like foreigners or beggars. They never gave us food or clothing, no matter how badly we needed them, and never treated us as children should be treated. Here is an instance. Often when we were playing Prince Ivan Vasilievich Shuisky sat on a bench, chin in hand, resting his leg on our father's bed. What can I say of our family's fortune? They devised cunning schemes to dissipate all of it. They pretended they wanted to reward junior boyars but took everything themselves. They never recompensed junior boyars for service nor rewarded them in accordance with their rank. They filched gold and silver vessels from the store belonging to my father and grandfather and inscribed the names of their own parents on them as though they had themselves inherited them. Everybody knew what they had done. While our mother was still alive Prince Ivan Shuisky had a coat of marten fur lined with mohair, whose skins were worn. If his family had really possessed ancestral wealth it would have been better to exchange the coat in order to obtain the wherewithal to inscribe the vessels.[3] They toured towns and villages and plundered the inhabitants mercilessly. No one can estimate how many times they attacked their neighbors. They made citizens their slaves and their slaves noblemen. They thought they were ruling effectively, but all they did was to encourage injustice and create dissension. Their cupidity knew no bounds; everything they said or did was designed to line their pockets."

Kurbsky believed the example the proud and mighty boyars set for Ivan caused their and their children's ruin. Each one strove to outdo the other in pandering to Ivan's every whim and appetite. When the young prince was twelve he took to killing animals by hurling them down from high towers. His attendants, unaware of the harm they were doing, encouraged and even praised him. When he was almost fifteen he transferred his attention to humans. Collecting a gang of young nobles he rode about the streets, beating and robbing any man or woman he encountered. No matter how outrageously he behaved his toadies constantly flattered him, crying: "What a brave and courageous tsar he will be."

If Kurbsky's allegations that Ivan manifested evil tendencies at twelve and his attendants made no efforts to restrain him be true, these purported incidents took place during the administration of Andrei Shuisky and his confederates. Earlier, when Ivan was younger, the Shuisky faction had not considered it necessary to pay the slightest attention to him; Prince Ivan put his feet on Grand Prince Vasily's bed in his son's presence, and Tuchkov kicked his mother's possessions. Both forgot that a child remembers such occurrences better than an adult. In those days many incidents offended the boy: he received inferior clothing, and was not given enough time to eat. When he matured those around him altered their mode of address. Seeing him now as a source of future largesse they abruptly stopped treating him like a child subject to lengthy tutelage, and began considering him the grand prince, whose favor must be cultivated.

Vorontsov decided that he would be well advised to acquire the good offices of the thirteen-year old sovereign. The Shuisky faction considered Vorontsov's action fraught with danger to its interests. Shuisky and his confederates probably changed their approach as well, and urged Ivan's attendants to encourage the sort of activities Kurbsky has described. The change in Ivan's situation when he became thirteen is further illustrated by the fact that the description of the fall of Prince Belsky and Metropolitan Ioasaf says only that Ivan was dreadfully frightened, whereas the report of the Vorontsov affair mentions that Ivan intervened with the Shuisky faction on behalf of his favorite.

SHUISKY TOPPLES

Shuisky's attack on Vorontsov proved to be the last independent action of the boyar regime. It is correct to say that directly after that the thirteen-year old Ivan struck Shuisky down, but it is not clear who prompted and encouraged him or what preparations he made. The young grand prince decided to aim his blow at the most prominent noble of the realm, and not surprisingly delivered it with as much force as the Shuisky faction was accustomed to employ against its opponents. On December 29, 1543 Ivan arrested Prince Andrei Shuisky, president of the boyar council, and handed him over to his kennelmen, who killed him and exposed the corpse in front of the prisons. His confederates, Prince Fedor Shuisky, Prince Yury Temkin, and Foma Golovin (who had ventured to insult the metropolitan as described above), were banished.

The attack was a success. The enemy was terrified and thrown into utter confusion. After that, the chronicler notes, the boyars grew afraid of the sovereign and obeyed him. A year later Ivan, now fourteen, laid his displeasure on Prince Ivan Kubensky and exiled him to Pereiaslavl under house arrest. He and his brother Mikhail had been ringleaders in the conspiracy against Belsky and Metropolitan Ioasaf that had brought Shuisky to power. He is mentioned among the boyars joining the Shuisky faction in the assault on Vorontsov. He was arrested December 16, 1544, but released in May of 1545. On the following September 10, Afanasy Buturlin had his tongue cut out for impudence, and in October Prince Ivan Kubensky again fell under official displeasure, together with Princes Peter Shuisky, Alexander Gorbaty, and Dmitry Paletsky, and Fedor Vorontsov. It is small wonder that the Shuisky faction and its chief partisans were alarmed and gave vent to their annoyance. Times had changed, and they had sustained severe losses, which included Prince Peter Shuisky, son of the former regent, Prince Ivan, Prince Kubensky, and Prince Paletsky, whose role in the conspiracy against Belsky and Vorontsov had been as important as Kubensky's. It is odd to find Fedor Vorontsov's name on this list, disgraced along with his inveterate enemies.

Fortunately, in this instance the chronicler provides an entirely satisfactory explanation. Immediately after Andrei Shuisky was slain the grand prince brought Vorontsov back from exile and showed him as much favor as he had earlier. Returning to court triumphant and fully vindicated Vorontsov conceived the notion that he could assume the position formerly held by Andrei Shuisky, take full charge of the government and distribute favors in the name of the ruler, who was still a minor. The chronicler reports that Fedor was angry whenever Ivan showed favor to someone without his approval. It may be that Ivan noticed these displays of temper, or others close to Vorontsov (perhaps Princes Mikhail and Yury Glinsky, Ivan's uncles) pointed out that Vorontsov was on his way to becoming another Shuisky. At any rate, Vorontsov was disgraced along with his former enemies. In his case the displeasure lasted no more than two months. The grand prince restored the boyars to favor in December of 1545 at the instance of his spiritual father, Metropolitan Makary.

It is necessary to notice the shifting relationships which are displayed in Ivan's invocations and revocations of displeasure involving the same persons from his thirteenth to his seventeenth year. It is misleading to assume that old animosities harbored against friends and relatives of the Shuisky family would lead the young Ivan to attack and forgive them for no reason. It is equally difficult to believe that the execution of Prince Andrei so weakened the powerful Shuisky faction that it abandoned the struggle entirely. The chronicles provide no clue as to

who stood behind the grand prince in the contest. Vorontsov is a prime
candidate. Others might be the Glinsky princes, whose power is attested
by the universal detestation the nobility entertained for them, but the
sources are unequivocal in their assertions that the Glinsky princes were
not responsible for the final downfall of Kubensky and Vorontsov.

In May, 1546 the grand prince led an army to Kolomna when he
learned the Crimean khan was on his way to the area. Once when he
went outside the town for a walk some Novgorod fusiliers stopped him
to submit a petition. He was not disposed to grant it and told his
attendants to clear the men out of his way. The chronicler does not say
how his attendants responded to his order; he merely says that the
fusiliers struck them with their helmets and threw mud at them. When
he saw what was happening Ivan summoned a squad of his personal
retainers to drive the fusiliers away, but the fusiliers resisted them too.
Units were preparing to attack in force when the fusiliers went on a
rampage, whacking with their clubs and firing their pieces. The retainers
fought back with bows and arrows and used their swords. No more than
five or six men survived on either side. The grand prince was unable to
return straight to his headquarters and had to take a circuitous route.

Ivan's reaction to such a scene is easy to imagine. He had been
terrified by similar occurrences as a child and he bore the scars the rest
of his life. He had not expected to meet enemies daring to challenge his
authority among the rank and file and his suspicions were immediately
aroused. He ordered an investigation to find out who had encouraged
the fusiliers to behave so rashly, for they would never have done what
they did unless someone had urged them on. To ascertain the truth of
the matter Ivan entrusted the investigation not to a prominent personage, but to his confidant, a state secretary, Vasily Zakharov. This action
reveals that Ivan, like his father before him, was quickly surrounding
himself with new men, ordinary officials who were not ambitious descendants of old houses. Zakharov reported that certain boyars, Prince
Kubensky and two Vorontsov brothers, Fedor Mikhailovich and Vasily
Mikhailovich, had tampered with the fusiliers. The grand prince verified
his official's allegations and in a rage had Kubensky and the Vorontsov
brothers executed for this fresh crime, as well as for their previous
transgressions and their venality in the conduct of his and the country's
affairs. Their confederates were exiled. As the chroniclers phrased it,
an ordinary official had ventured to calumniate princes of the realm.
Kurbsky assigns other executions to this period as well.[4]

IVAN'S CORONATION AND MARRIAGE

These events occurred when Ivan was sixteen. The following year he summoned Metropolitan Makary, on December 13, 1546, and told him he wished to marry. Next day the metropolitan said mass in the cathedral of the Assumption and invited all the boyars, including those in disgrace, to accompany him to the grand prince. Ivan said: "Placing my hopes in merciful God and the Virgin Mary and in the prayers and mercy of the mighty miracle-workers Peter, Alexis,[5] Iona[6] and Sergius, and all the Russian miracle-workers, with your blessing, my father, I have decided to marry. At first I thought of arranging a marriage with a foreign princess, the daughter of a king or tsar,[7] but I abandoned the plan. I do not wish to take a foreign bride because my parents died when I was very young. If I marry a foreign princess and our temperaments are incompatible our life together will be intolerable. With your approval I intend to marry one of my subjects, whomever God vouchsafes me."

The metropolitan and the boyars, so the chronicler reports, burst into tears of joy when they saw that their ruler, though still so young, was able to make up his own mind. Young Ivan astounded them further as he continued: "With your blessing, my father metropolitan, and with your counsel, my boyars, before I marry I desire to examine the ancient records and study the formula our ancestors, the tsars and grand princes, and particularly our relative, Grand Prince Vladimir Vsevolodovich Monomakh,[8] used at their coronations. I too shall use their formula and be crowned tsar and grand prince." The boyars were delighted to learn that their young ruler intended to scrutinize ancient titles. What naturally surprised them most and in some instances (according to Kurbsky's letters) considerably alarmed them was that the sixteen-year old grand prince had decided to adopt the distinctively Russian title of tsar for which no foreign precedents existed, and which neither his father nor grandfather had seen fit to adopt. Ivan's coronation took place on January 16, 1547, in circumstances reminiscent of the installation of Ivan III's nephew Dmitry.

In December, while preparations for the coronation were under way, local princes and junior boyars received a notice: "This, our rescript, requires each and every one of you who has marriageable daughters to bring them at once to your district town, where our governors will conduct a bride-show. You must produce your daughters. Anyone who conceals his daughter and fails to show her to our governors will incur our severest displeasure and be punished. Circulate this rescript among yourselves immediately."

The choice fell upon a girl belonging to one of the most ancient and distinguished boyar families of Moscow, which had successfully maintained its position close to the throne although the number of princely families had significantly increased. Ivan's bride was Anastasia, daughter of the late lord-in-waiting, Roman Yurevich Zakharin-Koshkin, and niece of the boyar Mikhail Yurevich, who had enjoyed Grand Prince Vasily's confidence. Her family connections probably influenced the choice; Grigory Yurevich Zakharin, who became head of the family on the death of another uncle of Anastasia, the boyar Mikhail, had not sided with the Shuisky faction and there is no record of this house's participation in any of the disturbances caused by the boyars during Ivan's minority.[9] The tsar was married on February 3.

THE GREAT MOSCOW FIRE

On April 12 a great fire broke out in Moscow, followed by another on the 20th. On June 3 the huge bell that summoned the people to church fell, and on the 21st occurred the fiercest conflagration Moscow had ever seen. The church of the Holy Cross in the Arbat quarter caught fire during a heavy wind; spreading as quickly as lightning the fire destroyed the entire Semchinsk sector to the west as far as the Moscow river. The conflagration next engulfed the Kremlin, raged through the cathedral of the Assumption, burned the palace roof, the treasury, and the cathedral of the Annunciation. The armory and its equipment, the chamberlain's residence with its storerooms, and the metropolitan's headquarters burned down. The iconostasis in several stone churches was consumed along with much personal treasure, which people used to hide in such places. The iconostasis and church vessels in the cathedral of the Assumption survived.

Metropolitan Makary almost suffocated. He emerged from the cathedral carrying the icon of the Virgin which had been inscribed by Metropolitan Peter, followed by an archpriest bearing a scroll which contained the cathedral's regulations. The metropolitan sought refuge in a secret passage which led from the Kremlin wall to the Moscow river but the smoke forced him out. As he was lowered from the passage to the river in a wooden cage the rope broke and the metropolitan was badly shaken up. When he recovered he was conveyed to the New Savior monastery. The Miracles and Ascension monasteries in the Kremlin and shops and merchandise in Kitaigorod were destroyed, and all the homes outside the city, including those in Rozhdestvenka and a large settlement on the river Neglinnaia, burned down as far as the Nikola Drachevsky monastery.

The fire followed the Miasnitskaia river to the monastery of St. Florus[10] and reached the church of St. Vladimir in Pokrovka. 1700 people lost their lives. The grand prince and his wife, his brother and the boyars sought refuge in the village of Vorobevo.

THE GLINSKYS FALL

The following day Ivan and his boyars went to the New Savior monastery to inquire after the metropolitan. The tsar's confessor, Fedor Barmin, archpriest of the Annunciation monastery, Boyar Prince Fedor Skopin-Shuisky, and Ivan Petrovich Cheliadnin declared that witchcraft was the cause of the fire that had destroyed Moscow. Wizards extracted people's hearts, soaked them in water, and scattered the water about the streets. This started the fire in Moscow. The tsar ordered the matter investigated. Here is how the investigation was conducted. On Sunday the 26th, five days after the fire, the boyars assembled in the Kremlin square near the cathedral of the Assumption, summoned the citizenry, and asked who had set fire to Moscow. People in the crowd shouted: "Princess Anna Glinskaia and her children are sorcerers. She extracted men's hearts and put them in water. She went all over Moscow scattering this water. This made Moscow catch fire."

The people said such things because the Glinsky family stood close to the ruler and enjoyed his favor, but men in the Glinsky service attacked and robbed ordinary citizens who were not connected with the family. Boyar Prince Mikhail Vasilievich Glinsky, master of horse and the tsar's maternal uncle, was with his mother in Rzhev, which the ruler had assigned to his estates, but his brother, Prince Yury, was present in Moscow with the boyars assembled in the Kremlin square. When he heard the people shouting abuse of him and his mother he realized what might happen and sought refuge in the cathedral of the Assumption. The boyars, who grudged the Glinsky family its privileged position, deliberately provoked the crowd. A mob stormed the cathedral, murdered Glinsky, dragged his corpse out of the Kremlin, and left it in the square where criminals were executed. Next the mob assailed Glinsky's men, beat many of them, and plundered his palace. Many innocent junior boyars from the Seversk region erroneously assumed to be in Glinsky's service perished in the fracas.

One Glinsky was not enough. Two days after Prince Yury was slain mobs appeared before the tsar's retreat in Vorobevo, shouting that the tsar must surrender his grandmother, Princess Anna Glinskaia, and her son, Prince Mikhail, who were thought to be hiding there. In retaliation

Ivan ordered the ringleaders seized and executed. This frightened the rest, who dispersed to the towns from which they had come.

The chronicle considers Fedor Barmin, archpriest of the Annunciation monastery, Princes Fedor Skopin-Shuisky and Yury Temkin, Ivan Petrovich Cheliadnin, Grigory Yurevich Zakharin, and Fedor Nagoy primarily responsible for the rising against the Glinsky family and the riot. During Ivan's minority the Shuisky faction and its supporters had singlehandedly crushed their opponents, but when Ivan grew up and the executions of Andrei Shuisky, Kubensky and Vorontsov showed them they could no longer rule as they pleased, they transferred their hostility to the tsar's intimates, such as the Glinsky family. They did not move against their opponents openly, but aroused the populace to do their work for them. Princes Fedor Skopin-Shuisky and Yury Temkin were behind the attack on the Glinsky family. The principal confederates of Andrei Shuisky, they had been exiled after their leader's execution, but subsequently returned to Moscow. On this occasion Shuisky and Temkin cooperated with Barmin, the tsar's confessor, and Grigory Zakharin, Anastasia's uncle, because, too weak to act alone, they were forced to form combinations with those among Ivan's confidants who had clashed with the Glinsky family in the rivalry for influence over the young ruler.

SILVESTER AND ADASHEV

Those responsible for the events of June 26 managed to evade detection after crushing the Glinsky family. Prince Mikhail Vasilievich Glinsky, the lone survivor, abandoned all hope of triumphing over his enemies and feared for his safety. He and his friend, Prince Turuntay-Pronsky, decided to flee to Lithuania, but were apprehended by Prince Peter Shuisky and spent a short time in confinement until they were pardoned. They were released under bond, on the assumption that their flight was occasioned by confusion and fear because of what had happened to Prince Yury Glinsky. The power of the Glinsky clan had been annihilated, but its enemies failed to replace it. Silvester, a simple priest of the cathedral of the Annunciation, and Alexis Fedorovich Adashev, the tsar's chamberlain, a man of humble origin, acquired Ivan's full trust and assumed direction of domestic policy.

As a child Ivan had been exposed to serious emotional pressures and frustration. He was encouraged to indulge his baser instincts, and he observed the unsavory behavior of others. These circumstances unquestionably had a deleterious effect on the formation of his character and, among other things, had tended to make him irritable. But the very irritability, impressionability and, as it were, feminine characteristics of his temperament also made him open and readily accessible to good influences, if they emanated from a model who possessed positive moral qualities, was a member of the church hierarchy, and had not incurred Ivan's suspicion.

The Moscow fire had made a profound impression on the young tsar. Here is what he wrote about it to an assembly convoked to deal with church problems: "It is impossible to describe or even to utter all the iniquities and sins I committed in my youth. God humbled me. He took away my father, who was shepherd and intercessor for all of you. The boyars and nobles pretended to support me, but they craved supreme power for themselves. In darkness of mind I presumed to arrest and slay my paternal uncles. After my mother died the boyars ruled my kingdom as they wished. I was a young sinner and orphan; many perished in the internecine quarrels, while I grew up neglected and without guidance. I became accustomed to the boyars' evil ways and since that time I have sinned mightily against God, and God has visited condign punishment upon me.

"Often I took up the cudgels to wreak vengeance on my enemies, but nothing turned out aright. I failed to realize that the Lord was inflicting mighty punishment upon me. I did not repent; indeed I myself tormented hapless Christians in the cruelest possible ways. The Lord punished me for my sins with flood and plague, but even then I refused to repent. At last God unleashed the dreadful fires; fear entered my soul and my bones trembled. My spirit grew humble and I acknowledged my transgressions. I begged the clergy's forgiveness and pardoned the princes and boyars." Kurbsky says that God devised a way to help Christian folk: when the people rose against the Glinsky family an elder recently arrived from Novgorod called Silvester came to Ivan, frightened him with God's authority by quoting Holy Scripture, and threatened him with the appalling dooms of God. Silvester also told the grand prince of miracles and other manifestations of God's power. "I do not know," Kurbsky adds, "whether he was telling the truth about the miracles or trying to find a way to frighten Ivan and induce in him a measure of restraint, but he achieved his purpose. With help from Alexis Adashev, Metropolitan Makary, and other holy men whom the clergy revered, Silvester healed and purged Ivan's soul and cured his debauched mind."

Kurbsky does not imply that Silvester was now suddenly appearing at court for the first time, or that the grand prince had not been acquainted with him previously. Silvester probably moved to Moscow from Novgorod much earlier to become one of the priests attached to the cathedral of the Annunciation in the Kremlin, a position that was bound to bring him to Ivan's attention. His qualities also attracted notice, and now his influence and authority increased. The Book of Degrees[11] states that Silvester was on excellent terms with appanage Prince Vladimir Andreevich and his mother and his efforts secured their release from prison. This is a most important piece of information. Prince Vladimir and his father were released from prison during the administration of Prince Belsky and Metropolitan Ioasaf. No source mentions a second arrest. It is unlikely that all the chroniclers, when discussing the disgrace and execution of certain boyars, would neglect to mention that the tsar's cousin was involved; thus, it is reasonable to assume that the Book of Degrees refers to the one time Prince Vladimir was released. Since this occurred during Belsky's administration, Silvester had clearly achieved a position of prominence by that time.

To explain Silvester's influence and Ivan's moral transformation it is necessary to recall certain events that took place late in Ivan's sixteenth and in his seventeenth year. One was the execution of the boyars Kubensky and Vorontsov, whom the tsar had deemed incorrigible. Another was Ivan's determination to be crowned with the title of tsar, an action that revealed the young ruler's remarkable mental and emotional precocity. A third was the profound change that marriage was bound to produce in a youth of sixteen. Finally there were the fires, and the popular rising against members of a family whom the young tsar had been led to trust fully by community of interest and close ties of kinship, but whose failure to punish their retainers for acts of lawlessness had aroused widespread discontent. These circumstances at last constrained Ivan to turn his back upon the princes and boyars to seek support among men of demonstrated integrity but of a different social origin. These factors initiated Ivan's significant moral transformation at the age of seventeen, but it was not until the young tsar reached twenty that he became mature and strong enough to make a complete break with the pernicious influences of the past.

Ivan's vivacious and passionate temperament stimulated his mind and imagination and drove him to find outlets for his enthusiasms. He was the most outstanding ruler of early Russia in the zest and capacity he displayed for speaking and disputation, oral or written, whether in public, or at a church council, with a defected boyar, or with foreign envoys. His abilities earned him the title of *master of spoken wisdom*. Ivan's unfortunate childhood made him feel he was always on the defensive both to himself and to others, and his speeches and letters are thus usually exculpatory or accusatory. His irritable emotional nature combined with his unhappy circumstances tended to make him go to extremes, and he lived in incessant fear of failure. This was why he was always ready to defend himself and blame others for his difficulties.

In his speech to the council on this occasion he justified his actions to the people and blamed the disasters that had occurred on those he considered his enemies. Earlier he would have disgraced or executed them, but in his new frame of mind he merely wished publicly to proclaim their guilt. At twenty Ivan understood that the violent and lawless actions of the powerful had reduced the state to a parlous condition. He tried to bring about a general reconciliation.

IVAN'S SPEECH TO THE LAND ASSEMBLY

After consulting the metropolitan about measures to end the rioting, prevent further lawlessness, and alleviate the climate of hostility, Ivan summoned representatives of every rank from all the towns in his realm. When the delegates arrived Ivan appeared on a Sunday on the Stone Platform,[12] which was adorned with crosses. He prayed and said to the metropolitan: "Holy father, I pray to you. Help me and foster love, for I know you desire good works and love. You know that I was four years old when my father died and eight when my mother died. My relatives showed no concern for me and my powerful, ambitious boyars and nobles had no interest in me. Using my name they strove to win rank and position for themselves and performed many selfish, cruel and brutal deeds. I was like a deaf mute; my youth and helplessness made it impossible for censure to pass my lips. They ruled arbitrarily. Unjust usurers, bloodsuckers, unrighteous judges, can you answer me? The world cries out against you. I never shed blood, but you await retribution."

Bowing in all directions Ivan continued: "Holy men, whom God has bestowed upon me, I pray for you to have faith in God and love for me. I cannot now redress wrongs, prevent dissension, or lower taxes. For a very long time I have been a feeble lad, and a dabbler in foolish things while my boyars and governors acted wickedly, rendered unjust decisions, and greedily extorted money from you. I beseech you to cease this ruinous strife, unless issues of the greatest moment are involved. In those cases and in future I shall judge and defend you as best I can. I shall root out injustice and restore what others have stolen."

This was a time when Alexis Adashev's influence with the tsar was very great. The day he spoke to the people Ivan made Adashev a

lord-in-waiting and said at the ceremony: "Alexis, I have raised you
from low and humble station. I have heard of your good qualities and I
have elevated you beyond your condition to be my helper. You have
not sought this position; it is I who have conferred it upon you and
upon others of like condition, to assuage my grief and to care for the
people, whom God has entrusted to me. I charge you to receive petitions from the poor and downtrodden and scrutinize them carefully.
Have no fear of the powerful and illustrious, who have filched away
honor and ruined the poor and the weak with their violence. Pay no
attention to hypocritical tears shed by a pauper who calumniates the
rich, pretending thus to be righteous. Fear God's wrath, scan everything
attentively, and tell us the truth. Seek honest judges among the boyars
and nobles." Ivan spoke with great earnestness, and added that he
intended to hear many cases personally and render just judgments. In
this way the boyar regime came to an end.

SIGNIFICANCE OF THE BOYAR REGIME

The boyar administration resolved a question fundamental to the existence of the Russian state. The princes of Moscow unified northeastern
Russia and created a state in that region. These princes, now sovereigns
of all Russia, were surrounded by a new group of state servitors, descendants of grand and appanage princes who had lost their hereditary
estates to the successors of Ivan Kalita and became Muscovite boyars,
attendant upon the princes. The new order now required the princes to
alter their relations with the sovereign head of the state. As the leading
exponent of change the grand prince of Muscovy was determined to
strengthen and expand the new system, but he was surrounded by men
living in recollection of past glories, who had no sympathy with his
ideas. Their positions and titles served only to remind them of the
higher rank and dignity they had possessed in the recent past, which
remained very real to them. The operation of these two contrary principles, the first seeking a further, fuller development, the second striving
to check the first and preserve the outmoded relationships of the past,
rendered a struggle inevitable.

The clash occurred during the reigns of Ivan III and his son, and was
reflected in the fate that overtook members of the Patrikeev and Riapolovsky families, Kholmsky, Bersen and others. The grand princes had
to separate themselves from men who lived in the past and allowed
their attachment to it to interfere with change and development. They
were also determined to advance new men who would look forward

rather than backward. Since the new order created and endowed these men with influence they were bound to be its docile servants.

Grand Prince Vasily Ivanovich was suddenly succeeded by Ivan, a child who was still a minor when his mother, the regent, died. Those who took control of the government at her death had no sympathy for the policies of the rulers of Muscovy. It was not difficult to surmise what they would do as soon as their hands were free and they acquired unrestrained power to follow their own bent and act in accordance with their own notions. They would justify their opposition to the new order with pious phrases about the country's welfare. They would never understand that it was senseless to resurrect the outmoded and obsolescent appanage relationships of the past, or that such an attempt would evoke no more than shadows bereft of substance. They lacked sufficient perception to recognize that the new order was inevitable. They were incapable of transferring what was best from the old system to the new in order to benefit and strengthen the state, nor could they see that a judicious blend of the past and the present would enhance the national interest.

What use the Shuisky faction made of its opportunity has been seen. Its members strove to achieve personal goals and confused the interests of the state with their own. They failed even to identify the concerns of their own corporate body. Their behavior actually reinforced the power of the system they opposed, thanks to their belief that they were championing traditional rights. Their ties with their own home sources of power had grown weak. The actors fighting, triumphing and perishing upon the stage are descendants of Rurik and princes of Suzdal, Rostov, Yaroslavl, and Smolensk, but the inhabitants of these regions never displayed sympathy for them. There is no record that people in Suzdal or Nizhegorod strongly supported the Shuisky faction because they considered them descendants of their earlier rulers. The Shuiskys received wholehearted support from Novgorod, and it is surely strange that only Novgorod was prepared to support a new movement to reinstate the old norms. Recent arrivals from Lithuania, such as the Belsky and Glinsky princes, understandably received even less support.

These factions might have evoked genuine support only had they identified their personal interests closely with those of the country at large. They failed to do so and society knew they cared for nothing but asserting their traditional prerogatives. They were convinced that they possessed an inherent right to wring every penny from the people it was their duty to protect. The people naturally gave their full support to the one institution capable of protecting them from such individuals and checking their rapacity. The young tsar took advantage of the mistakes made by these men, whom he considered his enemies. In the presence of representatives from the entire country he declared from the Stone Platform that the regime of the selfish, extortionate, and unjust boyars and princes had come to an end, for he intended to become universal judge and protector and had assigned a man from the ranks of the poor and humble to scrutinize petitions. Adashev took the place formerly held by the Shuisky, Belsky and Glinsky families. Esau had sold his birthright to his younger brother for a mess of pottage.

RELATIONS WITH LITHUANIA

It was fortunate for the boyar regime that the difficult war with Lithuania had ended earlier. The aged Sigismund planned no new offensive and devoted all his efforts to defense in case Moscow decided to attack when the truce expired. In September of 1538 Sigismund reminded the council of Lithuania that the truce had but three years to run and urged it to consider what steps to take in the event of a new conflict: "The vital question of war with our Muscovite enemy requires careful consideration. I do not think our grand duchy can fight a war unaided; we need the assistance of a mercenary army. You members of council are aware that we rushed into the last war without adequate preparations. We held a general assessment, but it failed to produce sufficient revenue. What was the result? When our money ran out we were forced to come to humiliating terms. If we are not careful this time, the truce will expire; our Muscovite enemy will note our disarray and lack of preparedness, see our frontier fortresses in ruins, and probably send an army to attack us. To make ready for war with Moscow, I proclaim my will to your excellencies. During each of the three remaining years of the truce we should levy assessments on each 800 acre unit in the amount of 1 ruble 60 kopecks the first year, one ruble the second, and eighty kopecks the third. After collection this money should be deposited in the treasury and used exclusively to pay mercenary troops."

When the truce expired Lithuanian envoys, Jan Glebowicz, governor of Polotsk, and Nikodim Tekhanovsky, came to Moscow in March, 1542. The escorts designated to accompany them were instructed thus: "Meet the envoys at the frontier and spend the night with them at least six miles distant from Smolensk. Do not let them spend the night in Smolensk under any circumstances. Conduct them carefully around Smolensk, so that they will have no opportunity to speak to anyone in the city." As before, all attempts to achieve permanent peace were frustrated by the problem of Smolensk, and as before, all efforts made by the Muscovite boyars to free the prisoners proved abortive. The envoys demanded Chernigov and six other towns in exchange for them, and told the boyars: "You cannot expect our ruler to free prisoners and get nothing in return. You know that our sovereign king captured them honorably in war and that traitors robbed him of parts of his patrimony. You want the best of both worlds, to keep Smolensk and recover your prisoners." The boyars replied that it was God Who had permitted Grand Prince Vasily to take Smolensk.

Both sides finally agreed to extend the truce for seven years, but a dispute promptly arose concerning boundaries. In an attempt to resolve the issue Sukin was sent to Lithuania; among his instructions was: "If you are asked whether our sovereign grand prince plans to marry, you are to reply: 'God has approved his present intention to enter the state of matrimony. We understand our sovereign has sent scouts everywhere to find a bride for him. He will hold bride-shows and make his choice. He desires to be entirely free in this matter.' Note what they say to this and, when you return, tell the sovereign grand prince about it." Nothing happened, because the Lithuanians made no inquiries concerning young Ivan's marriage plans.

Seeking to provide against every contingency in the event of war with Moscow, Sigismund devoted increasing attention to the Crimea, where Semen Belsky was actively intriguing on his behalf against Moscow. In fall, 1540, Belsky informed the king that he had succeeded in diverting the Crimeans from a planned raid into Lithuania and had obtained the khan's assurance that he would attack Moscow in the spring. The king thanked his loyal and devoted servitor for his efforts and sent him fifty rubles. The queen added a modest sum on her own account. In July of 1541 Belsky told Sigismund: "The khan could not attack Moscow early in the spring because he was taken ill. When he recovered and was preparing to set out his princes and nobles tried to persuade him not to go because Moscow had assembled a large army. When I heard of this I went with three noblemen in your majesty's service to urge the khan to honor his commitment. Calling upon God to aid me I, your majesty's servant, took my life in my hands by arousing the tsar to attack me, in order to render your majesty a service.

"Before I departed, envoys from Moscow arrived to see me. They had been sent by the grand prince, my brothers, the metropolitan, and the entire council. They brought many gifts and duly attested letters begging me not to arouse the khan against Moscow. The grand prince and all his people vowed complete subservience to me until the grand prince attained his majority. Mindful of the oath I swore to your majesty, I refused to have anything to do with the grand prince." The impression such boasting made on Sigismund's shrewd mind can readily be imagined, and Belsky soon realized that the king and his court were ridiculing his claim to be the grand prince's guardian. He wrote again to Sigismund, enumerating his services: three times he had tried to persuade the Nogays to attack Moscow, and he had prevailed on the Crimean khan to raid the countryside, where he had captured, enslaved and carried off many prisoners, acquired huge booty, and inflicted enormous damage while he stormed, sacked and destroyed towns, seized artillery, twice defeated Muscovite armies, and forced the grand prince and his boyars to flee from Moscow.

THREATS FROM THE CRIMEA

When Sahib-Girey became sole ruler of the Crimea his threatening attitude placed Moscow in a difficult position. To avoid war on two fronts the government had allowed Safa-Girey to remain ruler of Kazan as long as he maintained friendly relations with Moscow, but the Crimea was determined to disrupt the relationship. When he received a communication from Ivan asserting Moscow's right to control the destinies of Kazan, Sahib arrested a courier whom the grand prince had dispatched to the hospodar of Moldavia and wrote to Ivan: "Your father failed to observe the etiquette proper among rulers. No sovereign ever did what he did. He killed our representatives at his court. Two years ago I sent men to Kazan. Your soldiers intercepted them, brought them before you, and your mother had them put to death. My army is more than 100,000 strong. If I lead all my forces at once to attack your country, what losses do you think you will suffer and how much will my treasury benefit? I am on my way; you had better prepare for me, as I shall appear unexpectedly. I shall do what I want in your country, but no matter how much you wish to harm me, you will not get near my country."

The boyars decided to send a lord-in-waiting, Zlobin, with handsome presents to the Crimea in an effort to persuade the khan to respect the existing understanding that the grand prince would not attack Kazan as long as Safa-Girey remained subservient to Moscow. The khan responded by sending Divi-Murza, his ambassador, to Moscow with a letter containing the observation: "You sent your ambassador Stepan Zlobin to us with fine gifts. God help you, this is the least you can do." The khan demanded that the grand prince make an advance guarantee in

Divi-Murza's presence to observe any alliance concerted between them and then send an ambassador to receive the khan's covenant. Peace between Moscow and Kazan would form an essential condition of any agreement. In another letter the khan specified who were to receive presents: "Gifts are authorized for members of the royal house, including my brothers and children. Besides these nobles and princes gifts should be sent to one man in each clan, totalling 124, and fifty other tribesmen. See that the latter receive gifts; fifty is no large number. If you oblige, your land will be tranquil and you will rejoice."

Zlobin obtained a covenant from the khan, but when he brought it to Moscow the boyars at once discovered that it contained an unexpected clause. The document specified the gifts the grand prince was to remit regularly to the Crimea, a condition which the Muscovite government, as has been seen, steadfastly refused to accept, for it was the equivalent of agreeing to pay tribute. In a final effort to resolve the dispute the khan sent Sulesh, a nobleman, as ambassador to Moscow. A son of Magmedin and a nephew of Appak, he had long been a supporter of Moscow. Sulesh agreed to reword the covenant along the lines the boyars desired and it was returned to the khan for revision. The khan replied with a letter containing unflattering expressions; he wrote that the grand prince was too young to have acquired understanding. The boyars were moved to tell Sulesh, when he asked to depart: "Consider what answer we can give you to take to your ruler. The khan has written uncivil words to our sovereign. How is our sovereign to address your khan? Is he to beseech or scold him? Our lord wishes to be on terms of fraternal friendship with your ruler, but he has no choice. He must go to war to avenge such an insult." The khan passed from offensive words to deeds and ravaged areas around Kashira and Rostov. When Moscow learned of his actions the government confiscated Sulesh's horses, placed the envoy under house arrest, and confined Egup, the khan's courier, and his men in various places. Later dispatches seized from some Tatars revealed that the khan had deliberately sent forces into the field to force the grand prince to disgrace Sulesh. Sahib was angry with him because Sulesh had consented to revise the section about gifts in the covenant. The grand prince persuaded the boyars to restore Sulesh to favor; he was the son and nephew of men who had consistently supported Moscow.

Meanwhile, in expectation of assistance from the Crimea the people of Kazan raided adjacent areas in Muscovy. In 1539 they advanced to Murom and Kostroma and slew four Muscovite commanders in a stubborn battle south of Kostroma, that lasted until they had to flee after suffering defeat at the hands of Khan Shig-Aley and Prince Fedor

Mikhailovich Mstislavsky. In December, 1540 Safa-Girey, accompanied by his own forces, Crimeans, and Nogays, approached Murom, but withdrew on learning that commanders were on their way from Vladimir and Shig-Aley had set out from Kasimov. Safa-Girey owed his throne to Prince Bulat, but, as has been seen, a faction opposing the Crimea existed in Kazan. Originally this faction was weak and could count on little effective support from Moscow, but within a few years the situation changed. Safa-Girey surrounded himself with men from the Crimea, placed extraordinary trust in them, and showered them with favors, a policy that served to alienate even the nobles who previously had favored a Crimean orientation. Bulat now assumed leadership of the opposition and in the name of the people of Kazan sent representatives to Moscow in 1541 to ask the grand prince to forgive them and send forces into the area: "We shall serve the grand prince, assassinate the khan, or arrest and hand him over to your officers. The khan oppresses the people of Kazan; estates belonging to our princes are confiscated and assigned to Crimeans, the people are robbed, and all funds we acquire are shipped to the Crimea."

The grand prince told Bulat and the people he forgave them and would dispatch troops. Boyar Prince Ivan Vasilievich Shuisky, the man formerly in charge of the government, other officers, and substantial forces drawn from many rural districts and seventeen towns were immediately moved to Vladimir with instructions to observe events in Kazan and communicate with the opposition. Realizing that war with Safa-Girey and Kazan meant war with the Crimea the administration, which at the time was composed of Prince Ivan Belsky and Metropolitan Ioasaf, also sent troops to Kolomna to guard the southern frontier. Their foresight was justified. Two prisoners escaped from the Crimea told Moscow that Safa-Girey knew of the deployment of this army and had informed Sahib-Girey. The latter invaded Russia with all his forces, leaving behind only those too young or too old to serve. He was accompanied by Prince Semen Belsky, Turkish artillerymen and musketeers, Nogays, and men from Kaffa, Astrakhan, Azov and Belgorod (Akkerman). Boasting what he would do, the khan marched to attack Russia.

When this news reached Moscow the administration ordered the governor of Putivl to plant a cossack formation across the enemy's line of march. A scout reconnoitred and reported he had found many tracks, which showed that a huge army of 100,000 or more men was on its way to Russia. Boyar Prince Dmitry Fedorovich Belsky hastened from Moscow. He and the officers stationed in Kolomna were ordered to take a stand on the Oka at the place where previous Muscovite commanders had met the khans, while Prince Yury Mikhailovich Bulgakov-Golitsyn and one of the Tatar princes took up positions at Pakhra. Moscow feared that the khan of Kazan might launch a simultaneous attack; thus, Khan Shig-Aley was told to quit Kasimov and other commanders to leave Kostroma in order to converge on Vladimir and assist Prince Shuisky.

In July another scout reported to the grand prince that he had observed an enormous army moving north of the Don. It had taken much more than a day to pass. Sahib-Girey approached the town of Osetr on July 28, and Commander Glebov engaged him at its outskirts. Many Tatars were killed and nine, who were taken prisoner, were sent to Moscow. Prince Bulgakov was told to advance from Pakhra to the Oka and other officers were sent in to take up the position he had vacated. In Moscow the grand prince and his brother went to the cathedral of the Assumption, where they prayed before the icon of the Virgin of Vladimir and at the tomb of Miracle-Worker Peter. They asked the boyars and Metropolitan Ioasaf whether Ivan should remain in Moscow or seek refuge elsewhere. Some boyars observed: "Hitherto whenever the khans threatened Moscow our rulers were not children and could flee quickly; they knew what was best for themselves and the country. When Edigey invested Moscow Grand Prince Vasily Dmitrievich placed his two brothers and Prince Vladimir Andreevich in charge of the city while he went to Kostroma. Edigey pursued him. The Tatars almost captured him; only God's grace saved him. Now our sovereign is young and his brother is younger. They cannot move quickly and are gripped by fear. No one can make haste with small children."

The metropolitan said: "The towns in which our sovereigns sought safety during previous Tatar incursions are menaced by Kazan. Our sovereigns have never withdrawn to Novgorod and Pskov because these cities lie too close to the Lithuanian and German frontiers. To whom could we entrust the protection of Moscow and the relics of the miracle-workers? When earlier grand princes withdrew from Moscow they left their brothers to defend it. When Grand Prince Dmitry quitted Moscow he did not leave his brother or any vigorous commanders there and a terrible disaster overtook the city. O Lord, forfend and preserve us from such horror! Our grand princes left Moscow to collect troops and succor the city and other towns, but now many are here to protect the grand prince and defend his capital. It is better to commend the grand prince to God, His Holy Mother, and Miracle-Workers Peter and Alexis, Who care for the Russian land and our sovereigns. Grand Prince Vasily commended his son to these miracle-workers." The boyars unanimously agreed that the grand prince should stay in Moscow.

Summoning the city prefects they instructed them to provision their districts, station cannon and muskets at strategic points, assign men to guard the gates, the apertures in the walls used to discharge arrows, and the walls themselves, and to erect barricades in the streets outside the walls. The people toiled incessantly and promised to stand firm and lay down their lives to defend the grand prince and their homes. Rumors circulated that the khan had reached the Oka and was preparing to cross. The grand prince exhorted his officers to avoid dissension and resist the khan when he tried to cross the river, no matter what they suffered, in order to preserve the holy churches and the Orthodox Christian faith. He, the grand prince, would gladly show his favor both to them and to their children. He would carve the name of anyone God took away on a memorial plaque and reward his wife and children.

The officers read the grand prince's letter, wept and said: "Brothers, let us display fortitude and devotion. Let us remember the favor Grand Prince Vasily showed us. Grand Prince Ivan, our sovereign, is still too young to bear arms. We shall serve our young ruler and he will honor us and our children after us when he is older. Let us sacrifice for our ruler and the Christian faith. If God fulfills our desire we shall win glory at home and abroad. We are but mortal. God will never forget anyone who suffers death defending the faith and our sovereign. Our sovereign will requite our children." Commanders who had been feuding humbly and and tearfully begged each other's pardon. Prince Dmitry Belsky and the other commanders read the grand prince's exhortation to the troops and the soldiers shouted: "We rejoice to serve our sovereign and lay down our lives for the Christian faith. We wish to drain the cup of death with the Tatars."

Sahib-Girey reached the Oka on the morning of July 30 and halted on the bank while the Tatars prepared to cross, exchanging volleys of arrows with the Russian advance guard led by Prince Ivan Turuntay-Pronsky. The khan ordered his artillery and muskets to open fire in order to drive the Russians back from the bank and allow his army to cross. Pronsky's advance guard wavered, but was speedily reinforced by Princes Mikulinsky and Serebriany-Obolensky, then Prince Kurbsky and Ivan Mikhailovich Shuisky, and, finally, Prince Dmitry Belsky. The astonished khan summoned Prince Semen Belsky and his attendants and angrily said: "You assured me the grand prince's forces had gone to Kazan and I would encounter little opposition. I have never seen so many soldiers in one place." Sahib retired to his camp to reflect on the situation. When he heard Russian artillery had come up he immediately withdrew from the Oka and retreated by the route he had come. Two officers, Princes Mikulinsky and Serebriany, set out in pursuit, killed Tatar stragglers, and took prisoners, who told them the khan had complained to his princes that he was humiliated. He had led a huge host to attack Russia but had failed to achieve the slightest success. The princes reminded him that Tamerlane[13] had invaded Russia with large forces but had taken only the single fortress of Elets. This moved the khan to say: "Pronsk, one of the grand prince's towns, lies on our line of march. We shall take it and treat it as Tamerlane once treated Elets, so that no one can say the khan invaded Russia and failed utterly of accomplishment."

The Tatars appeared before Pronsk on August 3. Vasily Zhulebin of the Sviblov family and Alexander Kobiakov, a boyar originally from Riazan, were in charge of its defense. The Tatars assailed the besieged town all day and princes and nobles kept riding up and shouting to Zhulebin: "Surrender and the khan will prove merciful. He will not depart until he has taken your town." Zhulebin replied: "The town will survive as long as God wishes. You cannot take it unless God allows you. Have your khan wait a little and the grand prince's officers pursuing him will overtake him."

The khan ordered his entire army to construct towers and other siege devices in preparation for a grand assault on the town. The commanders and all the inhabitants of Pronsk, including the women, responded by strengthening the fortress and piling heaps of stakes and stones and buckets of water on the walls. At that moment seven junior officers sent ahead by Mikulinsky and Serebriany reached Pronsk to urge the citizens to put up a stiff resistance, since large forces would soon arrive, which intended with God's help to attack the khan. The people of Pronsk were greatly encouraged. When a prisoner told the khan of their joy he burned his towers and hastily withdrew. Not finding him at Pronsk the commanders continued their pursuit towards the river Don, but when they approached the banks they saw that the Tatars had crossed. After detailing a small contingent to keep following the khan the commanders returned to Moscow, where there was universal rejoicing. The sovereign showed substantial favor to his boyars and commanders and gave them coats and caps.

The next spring, in 1542, Imin-Girey, Sahib's eldest son, attacked the Seversk region but was driven off. In August the Crimeans appeared in the vicinity of Riazan, but as soon as they saw their way was blocked by Russian forces under Prince Peter Pronsky they grew alarmed and retired. Units from various frontier towns followed them as far as Mecha, while Russian guard detachments defeated Tatar units at Kulikovo.

Imin-Girey enjoyed better success when he attacked the area around Belaia and Odoev in December, 1544. The Tatars carried off enormous booty because the three commanders, Princes Shcheniatev, Shkurliatev and Vorotynsky, quarrelled over precedence and failed to advance. The khan wrote the grand prince: "The king makes me an annual subsidy of 15,000 gold pieces; your gift is smaller. It is up to you: if you give me what I want we can come to terms, but if you refuse we shall go on fighting. Heretofore you were a child, but you have now reached the age of understanding and are able to decide which is the more advantageous course for you to follow." Ivan concluded no benefit could accrue from maintaining relations with bandits. He decided not to send an envoy to the Crimea and placed the Crimean representative under official displeasure, because the khan had abused Liapun, a junior official who had been sent to him. He had slit his nose and ears and led him naked around the marketplace. The khan's men stole 39 gifts from couriers and impressed 55 Muscovites into slavery.

CAMPAIGNS TO KAZAN

Negotiations with the Crimea were unlikely to produce results. It was essential to settle the problem of Kazan at any cost, and after Sahib-Girey's abortive campaign, Kazan too was anxious for peace. Bulat came to an understanding with Safa-Girey, who asked the boyars to sound out the grand prince on the subject of a peace treaty. His wife Gorshadna sent a note about it to Ivan personally, but the exchange went no further. Kazan affairs are not mentioned again until the spring of 1545. The domestic situation in Muscovy, Belsky's fall, the advent of the Shuisky faction, and the uncertain behavior of the new government after Andrei Shuisky was executed are ample reasons to explain the silence. The first major initiative Ivan's administration undertook after the young grand prince asserted his authority over the boyars was a campaign against Kazan. It began in April, 1545, but the reasons for it are unclear.

Prince Semen Punkov, Ivan Sheremetev, and Prince David Paletsky advanced on Kazan with a small river force. Prince Vasily Serebriany proceeded from Viatka and Commander Lvov from Perm. Coming down the Viatka and Kama rivers Serebriany killed many of the enemy and linked up with Punkov near Kazan at the same hour on the same day, just as though they both had come from the same estate. After effecting their junction the boyars killed many Kazan soldiers and burned down some of the khan's outbuildings. Junior officers went to Sviiag, where they also killed a number of the enemy. They returned home after these insignificant skirmishes and were lavishly rewarded. The commanders and junior officers got anything they asked for, because the young grand prince was delighted that the campaign had begun successfully and the two contingents had returned unscathed. The third was less fortunate. Lvov and his men from Perm were late and arrived after the other Russian forces had left the area. Troops from Kazan surrounded them. The army was defeated and wiped out.

Although the campaign achieved few gains it proved useful in that it redoubled the domestic discord and factional strife in Kazan. The khan suspected his princes had helped the Muscovite forces. He executed a few of them, and many sought refuge with the grand prince in Moscow, while others went elsewhere. On July 29 two noblemen, Prince Kadysh and Chura Narykov, told the grand prince they would hand over Safa-Girey and thirty of his Crimean supporters to him if he sent a force to Kazan. Ivan told them to seize and detain the khan and then he would send a force. In December the grand prince went in person to Vladimir. He probably did so in order to get news from Kazan more quickly, and on January 17, 1546 he learned that Safa-Girey had been expelled and many of his Crimean supporters slain. The people of Kazan petitioned Ivan to show his favor to them, lay aside his wrath, and allow Shig-Aley to become their ruler. In June Boyar Prince Dmitry Belsky installed Shig-Aley as khan. The expulsion of Safa-Girey and the accession of Shig-Aley were the work of a single faction. No sooner had Prince Belsky returned from Kazan when word arrived that the people had tricked the grand prince and Shig-Aley and summoned Safa-Girey to the Kama river. Shig-Aley fled, obtained horses from the Gorodets Tatars on the Volga, and rode off into the steppe to meet a Russian unit sent by the grand prince to encounter him.

The Crimean party had triumphed and Safa-Girey immediately executed the leaders of the opposition, including Princes Chura and Kadysh. Chura's brothers and seventy others who favored Muscovy or Shig-Aley managed to escape to Moscow. A few months later the Hill Cheremis asked the grand prince to send forces to attack Kazan. They promised to serve him and join the campaign. Ivan complied by sending Prince Alexander Borisovich Gorbaty, who cleared the way to the mouth of the Sviiag river and returned accompanied by 100 Cheremis. Late in 1547 the new tsar of Muscovy decided to lead an army to attack Kazan himself. He proceeded to Vladimir in December, ordering the artillery to follow. The guns were moved up early in January, 1548. It was a difficult undertaking, for the winter was mild, with constant rain and no snow.

In February Ivan moved from Nizhny Novgorod to take up a position on the island of Robotka. A heavy thaw occurred. The ice on the Volga was covered with water; many cannon and muskets sank into the river and many soldiers fell through holes in the ice which were hidden by the water. The tsar waited three days on Robotka, hoping to cross, but was unable to do so. He sent Prince Dmitry Fedorovich Belsky to meet Shig-Aley at the mouth of the Tsivil river and returned to Moscow weeping bitterly because God had not allowed him to finish the campaign. His tears are noteworthy. He wept because he was only seventeen, and because he had an irritable, passionate and impressionable temperament.

Belsky effected a junction with Shig-Aley and both approached Kazan. Safa-Girey came out to confront them at Arsk but rushed back into the city before the charge of the advance guard led by Prince Semen Mikulinsky. The commanders remained a week before Kazan, ravaging its environs, before they withdrew. The nobleman Grigory Vasilievich Sheremetev was a casualty. In the fall the people of Kazan, led by Arak-Bogatyr, attacked the Galich district, but Yakovlev, governor of Kostroma, inflicted a crushing defeat on them and killed Arak. In March of 1549 Moscow learned that Safa-Girey had died. During Ivan's minority Moscow's lack of initiative in the war with Kazan stemmed largely from fear of the Crimean khan. It proved very costly to the border areas, which were exposed to constant raids from Kazan. Other testimony of the time indicates that districts within the grand duchy endured equally severe devastation during the boyar regime.

BOYAR INJUSTICE

The tsar's speech from the Stone Platform sheds light on the administration of justice in Muscovy. The Pskov chronicler has much to say about the rapacity of the governors in his city. The people were delighted when a state secretary, Koltyr Rakov, who had introduced many new imposts, was removed during Elena's administration, but their joy was short-lived. The first Shuisky administration sent Prince Andrei Mikhailovich Shuisky, who has figured in these pages, and Prince Vasily Ivanovich Repnin-Obolensky to govern Pskov. In the chronicler's phrase, these governors were as savage as lions and their people behaved like wild beasts towards Christian people. Their informers slandered decent men and caused them to move to other towns. Righteous abbots of monasteries took refuge in Novgorod. Prince Shuisky was a wicked man, whose lawless actions afflicted city and countryside alike. He revived old cases and assessed fines of 100 rubles and more. Craftsmen worked for him without pay and rich men gave him presents. It is curious, the chronicler says, that the abbots sought refuge in Novgorod. Conditions were admittedly better there, but it may be remembered that Novgorod wholeheartedly supported the Shuisky faction.

When the Shuisky faction was superseded by Belsky and Metropolitan Ioasaf changes occurred in Pskov and, very likely, in the other towns oppressed by the previous administration. The change at the top inevitably led to removal of relatives and friends of the previous rulers holding posts outside the capital. Complaints now received attention because, unlike the powerful Shuisky faction, which comprised many noble families and remained vigorous even after losing its leaders, Prince Ivan Belsky and Metropolitan Ioasaf had to cultivate goodwill among the people by introducing improvements and rely on popular support to counter the challenge of their powerful rivals. Belsky's previous behavior is no proof that he harbored good intentions, but it should not be forgotten that his principal coadjutor was Metropolitan Ioasaf, who had intervened on behalf of men under official displeasure.

PSKOV PROTESTS

The administration of Belsky and Ioasaf issued charters to major towns, their environs, and their districts which granted inhabitants the right to apprehend criminals who had sworn not to perpetrate crimes but committed a second offense, and inflict capital punishment upon them without referring such cases to the governors or their officials. When Pskov acquired such an authorization the local authorities were empowered to try criminal cases at the prince's palace and in the courthouse on the bank of the Velikaia river, and condemn culprits to death. When Prince Andrei Shuisky returned to Moscow, Prince Repnin-Obolensky remained in sole charge. The chronicler reports that he was furious because Pskov had obtained the statute. The people were delighted to be rid of criminals and informers, as well as of governors and their officials touring the districts. For the first time they uttered prayers for the sovereign. Criminals disappeared and calm prevailed, but this state of affairs did not last long. The power of the governors was quickly restored when the administration of Belsky and Ioasaf fell and the partisans of the Shuisky faction resumed their former practices. It is asserted that Prince Andrei Shuisky resorted to violence to drive out landowners and force them to sell their lands at low prices. He ruined peasants by compelling them to provide excessive maintenance for men travelling on his business to and from his estates. Every servitor and every peasant under his protection engaged in acts of lawlessness.

The unjust behavior of the Pskov governors exacerbated the tension between the powerful and the poor. Such friction had been a condition of life in Novgorod during its independent existence, but it had a different origin in Pskov at this time. In Grand Prince Vasily's reign the original ruling class in the city had been expelled and replaced with settlers from Moscow. This action superimposed hostility between native citizens and the unwelcome arrivals on the traditional enmity that had existed between the higher and lower orders. In an entry for 1544 the chronicler states that Pskov was gripped by tension between the powerful and the poor; men made frequent visits to Moscow and spent large sums of money. Late in 1546, on one of the pilgrimages of which he was fond, Ivan made a brief visit to Pskov. He assigned a number of villages to the Pechersky monastery but, says the chronicler, he did not alleviate conditions in his ancestral realm of Pskov; he laid heavy burdens on the courier service and caused Christians to sustain heavy losses. In summer, 1547, seventy men from Pskov went to Moscow to lodge a complaint against the governor. Ivan's treatment of them reveals the young tsar's tendency to fly into fits of passion. The delegation found Ivan in the village of Ostrovka. Growing angry with the men for some reason he poured boiling wine over them, plucked out their beards, set fire to their hair with a candle, and ordered them stretched naked on the ground. The affair might have ended in tragedy, but word suddenly arrived that the great bell in Moscow had fallen down. The tsar left for the capital immediately, and the members of the delegation were spared further indignity.

LOCAL CRIMINAL STATUTES

The Pskov chronicler's assertion that Prince Belsky's administration gave his city respite from the exactions of the governors may be applied to other areas. The relaxation contributed to a general improvement in the administration of justice, but it is unfair to assign Prince Belsky's administration exclusive credit for promulgating the local criminal statutes to which the chronicler attaches such great importance. Similar statutes have come down from the Shuisky princes' first administration. In October of 1539 two charters were issued to the inhabitants of Belo-ozero and Kargopol: "To the princes, junior boyars, hereditary landowners, service landowners, serving men, elders, hundredmen, and decurions; and to the peasants belonging to me, the grand prince, or the metropolitan, archbishop, princes, boyars, service landowners, and monasteries; and to the free cultivators, kennelmen, woodsmen, drovers, beekeepers, fishermen, beaver trappers, and men paying quitrent; and to all men without exception. You have informed us that bandits rob hamlets and villages in your districts, plunder your estates, burn down your hamlets and villages, commit frequent robberies on the highroads, and attack, maim and kill numerous victims. You have also told us that individuals shelter bandits in their homes and that bandits conceal their loot in the homes of individuals. We have sent investigators, but you complain that our investigators do great harm and you refuse to cooperate with them in apprehending bandits. Because of the numerous formalities you are afraid to track down and seize bandits without our approval. You should form an association headed by three or four local junior boyars who are literate and capable. Your elders, your decurions, and five or six prominent local peasants should cooperate with them in discovering bandits hiding in your villages and districts. You have our full authority to apprehend them. You must punish any robbers you catch most severely, as well as those who harbor them and receive stolen goods. You may torture, knout and execute them. I have assigned you this responsibility; you will not incur my displeasure by exercising it, and our governors will not interfere.

"If under torture a robber implicates confederates in other towns you should inform the junior boyars in charge there and forward the evidence as soon as possible. Whenever you apprehend, try and execute a thief, prepare a report, including the name of the arresting officer and a list of the charges of which the defendant was found guilty. Those of you who are literate should sign the report. You should conduct strenuous investigations, but you must refrain from acts of private vengeance and never harass or punish innocent persons. If you fail to apprehend and try known criminals; if you fail to pursue, arrest and punish them, or if you release such men or treat them with laxity, I authorize those who complain that thieves remain free to commit robberies in your districts to recover double their losses from your corporations, which will have to pay an additional fine and costs. Whenever you apprehend, try and execute known criminals you must consign any property recovered from such persons to the authorities in charge of your corporations, who will distribute the proceeds proportionately among the victims of thieves who have been executed. You must keep a record of amounts you recover from thieves and distribute among claimants, and make a note of any remainder. Keep your records in a safe place, and inform our boyars in Moscow in charge of the criminal bureau."

Belsky's administration issued a criminal statute in the following form to the inhabitants of the Galich district: "You are to establish a system of watchmen—a decurion for each ten houses; a fiftyman for each fifty, and a hundredman for each hundred. Whenever a traveller puts up at your domicile or enters it to buy salt or sell wares, you must inform the decurion of his presence. The decurion will inform the fiftyman, who will inform the hundredman. All these officials will examine and register such individuals. If an unknown person appears, who is evasive and refuses to give his name, they will apprehend and bring him before the town prefects and cooperate in an investigation to determine his identity. If you determine he is a respectable man you may register and release him. You and the town prefects are to torture severely any such persons found to be criminals. A representative of the crown, constables and leading citizens are to be present when torture is applied. A scribe should take down anything such men say under torture, and you are to attest the document with your signatures. A convicted thief is to be knouted in the square and executed."

At the request of Abbot Alexis, in 1541 similar charters were issued to the hamlets and villages belonging to the Holy Trinity-St. Sergius monastery. The peasants were to choose a prefect and elect hundredmen, fiftymen and decurions. The villages belonging to the Kirillov monastery received a charter in 1549: "In response to their petition I, tsar and grand prince, have ordained that junior boyars (listed by name), constables, and local peasants (listed by name) are to cooperate with their local elders and elected leaders in criminal matters." This charter provides more detail than previous ones: "When a thief is charged with a first offense his accusers are to come forward. He is to pay a fine to the governor, the district administrators and their officials. As soon as the governor, district administrators and their officials collect the fine from the thief, you, the district elders, are to have him knouted and whipped out of your district. On commission of a second offense the thief is to be knouted, have his hand cut off, and whipped out of the district. On commission of a third offense the thief is to be hanged. A quorum of elected leaders may decide minor cases, but all must come in from their villages and districts and assemble in Beloozero in order to decide major cases. If they cannot resolve an issue they are to communicate with the boyars in charge of the criminal bureau. District elders may not enter the governor's court, and the governor may not enter the district elders' court. In cases of robbery and theft district elders are not to accept gifts or take bribes and must watch that others do not accept or take them."

JUNIOR BOYARS IN COUNCIL

As noted above, a reference to junior boyars in council was made during Elena's regency. A similar reference, with an interesting addition, is found for the boyar regime. The description of the reception accorded the Lithuanian envoys Glebowicz and Tekhanovsky states: "Guarding the grand prince on his right stood Boyar Prince M.I. Kubensky, and on his left Lord-in-waiting I.S. Vorontsov. Boyar Prince Dmitry Fedorovich Belsky and other boyars sat to the right of the grand prince, and Boyar Prince Ivan Vasilievich Shuisky and other boyars sat to his left. The chamber contained princes and junior boyars who *lived* in council and those who did not. Princes and junior boyars not living in council but present in chambers when envoys were received were: Prince Odoevsky, Trubetskoy, members of the Vorotynsky and Obolensky families, and others from Rostov, Yaroslavl, Suzdal, Starodub, Moscow (Laskirev, Morozov and several members of the Shein family), Pereiaslavl (Prince Kurakin, Buturlin, and others), Yurev, Volok (several princes Khovansky), Mozhaisk (Prince Nogtev), Viazma (Godunov), the court at Tver (Princes Mikulinsky and others), Kaluga, Dmitrov (Prince Okhliabinin), Staritsa (Umny Kolychev), and the masters of the hunt, Nagoy and Diatlov."

FLIGHT OF PETER FRIAZIN

The disorders following the death of Grand Princess Elena forced the distinguished Italian architect Peter Friazin to flee from Moscow. He had come from Rome in Grand Prince Vasily's time, adopted the Orthodox faith, married in Moscow, and had been granted service estates. In 1539 he was sent to fortify the new town of Sebezh. He took advantage of the opportunity to cross the frontier into Livonia. When the bishop of Dorpat asked him why he had left Moscow, Peter replied: "The grand prince and grand princess are dead. The present ruler is a child. The boyars do as they please and behave unconscionably. There is no order in the land and the boyars are at each other's throats. I left because a serious disturbance broke out. The state scarcely exists."

NOTES

CHAPTER I

1. Ivan III had set Mohammed-Amin on the throne of Kazan in 1487, and Moscow had every reason to believe he would prove a docile vassal. However, Mohammed-Amin successfully revolted in 1504, just before Ivan's death. This marked the beginning of the serious deterioration in relations between the two states with which Vasily was so much preoccupied.

2. The *Tale of the Kingdom of Kazan* relates that the people of Kazan pitched tents in the field of Arsk to hold a fair, which many attended. When all were happily engaged in the festivities the Muscovite force made a sudden descent and destroyed them. Kazan would have been taken if the victors had occupied the city instead of scattering to plunder, riot and drink in the tents. Their action allowed Mohammed-Amin to rally his forces, attack and rout them. This incident is comprehensible in the *Tale*, whose author describes this event only and creates the impression that the Russians went to attack Kazan directly from their boats and came upon the celebration. However, when one considers the information supplied by more trustworthy chronicles, which refer to two descents on Kazan, it becomes impossible to accept the narrative in the *Tale*, as Karamzin does. The people of Kazan must have known that the Russians, after suffering initial defeat, had not embarked on their boats and departed; thus, they would never have opened a fair. Juxtaposing the story of the rout the people of Kazan suffered in their tents to the chronicle narrative, one is obliged to accept Herberstein's account, which forms the basis for the present narrative. In general, Herberstein's account deserves much greater credence than the *Tale*, a highly untrustworthy source which, for example, declares that Commander Kiselev died, although the chronicles number him among the victors withdrawing to Murom. (Soloviev's note)

3. In 1470 Ivan III named his son, Ivan Ivanovich (b. 1456), by his first wife, Maria of Tver, as his heir. Maria died in 1467, and in 1472 Ivan married Sophia, niece of the last Byzantine emperor, Constantine XII. Sophia's first son, Vasily, was born in 1479. In 1490 Ivan Ivanovich died, leaving his widow, Elena of Moldavia, and his son, Dmitry, born in 1483. An intense power struggle developed during Ivan's last years between Sophia and Vasily on one side and Elena and Dmitry on the other. Early in 1498 Ivan formally installed his grandson, Dmitry, as his successor, signalizing a defeat for Sophia and Vasily. Sophia fought back in a round of court intrigues, apparently with increasing success. She and Vasily were gradually restored to favor, and early in 1502 Ivan disgraced and arrested Elena and Dmitry and appointed Vasily grand prince and co-ruler. Sophia died in 1503, and Ivan himself died in 1505, when Vasily ascended the throne. Elena of Moldavia died the same year, and Dmitry died, a closely-guarded prisoner on his estate, in 1509. Vasily had triumphed over all opposition.

4. In 1493, in an attempt to settle a border war, Lithuanian envoys suggested that a marriage of Elena, daughter of Ivan III and Sophia, and elder sister of Vasily, to Alexander, who had become grand prince of Lithuania in 1490, would

lead to better relations between the two kingdoms. Ivan agreed, and the marriage was celebrated in Vilna early in 1495. A principal clause in the marriage articles was the insistence that Princess Elena remain Orthodox, but the Catholic clergy of Lithuania brought substantial pressure upon her to change her faith. The marriage brought about no improvement in relations and each side used Elena as a pawn to advance its own interests. She died in 1513.

5. Most available Muscovite chronicles, Mitya as well as Herberstein and Stryjkowski, assert that Glinsky took the initiative and sent a petition to Moscow. The work known as the *Russian Diary* states: "When Grand Prince Vasily Ivanovich heard that the Glinsky family had broken with the king and retired to their estate, he sent his junior official, Mitya Ivanovich Guba of Kolomna, with a letter urging members of the Glinsky family to enter his service and entrust their holdings to him. Glinsky and his men waited until Easter to hear from the king, but they heard nothing from him during that time. Then they released and sent the junior official, Mitya Guba, back to the grand prince, and with him they sent their own junior official, Ivan Priezhdy, to the grand prince with a letter in which they asked the grand prince to show his favor to them, take them into his service, and grant them estates." One version has Glinsky say to the grand prince: "Sovereign, show mercy, generosity and favor *to my petition;* intercede on my behalf, etc.," but Glinsky here might have been thinking of the petition he sent in answer to the offer conveyed by Guba. It is safe to assume no more than that Glinsky's relationship with the grand prince was of long standing and that, as the above citation indicates, Glinsky was initially concerned only with the aid the grand prince had promised him. (Soloviev's note)

6. The principal importance of this letter lies in the fact that it gives the month and year (June, 1507) in which it was composed. It proves that Glinsky's negotiations with Moscow began in the spring of 1507. (Soloviev's note)

7. The Golden Horde, whose rulers were the last descendants of the house of Genghis-Khan, and whose territories lay athwart the lower Volga steppeland, between the enclaves of the Crimeans to the west and the Nogays, along the Yaik river, to the east, was in a state of precipitate decline. Fear of the Golden Horde had caused Mengli-Girey to esteem and observe the alliance he had forged with Ivan III, but by the beginning of the sixteenth century leadership among the Tatar enclaves clearly had passed to the Crimea. This meant a profound shift of policy. The alliance with Muscovy became less valuable, and Mengli-Girey denounced it in 1512. This inaugurated the period of intensified hostilities between Moscow and the Crimean Tatars, of which Vasily was required to bear the first brunt, that lasted well into the eighteenth century.

8. Abdul-Letif was a son of Ibrahim, khan of Kazan, and the brother of Mohammed-Amin. Their mother was Nur-Saltan, who married Mengli-Girey three years after Ibrahim died in 1482. An able and vigorous woman, she encouraged the khan of the Crimea to maintain a pro-Moscow orientation. In 1495 disturbances broke out in Kazan; Ivan III recalled Mohammed-Amin and set Abdul-Letif on the throne in his place. Then in 1504 Abdul-Letif was recalled in his turn and confined to his holdings in Muscovy, while Mohammed-Amin was restored to the throne of Kazan. It is highly probable that Ivan's actions provoked resentment and triggered Mohammed-Amin's revolt the year he returned to Kazan.

9. The trading republic of Pskov needed the support of Muscovy against the Germans of Livonia, and thus was glad to acknowledge the overall suzerainty of the grand princes. At the same time Pskov enjoyed a substantial degree of

independence in the conduct of its affairs. Moscow had to negotiate a variety of agreements with Pskov as though with a foreign power, and the city had supported Ivan III's grandson, Dmitry, in the succession crisis. Vasily thus had strong personal incentives to proceed against Pskov; in addition, he feared that Lithuania might seek advantage there to the serious detriment of Moscow's fundamental strategic position.

CHAPTER II

1. The Livonian Order originated in the mid-twelfth century. Its emphasis on religious conversion was moderate; Germans, attracted by the possibilities of land and trade, gradually settled the northeastern Baltic littoral, and Riga eventually became their headquarters. The genesis of the Teutonic Order was different. Originally a band of German knights who took the Crusaders' vow, its members had served in the Levant but were obliged to withdraw when Christian fortunes in the east declined. Their military skills and proselytizing zeal attracted Prince Konrad of Mazovia, and he invited them to assist him against the Prussians, a pagan tribe constantly raiding his kingdom. Accepting the commission the knights established themselves in territory on the lower Vistula river and commenced so successful a campaign of fire and sword against the Prussians that by 1234 the pope rewarded their enterprise with permission to retain the Baltic lands where they had exterminated the Prussians as their own sovereign territory. Domiciled in its new realm the Teutonic Order rapidly became one of the foremost military powers of the entire region and embarked on a series of savage campaigns to subjugate the peoples of the interior. The emergence of Lithuania in the fourteenth century and its subsequent rise to empire were results of the Order's activity; the knights' raiding first forced the tribes of the interior to band together and form a state in self-defense, and then encouraged the cooperation between Poland and Lithuania that was to prove so fateful for Lithuanian-Muscovite relations. The forces of Poland and Lithuania combined to fight the battle of Tannenberg in 1410, at which the knights suffered a decisive defeat. After that the initiative passed to the victors, and although the Teutonic Order remained a constant irritant, its power steadily declined until it reached its nadir in the events described in this chapter.

2. Andrei Vasilievich Saburov appeared before Roslavl in 1514 and pretended he was fleeing with his retinue to the king. He and his men received food and other support from the citizenry. The day after he arrived Saburov attacked and occupied the city while a trade fair was in progress, and captured eighteen German merchants present at the event. Vasily freed the merchants but was delighted with the initiative Saburov had displayed. The zest with which the chroniclers describe this incident is occasioned by their desire to offset the disaster that had just occurred at Orsha, although such a raid could not ameliorate the Muscovite position.

3. Vasily knew something of the complexity of contemporary Italian politics. In 1508 the League of Cambrai encouraged the emperor to seize territory from Venice to punish the maritime community for making an alliance with France. In 1509 Maximilian occupied Verona and refused to give it up. France won a decisive victory at Marignano in 1515 over the forces of the Holy League, which Maximilian strongly supported. The emperor thus had little choice but to negotiate with

France and agree to cede Verona to the French king with a stipulation that the city would revert to Venice, as it eventually did. "High principles" played a very small part in this transaction.

4. The Northern Territory was an enormous tract of sparsely-populated land rich in furs and other valuable natural resources extending eastward roughly from the Onega beyond the Northern Dvina to the Pechora river. Loosely administered from Novgorod since the early thirteenth century the Northern Territory passed under Muscovite control when Ivan III acquired Novgorod in the 1480s.

5. An allusion to events occurring in 1382. In 1380 Grand Prince Dmitry (1359-1389) achieved great fame when he defeated Khan Mamay of the Golden Horde at the battle of Kulikovo Pole on the Don river, where he won the title of *Donskoy,* but shortly afterwards he had to face Toktamysh, who had expelled Mamay. Toktamysh occupied and destroyed Moscow.

6. The Golden Horde was still powerful when Edigey was its supreme khan. In retaliation for dilatory payment of the regular tribute Edigey ordered the raid mentioned here in 1408. The khan's forces passed through Muscovite territory and closely besieged Moscow for three weeks before retiring in possession of substantial booty.

7. Herberstein adds: "Realizing he could not repel so powerful an enemy, Vasily temporarily despaired of his cause and, overcome with terror, hid in a haystack." (Soloviev's note)

8. The commanders' quarrel over precedence may have caused them to forfeit a good opportunity, for the loss of a detachment might be deemed sufficient reason for them to accept Kazan's terms. Therefore Belsky need not again be suspected of taking bribes, as the author of the bombastic *Tale of the Kingdom of Kazan* charges. (Soloviev's note)

9. When Islam invaded the borderlands he ordered Chabyk, the Crimean envoy, and his associates, to be drowned. Here is Vasily's instruction to Ambassador Zlobin: "When Islam invaded our sovereign's borderlands, our sovereign proceeded in person to defend them . . . he consigned Chabyk and his associates to his retainers with orders to protect them. The people fell upon his retainers, seized Chabyk and his associates, murdered them, and divided up all their possessions. Although they appropriated his belongings, they concealed Chalpan and his associates. Our sovereign has now released Chalpan and his friends to return to you, but we cannot ascertain where his goods have gone. Ivan Kolychev, our sovereign's envoy, was robbed here, and it cannot be learned where his goods have gone." (Soloviev's note)

10. Soloviev discusses Maxim the Greek and his contributions to the intellectual life of Muscovy in the next chapter.

CHAPTER III

1. These two incidents, although inadequately treated in the sources, illustrate the declining prestige of appanage princes, including the grand prince's brothers. Ivan Ushaty, a commander of the second rank, had in some way affronted Prince Dmitry, who retaliated by raiding his estates without securing the grand prince's prior approval. Dmitry controlled the town of Mezetsk, near Kozelsk, which was part of the grand prince's personal estate. Probably in 1520 soldiers from Kozelsk attacked Mezetsk, an action they scarcely would have undertaken without Vasily's approval. The ensuing exchange between the two principals is lost, but the present

reference indicates that Dmitry lodged a formal protest concerning both incidents with his brother, of which Vasily took advantage forcefully to remind Dmitry of his status as a subordinate.

2. This is Joseph Sanin (1439-1515), to whom Soloviev refers frequently in this chapter. Founder and first abbot of the monastery in Volokolamsk that bore his name, he was a prominent political figure and a leading exponent of the view that monasteries should have the right to acquire and possess landed property.

3. Ivan Saburov reported: "The grand princess told me: 'A woman from Riazan named Stefanida is now in Moscow. Find her and send her to me.' I located Stefanida, had her brought to my residence, and had my woman, Nastya, take her to the grand princess' palace. Stefanida stayed with the grand princess. Later, when I went to the grand princess, she said to me: 'You sent Stefanida to me. She examined me and told me I could not have children. She sprinkled some water and moistened me with it to make the grand prince love me.' The grand princess asked for her shifts, skirts and dresses. 'Stefanida told me to moisten my hands with water from the washstand and dampen my shifts, skirts, dresses and all my white garments with it.'. . . A nun sprinkled some kind of oil and fresh honey on her and told her to rub herself with the mixture to make the grand prince love her and enable her to conceive." Ivan went on to say: "I simply cannot remember how many men and women came to me on such errands." (Soloviev's note)

4. Prince Andrei Mikhailovich Kurbsky (1528-1583) was one of Moscow's leading generals until he defected to Lithuania in 1564. He corresponded with Ivan the Terrible and is the author of a history of Muscovy that constitutes an important primary source document.

5. Later in this chapter Soloviev provides considerable detail concerning this prominent figure in the intellectual life of sixteenth-century Muscovy.

6. The chronicles state that Vasily was advised to act because she was troublesome, sickly and barren. Herberstein provides a description: "As soon as she was tonsured in a nunnery where she lay weeping and crying the metropolitan brought her a cowl and tried to put it on her, but she resisted violently. Seizing the cowl she hurled it to the ground and trampled on it. Offended by the unseemly action Ivan Shigona, one of the leading councillors, sternly upbraided her and struck her with his staff: 'How dare you oppose our lord's will or delay to execute his behests?' Solomonia asked him who had decreed her doom, and he replied that it was the sovereign's command. With humbled spirit she then declared before everyone that she was forced to take the veil against her will, and called on God to avenge the monstrous wrong that had been inflicted upon her. . . .

"Straightway a tale arose that Solomonia was pregnant and about to give birth. Two women confirmed the rumor, the wives of leading councillors, Georgy Maly, a treasurer, and Yakov Mazur, a chamberlain. They declared Solomonia had openly told them that she was pregnant and about to give birth. When he heard the story the prince was greatly aroused, denied both of them his presence, and went so far as to have one of them, Georgy's wife, beaten for failing to report the matter to him seasonably.

"Next, to get to the bottom of the affair, he dispatched a councillor and one of his state secretaries [whom Herberstein calls, respectively], Theodore Rack and Potat, to the nunnery in which she was confined with instructions diligently to sift the entire matter. We were in Moscow at the time, and certain people swore to us that Solomonia had born a boy named Georgy but refused to show the tiny baby to anyone. They claimed she told those who had been sent there to ascertain the truth that they were unworthy to behold the child, who would, when he grew up, avenge the wrong which had been done to his mother. There were others who stoutly denied that Solomonia had ever had a child, and thus the story is suspect." Herberstein also tells of efforts undertaken by Georgy Maly (of Greek origin) even prior to Vasily's first marriage. Georgy had managed to dissuade Vasily from marrying a foreign princess and to take a Russian bride. He had calculated that the grand prince would marry his daughter, but he was deceived in his expectation.

A chronicle narrative contradicts Herberstein's account of Solomonia's tonsure: "The pious Grand Princess Solomonia, knowing that she was barren, like Sarah of old entreated sovereign Grand Prince Vasily Ivanovich of all Russia to allow her to enter the cloister. The tsar and lord of all Russia said: 'How can I sunder my marriage and take another? I am a pious sovereign who fulfills God's commandments and the prescribed law.' The Christ-loving grand princess tearfully and earnestly entreated the sovereign to permit her to act as she desired, but the tsar refused to grant her request and angrily spurned the overtures of the nobles she sent to urge her case. Realizing that the grand prince would never agree, the grand princess begged Metropolitan Daniel to intercede with the sovereign and incline him to grant her request. The grand prince obeyed the metropolitan." (Soloviev's note)

7. Ivan is the future tsar, Ivan IV (the Terrible), who lived 1530-1584. Her second son, Georgy (1533-1563), born feeble-minded, played no part in affairs. He lived quietly on his estates near Dmitrov until his death.

8. Sergius (c1324-1392), canonized by the Orthodox church in 1452, in the village of Radonezh founded and served as the first abbot of what became the Holy Trinity-St. Sergius monastery, located some sixty miles northeast of Moscow, the largest and most influential monastic establishment in the grand duchy. Strongly supporting the grand princes of his time, Sergius inspired Dmitry Donskoy before the latter successfully engaged the Tatars at the battle of Kulikovo Pole in 1380, an encounter which, although not decisive in itself, shattered the myth of Tatar invincibility.

9. A churchman, not to be confused with the monk Vassian Patrikeev.

10. In the Orthodox church the lesser parish clergy, who were allowed to marry, wore white garments. Black garb was restricted to the celibate monks, to whom alone the higher church offices, including that of metropolitan, were open.

11. The most famous act of Vladimir (grand prince of Kiev, 978-1015), son of Sviatoslav and a patron saint of the Orthodox church, was to introduce Christianity into Russia from Byzantium.

12. Peter, a saint of the church, was an early metropolitan. Born in Volynia in the second half of the thirteenth century, he moved to Vladimir about 1306, where he found a contest for primacy in the region under way between Moscow and Tver. Peter unswervingly supported Moscow and in 1325, a year before his death, he transferred the metropolitan see, with the great power and prestige attached to it, from Vladimir to Moscow. This marked the beginning of Moscow's supremacy in spiritual matters and proved to be of great assistance to subsequent grand princes in their struggles for temporal hegemony.

13. This is doubtless the saint of the church who founded and served as first abbot of the Intercession monastery in Uglich. He is supposed to have died in 1504 at the age of 107. His feast day is June 6.

14. A doubtful tradition relates the tale of St. Catherine of Alexandria. Of royal birth, she was baptized and became a Christian mystic. She discoursed with, confounded, and converted pagan philosophers at an audience with the Roman emperor in Alexandria, but when she converted the empress she was supposedly

tortured on a wheel and beheaded in November, 305. Angels then transferred her relics to Mt. Sinai, and a considerable cult in her honor soon arose in the eastern church.

15. Yury Danilovich (grand prince, 1304-1325) ruled Moscow while the Tatar yoke still held sway over Russia. Quietly acquiring adjacent petty principalities he gained control of lands all along the Moscow river. Not hesitating to resort to intrigue and bribery when necessary, he persuaded the khan of the Golden Horde to transfer his patent of authority from the prince of Tver to Moscow. He increased his revenues by levying tolls on the river trade. Prince Daniel's second son, Ivan Kalita (grand prince, 1325-1341) continued his brother's policies. He wooed the khan so successfully that the latter designated him the Horde's official tax-gatherer for the region, a position Ivan employed to Moscow's advantage by occasionally attacking his rivals in the khan's name. Effectively using the devices of purchase and marriage alliance he incorporated an ever-widening circle of territory in northeastern Russia into his realm. Soloviev has discerned correctly that these two rulers laid the foundation of Moscow's subsequent rise to power.

16. Vasily I (1389-1425), the elder son of Dmitry Donskoy, on succeeding his father profited from the decline and fragmentation of the Golden Horde to intensify Moscow's territorial acquisitions. His son followed him as Vasily II (1425-1462), but Vasily I's surviving brother, Yury, also claimed the succession. Neither side could prevail until after 1430, when Vasily's maternal uncle, Vitovt, the powerful grand prince of Lithuania, died and his protection was removed. To compensate for this loss Vasily II bribed the khan of the Golden Horde to support him, but Yury and his son, Dmitry Shemiaka, continued their harassment. Once a band of Tatars in the service of Yury and Dmitry captured Vasily and blinded him, the origin of his sobriquet Vasily the Dark. Undeterred, Vasily continued the struggle and by 1450 had succeeded in expelling his uncle and cousin from Moscow. Shemiaka sought refuge in Novgorod. This is one of the reasons why Vasily's son, Ivan III, was hostile to the place.

17. Herberstein says: "Stefan the Great, Palatine of Moldavia, often mentioned his name at banquets and would add: 'While sitting at ease at home he increases his dominions, whereas I am fighting every day of my life but I can barely manage to protect what I have.' " (Soloviev's note)

18. Joseph Sanin, mentioned in Note 2 above.

19. St. Sergius, mentioned in Note 8 above.

20. St. Nicholas was the most venerated saint in Russia; shrines and icons in his honor abounded everywhere. Nicholas had been bishop of Myra in Lycia and the beginnings of his popularity coincided with the translation of his relics from Asia Minor to the south Italian town of Bari in the late eleventh century, but it is difficult to explain precisely why his cult became so widespread in Russia.

21. Ivan Nikitich Bersen-Beklemishev, who began his service career in 1490, was a gadfly in Vasily's reign. Favoring greater independence for appanage princes he opposed the tendency toward centralization he believed he detected in Ivan III's and particularly during Vasily III's reigns, and he never hesitated to give trenchant expression to his views. Supporting a policy of peace with Moscow's neighbors he voiced the opinion that Vasily should restore Smolensk to Lithuania, the cause of the grand prince's wrath on this occasion. Soloviev has more to say later in this chapter about Bersen-Beklemishev's activity, which culminated in his execution in 1525.

22. Gedimin (grand prince, 1316-1342) founded the ruling house of Lithuania, which soon came to include much territory formerly ruled by Russian appanage

princes tracing their descent to the house of Rurik. Gedimin's descendants considered themselves and were acknowledged to be on a par with their counterparts in Muscovy. The denial of what these princes deemed their time-honored right to decide which royal house they might choose to serve, which Ivan III and Vasily III had begun to enforce with increasing success, was a constant source of friction in Moscow.

23. The chiliarch originally had been commander of a citizen militia unit of 1,000 men distinct from the personal retinue of the grand prince, a practice originating in Kievan times. In Moscow Vasily Veliaminov, the last independent chiliarch, died in 1374; Dmitry Donskoy refused to make another appointment, and the office was allowed to lapse. This is a small but significant sign that during the latter half of the fourteenth century control of all available military force was becoming concentrated in the hands of the grand princes.

24. It is difficult to render Soloviev's point effectively; it involves the use of diminutive forms of Christian names and abbreviated patronymics in a pejorative manner.

25. Clearly a ceremonial office, to be differentiated from the chiliarch as defined in Note 23. "It was said that the chiliarch was Andrei, the grand prince's brother, but the latter was not married until 1534. It may reasonably be assumed that a boyar's wife was designated the wife of the chiliarch for the purposes of the ceremony." (Soloviev's note)

26. See the Book of Joshua, 10, 12-14.

27. The *Life of St. Daniel of Pereiaslavl* contains information that the settlement of Vorgusha, located near the monastery which Daniel had built, was owned by a German named Johann, who had an extremely fierce wife called Natalya. These people attacked Daniel in fear that he might try to acquire their lands.

28. The charter Grand Prince Vasily granted the peasants of the village of Morevo establishes that workmen and individuals without land of their own were known as cossacks in northeastern Russia: "They are free to move wood and building timber by water, and they and the *cossacks* are not required to pay taxes or tribute on them." (Soloviev's note)

29. This introduces the first of four persons (Aleviz, Ivan (Gian-Battista della Volpe), Peter and Bon) called *Friazin*. Soloviev fails to make clear that the term is not a surname but a word Muscovites regularly applied to denote anyone residing among them who had come from Western Europe. In the sixteenth century, these were usually experts in various technical fields. The epithet *Friazin* thus by no means implies that an individual was a member of a single family, was related to others so called, or even came from the same country as the others. In this instance the reference is to an Italian architect, Alevisio the Younger, whom Ivan III hired in 1493 at the court of Ludovico il Moro in Milan to come to Moscow.

30. The concept of an autonomous municipal administration originated in Magdeburg, a prominent member of the Hanseatic League, in the thirteenth century. It is worth noting that this mode of procedure was confined to Russian towns under Lithuanian jurisdiction and did not spread to Muscovy.

31. This is Vasily I, mentioned in Note 16. The hunting master (or game warden) referred to in previous paragraphs was a court official who managed the lands, people and animals of a hunting area, a responsibility of considerable weight.

32. Herberstein reports: "Peasants work for their masters six days out of the seven but are allowed to work their own lands on the seventh day. They derive their sustenance from the plots they own and land and pasture which their masters have assigned to them. Everything else belongs to their masters. They have been

reduced to a wretched condition because nobles and soldiers regularly plunder their holdings." It is not clear whether by *peasants* Herberstein meant to designate free or unfree agriculturalists. In any event, it is difficult to believe what he says about the seventh day. (Soloviev's note)

33. The Muscovites confused two separate Parasceve. Great Martyr Parasceve, daughter of rich parents, dedicated herself to an ascetic life and perished during Diocletian's persecution, when she was summoned before the regional procurator and refused to renounce Christianity or get married. Parasceve the Younger was an anchorite of Constantinople in the tenth century, whose relics were transferred to Turnovo, the capital of Bulgaria, in the thirteenth century. This was the source of a legend that she was of Slavic origin, which helps account for the popularity of her cult in Russia. Thought to be a patron of merchants, she was frequently called *piatnitsa*, the equivalent of Friday, the day on which markets were commonly held.

34. Stefan, the son of a cleric, born between 1320 and 1340, became a monk in Rostov. A man of learning, he knew Greek and Finnish. The latter accomplishment led him to undertake a mission to the Finns and Ugrians inhabiting the remote northeastern region of Perm. He devised an alphabet for the local population and used it to translate the Gospels and essential liturgical material into the native language. The metropolitan of Moscow appointed him the first bishop of Perm. He died in 1396.

35. The heresy of the Judaizers, a movement with certain rationalist overtones, is thought to have begun in Novgorod with the appearance there of one Shkaria in 1470. Its members accepted the Old Testament while rejecting the New. Such a view prompted the Judaizers to consider Christ an ordinary prophet, not the Messiah. Their ideas inevitably led them to denounce the church, and there is considerable speculation that they became involved in various social protest movements designed to alleviate existing injustices. Two Novgorod priests transferred to Moscow disseminated these views in the capital and won converts in high places. This aroused the wrath of established churchmen such as Joseph of Volokolamsk and led to the convocation of a church council in 1503, which officially condemned the views of the Juadizers and demanded that members of the sect be punished.

36. "And at this time Prince Dionisy of Zvenigorod and Nil Polev, both formerly monks in the Josephan monastery, lived as elders in the wilderness around Beloozero, near the Kirillov monastery. Elder Dionisy, prince of Zvenigorod, approached a hermit and saw a cross under his couch. The latter joined the elder as an ordinary priest. On another occasion the elder and the priest approached another hermit. This hermit had a book in his hand and his cell was warm. When the hermit caught sight of Elder Dionisy he thrust the book in the stove and the book burned up. Elder Dionisy and the priest beheld this mighty heresy. Elder Dionisy sent Elder Serapion Krestechnik to Joseph with a letter in which he wrote that he had witnessed heresy among the anchorites. Joseph read the letter and forwarded it to Vassian, archbishop of Rostov, because the affair had taken place in his diocese.

"Archbishop Vassian was in Moscow at the time. Archbishop Vassian gave the letter to the grand prince. The grand prince showed the letter to the elder, Prince Vassian Kosoy, and asked him: 'Are your anchorites behaving properly?' Vassian said to the grand prince: 'Sovereign, this letter was written with intent to deceive; not a word in it is true. Question the priest, sovereign.' The grand prince had the priest brought before him and interrogated him. The priest said: 'Yes, it happened just as the letter says.' The elder, Prince Vassian, demanded the priest be tortured. The priest was tortured; his leg was broken and he died without repudiating his testimony. The grand prince was angry with the elder, Prince Dionisy, and Elder Nil, saying: 'They quarrel amongst themselves and have led me into sin.' The grand prince ordered Elder Dionisy and Elder Nil confined in the Kirillov monastery and their hermitage destroyed." (Soloviev's note)

37. Fedor Borisovich, Grand Prince Vasily's cousin, was the last independent appanage prince in Muscovy. He was hostile to the royal house because of what he considered its infringements upon traditional appanage prerogatives. His anger with Joseph stemmed not so much from a clash of individual personalities, as Soloviev seems to imply, but from the abbot's close political ties with Moscow.

38. Joseph stated: "Prince Fedor and Krivoborsky, his archimandrite, intrigued against me. Krivoborsky flattered and deceived Archbishop Serapion. . . . [Fedor] sent two monks with a letter for Krivoborsky, pretending he wished to buy salt and fish, but in the letter he wrote that Archbishop Serapion would become a second Chrysostom if he did what the prince asked, and if Krivoborsky succeeded in persuading the archbishop he would give him a share of his holdings. Now I had wounded Serapion's pride, and he saw this incident as an opportunity to prove to everyone that he was more righteous and intelligent than other men.

"He sent me a letter in which he wrote: 'When you placed your monastery under the protection of the grand prince you withdrew it from the protection of the Heavenly Father and placed under an earthly one.' Consider the wisdom Serapion displayed when he declared that Volok was Heaven, Moscow was Earth, Prince Fedor of Volok was of heaven, and the grand prince of Muscovy was of earth. Moreover, he failed to give a single citation from Scripture or the sacred canons . . . .

"The grand prince said to Serapion: 'You have said that Prince Fedor is of heaven and I am of earth. Indeed I am of the earth, but you must tell us why you have said that Prince Fedor is of heaven.' The archbishop, in an effort to curry favor both with the sovereign and all ranks of the higher and lower clergy, said: 'I know the reason why I did not give my blessing. Just as you all manage your own affairs, I am at liberty in my own diocese and Prince Fedor is free to rob or reward his own monastery.' " (Soloviev's note)

39. Soon after Joseph's death Vassian composed an exculpation of the charges Joseph had levelled against him and his teacher, Nil of Sorsk. Among other things Vassian wrote: "Joseph, you know very well that the sacred canons permit continent widowers to perform services, but scorning the sacred canons in your arrogance and hypocrisy you denied any widower the right to officiate. It is improper for monasteries to own villages. The sacred canons allow ordinary churches to possess lands, but no bishop nor priest may hold them. All church wealth must be under the administration of a steward, and bishops must give him express authority over all church servitors. Monks have no business growing rich and owning lands, for they leave forsworn all such vanity . . . . Joseph, you bear false witness against me and my elder, Nil, when you charge that we profane the miracle-workers of old and today. Elder Nil never excluded miracles from Scripture but rather exalted them by confirming them in other writings...." Vassian declared that it was wrong to adorn churches and icons with gold and silver. Finally, Vassian reproached Joseph: "You departed upon the everlasting road without seeking our pardon or bestowing your forgiveness upon us." (Soloviev's note)

40. These three examples are given to illustrate Maxim the Greek's conviction that ignorance of Scriptural authority led to error. Papias, a writer of the second

century, improving upon a reference in *Acts* to a "field of blood" where Judas Iscariot died, asserted that Judas lived in the field for many years but swelled to such an enormous size that he could not pass through an aperture large enough to admit a waggon. At last his stomach burst and his bowels scattered upon the ground.

41. Doubtless inspired by the story of Joshua, son of Nun (see above, Note 26), numerous tales expanded and embroidered upon the assertion found in all four synoptic gospels that the sun grew dark on the day of the Crucifixion.

42. This popular apocryphal story, of uncertain date and authorship (perhaps fifth century), enjoyed wide circulation throughout Europe from the tenth to the fifteenth centuries, and was known to the Slavs as *The Tale of What Happened in Persia.* It recounts a dispute about faith held at the court of the Persian king among Christians, pagans and Jews, over which High Priest Aphroditian presided. The Slavic recensions of the story, which are incomplete, relate miracles that purportedly occurred in a pagan temple in Persia the night Christ was born, and narrate the journey of the Three Wise Men, who were regarded as seers possessing magic powers. The part of the *Tale* that aroused Maxim the Greek's especial ire was its comparison of the Virgin with the Greek goddess Hera.

43. Appealing to Metropolitan Daniel, Maxim declared: "You condemned me as a blasphemous destroyer of Holy Scripture because of a few small items you discovered in my translation. I told your holy council at the time that I did not write as I did because I was careless, or absent-minded, or contumacious, or drunk. I affirmed this then and have since begged forgiveness three times." (Soloviev's note)

44. This is a *deisus,* a type of icon rather popular in Russia during the sixteenth and seventeenth centuries. It consisted of a single icon or series of icons which showed Christ enthroned on high, the Virgin on His right, and St. John the Baptist on His left. Various configurations of angels, apostles and saints could be added below.

45. These objects cannot be identified. This word is found nowhere but in this passage.

46. This Metropolitan Joseph should not be confused with other persons of the same name. After the separation of the Russian land into two regions, controlled by Lithuania and Muscovy respectively, two branches of the Orthodox church had developed there by the end of the fifteenth century: one under the jurisdiction of the metropolitan of Moscow, and the other administered by an Orthodox metropolitan residing in Kiev. As Soloviev points out, the burdens of the latter office were much greater than those borne by the metropolitan of Moscow, for its incumbents, such as Metropolitan Joseph, were constantly obliged to uphold the traditions of Orthodoxy in a realm where the chief secular authorities belonged to the hostile Catholic church.

47. The Russian Law was a distillation of Kievan legal experience, incorporated in three recensions made during the eleventh and twelfth centuries. Among its characteristics were diminished stress on physical punishment for crime, marked class distinction in the assessment of penalties, and a strong emphasis on property rights, commerce, and financial matters.

48. St. Basil the Great, bishop of Cappadocia (330-379), was a famous early church father, from whose precepts the Russian monastic tradition takes its origin. He was active in all phases of church life, but Nil Maikov (c1433-1508), better known as Nil of Sorsk, was attracted to the works Basil composed in praise of asceticism.

49. Barsanuphius, a seventh-century hermit, lived in Gaza in Palestine. His writings include a series of answers given to the faithful in which he extolled the contemplative life and advocated man's total and unconditional obedience to spiritual forces.

50. St. Isaac the Syrian, briefly bishop of Nineveh in the later seventh century, was an ascetic and mystic. He composed a number of treatises, the purport of which is revealed in the title of one of his books, *Contempt for the World.*

51. Nilus of Sinai (died about 430) was supposed to have been a rich and influential man who renounced the world at the height of his career to become a monk living in solitude on Mt. Sinai. He was a prominent early ascetic, of a strongly philosophical and mystical cast of mind, and a friend and pupil of St. John Chrysostom, the distinguished churchman whose works were popular in Russia.

52. Hesychius of Jerusalem, who also died about 430, was an important exegete of Scripture, but a good deal of the material that has been attributed to him, in praise of asceticism or otherwise, is considered of doubtful authenticity.

53. St. Symeon the New Theologian (949-1022), born in Paphlagonia, was abbot of the powerful Studite monastery in Constantinople. A stern mystic himself, he was a leading precursor of the revival of the mystical and solitary tradition in eastern monasticism associated with the name of St. Gregory of Sinai.

54. St. Gregory of Sinai (d. 1346), a Byzantine ascetic, founded a monastery at Paroria, a remote mountainous site in southeastern Bulgaria, which attracted Slavic novices. He was strongly influenced by the doctrine of Hesychasm (Quietism), which reemphasized the contemplative life. The monks in Gregory's monastery practised the devices which Nil of Sorsk commends in these passages.

55. This formulation has attracted a great deal of attention and has often been considered an early theory to justify Russian expansionism. Soloviev has placed it in its proper context. It was an ordinary communication to a local government official, expressing Filofey's conviction that Moscow must firmly uphold the traditions of Orthodoxy in a world full of snares for believers—a conservative, not a dynamic concept.

CHAPTER IV

1. Olga (died 969), a prominent princess of Kiev originally from Pskov, married Igor, son of Oleg, whose victory over Byzantine forces in 907 produced the first treaty in Russian legal history, to which Soloviev has referred in the preceding chapter. In 945 Igor was killed in a local altercation, and Olga served as regent for their minor son, Sviatoslav, until 962. A vigorous and capable ruler, she followed the aggressive policy her husband and father-in-law had begun, and introduced far-reaching fiscal reforms. Converted to Orthodox Christianity, Olga made a pilgrimage to its source, Constantinople, in 957, but failed to establish what she considered to be satisfactory relations with the emperor. Her son Sviatoslav refused to receive baptism, and the spread of Christianity among the Slavs of the Kievan state had to await the reign of her grandson, Vladimir. In popular culture Olga's name became a byword for resourcefulness and sagacity.

2. Only very late and fanciful accretions to the account of Vasily's death say: "He bequeathed the entire administration of the whole Russian tsardom to his [Ivan's] mother, Grand Princess Elena, who was to rule, administer and guide it in accordance with God's law until his son came of age." The Pskov

chronicle states: "He entrusted the grand duchy to his elder son, Ivan. While still alive he personally proclaimed him grand prince, and ordered a few of his boyars to watch over the boy until he attained the age of fifteen years." (Soloviev's note)

3. When the Lithuanian envoys suggested adherence to the terms of the treaty Casimir IV had made with Grand Prince Vasily II in 1449 they were thinking of the generous eastern boundaries for Lithuania the treaty had established. Casimir had intended the agreement to be merely a temporary arrangement until he was free to resume his predecessors' expansionist policy towards Muscovy. This never happened, and this treaty embodied Lithuania's greatest gains in the east. In the reigns of Ivan III and Vasily III the initiative passed to Moscow.

4. Pasha, the highest official title in the Ottoman Empire, was held by viziers of the central administration and frontier commanders. As the empire was stabilized, pashas served as provincial governors, who, as in the present instance, discharged both civilian and military responsibilities.

5. Shig-Aley's brother was Enaley. As Soloviev has noted, Enaley was the victim of a conspiracy led by the faction in Kazan favoring the house of Girey.

6. Gustavus I Vasa, king of Sweden, 1523-1560. He won Sweden's independence from Danish rule and established a strong centralized monarchy, but pressure from numerous foes made him anxious to maintain peace with Muscovy. He founded the Vasa dynasty, which was subsequently to play a major role in both Muscovite and Polish affairs.

7. This section reproduces original terms, since it is impossible to give exact monetary equivalents. Elena's currency reform, which was important and lasting, is another indication that her regime was able to attend to business amid distraction.

CHAPTER V

1. Andrei, appanage prince of Uglich, was one of Ivan III's four younger brothers. Taking advantage of the grand prince's struggle with Novgorod, he raised a revolt in 1480. Ivan repressed the outbreak but was obliged to make concessions to his brother. He added the important town of Mozhaisk to Andrei's holdings, but relations between the two remained strained. In 1491 Andrei ignored the grand prince's call to confront the Golden Horde and Ivan now felt strong enough to arrest him and his family on a charge of treason and confiscate his estates. Andrei died in prison in 1493, a martyr in some eyes to appanage principles. His son Dmitry remained a prisoner. Soloviev's comment implies that appanage rights were no longer the serious issue they had been in 1493.

2. Like all historians of sixteenth-century Russia, Soloviev relies heavily on an exchange of five letters between Ivan and Prince Kurbsky. Apart from direct quotations Soloviev bases many of his inferences and conclusions concerning the effect Ivan's upbringing had upon his temperament and character on incidents and details mentioned in the correspondence. As Richard Hellie has noted in his introduction to S.F. Platonov's *Ivan the Terrible* (ed. and trans. by Joseph L. Wieczynski, Gulf Breeze, Florida: Academic International Press, 1974, pp. xiii-xiv), Edward L. Keenan of Harvard University has challenged the authenticity of the correspondence. Keenan's hypothesis has by no means been universally accepted and has occasioned considerable controversy.

3. Ivan has failed to make the point of his ponderous joke clear. He seems to

be saying that Prince Shuisky would have behaved more honorably if he had deposited something he actually owned, such as his old fur coat, in the royal treasury, selected a new one, and sold it. With the money realized from the sale he could have bought gold and silver vessels, inscribed them, and then fairly claimed they were genuine family heirlooms.

4. "Then he killed Fedor Nevezha, a wealthy and esteemed landowner. Some two years earlier he had strangled Prince Mikhail Bogdanovich Trubetskoy, a young man fifteen years of age, and it is recorded that the same year he killed some noble princes--Prince Ivan Dorogobuzhsky, and Fedor Ovchina, Prince Ivan's only son, who were descended from the line of the Torussky and Obolensky princes. Like innocent lambs, they were slaughtered in the first bloom of youth." (Soloviev's note)

5. Alexis (1292/1298-1378) is logically linked with Metropolitan Peter. From a prominent Moscow boyar family, he became archbishop of Vladimir in 1345 and, on the death of his mentor, Metropolitan Feognist, metropolitan in 1354. Strongly supporting the grand princes of Moscow he served as regent during the minority of Dmitry Donskoy, the first grand prince successfully to challenge the hegemony of the Golden Horde, and voluntarily relinquished authority when the grand prince came of age.

6. Iona became bishop of Riazan and Murom in 1437. The Florentine Union, to which Metropolitan Isidor committed Moscow the following year, ushered in a critical decade for the Russian church. In 1442 Grand Prince Vasily II rejected the covenant and deprived Isidor of his office. After much soulsearching a church council five years later elevated Iona to the metropolitanate in 1448. He held office without the sanction of the patriarch of Constantinople. The fact that he was the first de facto head of a now autocephalous Russian Orthodox church may account for his popularity with Ivan, and he was canonized in the coronation year of 1547. Iona helped defend Moscow during a Tatar attack in 1451, and acquired a reputation as a miracle-worker during his lifetime. After his death frequent miracles were reported occurring at his tomb. His is symptomatic of the increasing power, prestige and independence of the Russian church.

7. Here the title tsar means khan, as rulers of Tatar principalities were frequently designated in documents of the time.

8. Vladimir Monomakh, a popular, effective and successful grand prince of Kiev (1113-1125), was the grandson of the Byzantine emperor Constantine IX Monomachos. In the late fifteenth century a legend arose, as part of Moscow's quest for an imperial ideology, that Constantine had sent Vladimir a cap and collar, royal regalia which he wore at his coronation. Ivan was crowned with a Cap of Monomakh, as were succeeding rulers until 1724. The cap, of uncertain but probably Central Asian origin, is preserved in the Kremlin Armory.

9. The Life of St. Gennady of Kostroma states: "Once it chanced the saint came to Moscow, where he was honorably received by Yuliania Fedorovna, wife of the boyar, Roman Yurevich, in hopes that he might bless her sons, Daniel and Nikita, and her daughter, Anastasia." The Life goes on to relate how Gennady foretold Anastasia would marry the tsar. This source thus supplies the name of Tsar Mikhail's great-grandmother. (Soloviev's note)

10. Tradition relates a story of twin brothers in the second century, Florus and Laurus, stone masons in Illyria who built a pagan temple, and consecrated it as a church. For punishment they were buried alive in a dry well. Hailed as martyrs, their relics were credited with performing miracles.

11. The Book of Degrees also reflected the new awareness of their status on the part of the rulers of Moscow. Probably compiled in the 1550s by men close to Metropolitan Makary the book consisted of laudatory biographies of certain grand princes (including Vladimir Monomakh and his coronation), determined by and grouped around their genealogical pedigrees.

12. An elevation facing the Spassky gate in the Kremlin, where executions sometimes took place. The platform was most frequently utilized as a place from which the tsar or the metropolitan might address the people on ceremonial occasions, and officials read proclamations.

13. Tamerlane (1336-1405), a superb military strategist and tactician, formed a powerful coalition of Central Asian tribes and embarked on an extraordinary career of conquest. During his lifetime his empire, with its capital at Samarkand, stretched from the borders of China to Turkey. Tamerlane thoroughly humbled both the Golden Horde and the khanate of the Crimea. He was not interested in attacking Russia, and his actions helped rather than hindered Moscow.

INDEX

Abdul-Letif, ruler of Kazan, 53, 54, 61, 80, 93; agreement with Vasily III, 39-41
Abdur-Rahman, 61
Absalom, 95
Adashev, Alexis Fedorovich, 220, 221, 223, 224, 226
Agrafena Vasilieva Cheliadnina, nurse of Ivan IV, 109, 182, 207
Agrinov, Tatar family, 41
Ahmad, 38, 73, 80, 114
Ahmad-Girey, 42, 53, 62, 63; cited, 42, 62
Albert, duke of Saxony, 74
Albert, margrave of Bradenburg, 75, 76, 77, 92; alliance with Muscovy, 63-65; attacks Poland, 78; declares war on Sigismund, 54; cited, 64, 76, 77
Alexander, grand prince of Lithuania, 29, 34, 35, 37, 42, 51, 53, 64, 73, 132, 140, 158, 181, 182, 189, 192; death (1506), 29; policy, 28
Alexandra, princess of Slutsk, 173
Alexeev, envoy to Constantinople, instructions to, 93
Alexis, abbot, 210, 240
Alexis, archpriest, 106
Alexis the Miracle-Worker, 217, 231
Alexis the Younger of Pskov, icon painter, 147
Alexsin, 32, 53
Alferiev, Ivan, will of, 161
Alp-Saltan, son of Mengli-Girey, 60
Ambassador, Turkish, 66
Anastasia, princess of Slutsk, 35
Anastasia, wife of Ivan IV, 218, 220
Andreev, Dobrynka, peasant, 169, 170
Andrei, prince of Staritsa, brother of Vasily III, 55, 81, 90, 104, 105, 106, 107, 108, 109, 110, 111, 112, 127, 178; arrested, 186; death, 187; fall, 183-187; flight, 185; marriage, 127-128; cited, 109 110, 184, 185, 208

Andrei Vasilievich, prince of Uglich, 209
Aphroditian, 152
Apocryphal writings, 152
Appak, Tatar nobleman, 41, 61, 62, 80, 82, 229; cited, 41, 61, 62
Arak-Bogatyr, 236
Armenia, 145
Army, see Military forces
Arsk, 236
Arta, town, 151
Artemovo, 141, 144, 204
Artiush, undersecretary, 170
Assembly of the Land, 223; speech of Ivan IV to, 223-224
Astrakhan, 39, 40, 63, 80, 81, 83, 84, 85, 94, 96, 230
Astrology, 175
Athos, Mount, 151, 157, 173
Austria, 54, 75
Avram, treasurer of Vilna, 73
Azov, 81, 94, 96, 145, 230; Tatar cossacks, 136

Baarynov, Tatar family, 41
Babur, Indian king, 96
Balakhna, 201, 202
Basmanov, Alexis, 210
Barmin, Fedor, 219
Barsanuphius, 174
Bartolomeo, Italian bombardier, 131
Beaver fur, 144
Beaver trappers of Vladimir, charter, 205
Belaia, 36, 53; Tatar attack on, 233
Bele, 71
Belev, 39, 53
Belgorod (Akkerman), 19, 197, 230; cossacks, 136
Beloozero, 90, 122, 144, 199, 209, 238, 240
Belozersk, 147, 170; charter, 204, 205
Belsk, district, 139, 140; duchy of, 196, 207
Belsky family, 207, 225, 226
Belsky, Prince Dmitry Fedorovich, 80, 81, 105, 120, 182, 187, 207, 230, 232, 235, 236, 241

THE EDITOR AND TRANSLATOR

Hugh F. Graham is Professor of History at California State College, Bakersfield, to which he came as a charter member seven years ago after service in other institutions of higher learning. Originally trained as a Classicist, he received his degrees from the University of Toronto, Princeton, and the University of Southern California. To satisfy his growing interest in the field, in the mid-1950s he became a post-doctoral scholar of Slavic studies at the University of California, Berkeley, where he worked closely for three years with the late Professor George V. Lantseff.

His interests are not confined to history in the narrow sense. They span numerous fields and various areas. He has published articles on such disparate topics as "The Escape Ode in Euripides' *Hippolytus;*" "Ivan P. Kotliarevskii, the Ukrainian Vergil;" "The Classics in the Soviet Union," and "The Tale of Devgenij." During a four-month's sojourn in Leningrad in 1975 he investigated the rich holdings of Greek and Latin materials pertaining to the early history of Muscovy in the State Public Library. This is now his primary focus of interest, as may be seen from his article, " 'A Brief Account of the Character and Brutal Rule of Vasil'evich, Tyrant of Muscovy,' " published in *Canadian-American Slavic Studies* (1975).

Stemming from his classical studies as an undergraduate Dr. Graham has been wedded to the proposition that translation is an important function, not one to be regarded as a handmaiden of serious scholarship undertaken by those automatically classed as unfit for higher aspirations. He proudly identifies himself as one of those "anonymous" individuals who, after all, stand between 99 percent of the reading public and those writers in foreign languages whose thought they wish to learn about. He considers this calling high and one to which he intends to devote the remainder of his scholarly life.

Dr. Graham hopes that his intermediation will enable a wide selection of interested individuals to become familiar with Sergei M. Soloviev, recognized as one of the great historians Russia has produced. He is delighted to have played a modest part in making Soloviev's seminal work available to a greater number of readers.

Academic International Press

The Russian Series

The Central and East European Series

Forum Asiatica